CustomerCentric Selling

CustomerCentric Selling

Selling

SECOND EDITION

MICHAEL T. BOSWORTH,
JOHN R. HOLLAND,
AND FRANK VISGATIS

New York   Chicago   San Francisco   Lisbon   London   Madrid   Mexico City
Milan   New Delhi   San Juan   Seoul   Singapore   Sydney   Toronto

The McGraw·Hill Companies

2 3 4 5 6 7 8 9 0   DOC/DOC   1 5 4 3 2 1

ISBN   978-0-07-163708-4
MHID   0-07-163708-7

Product or brand names used in this book may be trade names or trademarks. Where we believe that there may be proprietary claims to such trade names or trademarks, the name has been used with an initial capital or it has been capitalized in the style used by the name claimant. Regardless of the capitalization used, all such names have been used in an editorial manner without any intent to convey endorsement of or other affiliation with the name claimant. Neither the authors nor the publisher intend to express any judgment as to the validity or legal status of any such proprietary claims.

McGraw-Hill books are available at special quantity discounts to use as premiums and sales promotions, or for use in corporate training programs. To contact a representative please e-mail us at bulksales@mcgraw-hill.com.

This book is printed on acid-free paper.

To my children, Brendan, Brian, and Shiloah. To my brothers, Steve, Sam, and Dick. To those who are helping me grow, Madeline, Judy, and especially Jennifer.

Michael T. Bosworth

To Linda who gracefully handles being married to a road warrior, our three children, and the memory of Dick McManus, the best salesperson I ever knew. To practitioners of CustomerCentric Selling®, who all understand that selling is dead. Long live buying!

John R. Holland

I dedicate my contribution to this book, first and foremost, to my personal Lord and Savior, Jesus Christ. Secondly, to my wife, Nancy, the one person who has always believed I was better than I thought I could be even when I didn't. Finally, to my legacy—Jenna, Christian, Nicholas, and Luke. May God bless you and keep you and make His face to shine upon you, now and for all of the days of your life.

Frank S. Visgatis

Contents

Acknowledgments

This book is the culmination of a 16-year professional and personal relationship between Mike Bosworth, John Holland, Frank Visgatis, and Gary Walker, the cofounders of CustomerCentric Selling®. Many of the ideas and concepts in the book were hashed out over meetings, lunches, and conversations spanning several years. We have come to value the power of clear communication. We have come to value the difference between sales training and process and hope this book will help our readers realize and appreciate the difference. Each of us shares a passion to improve the perception of sales as a profession.

Chapter 1

What Is CustomerCentric Selling?

What is this book about, and how can you use it to your benefit?

The main focus of this book is helping individuals and organizations involved in sales to migrate from one kind of selling to another. Specifically, we seek to help people move from traditional sales techniques to "customercentric" selling behavior. We believe that our methodology—CustomerCentric Selling—can help you become more customercentric, and therefore more successful.

We are in the sales process, messaging, and training business. The ideas in this book are the result of many years of field testing—first as salespeople ourselves, then at multiple levels of sales management, and subsequently as principals in a firm that teaches our methodology to our clients.

As teachers, we work with all levels within our client organizations. We teach chief executive officers (CEOs) how to own and shape their customers' experience. We teach sales executives how to define and manage their revenue engines. We teach marketing executives how to own and manage their content and create Sales-Ready Messaging. We teach first-line sales managers how to assess and develop the talent of their salespeople, manage a sales process, and build a quality pipeline. Last—but certainly not least—we teach salespeople customercentric behavior. In doing so, we focus on how to influence the words sellers use when developing buyer needs for their offerings.

What Is CustomerCentric Behavior?

What is this customercentric behavior? It has eight basic tenets. These are summarized in Table 1.1 and are explained in order in this first chapter. As you read these descriptions, we invite you to imagine a spectrum of selling behavior ranging from traditional on one end to customercentric on the other. Try to locate yourself on that spectrum. Are you where you want to be, to be as successful as you can be?

If not, what needs to change?

1. Having Situational Conversations Versus Making Presentations

Traditional salespeople rely on making presentations, often using applications like PowerPoint. Why? Because they believe that this approach gives them the opportunity to add excitement, in the form of highly polished graphics, animation, and so on. It gives them the opportunity to turn down the lights and increase the dramatic effect of their presentations.

In selling, we find that conversations are far more powerful than presentations. And yes, it is possible to converse with audiences using PowerPoint—as opposed to presenting to them—but it is far more difficult. Have you ever had a conversation with a friend or a colleague that was based on a pre-scripted slide show? Of course not. So it shouldn't be a surprise that when senior executives see salespeople enter their offices with a laptop under their arm, many roll their eyes and sneak a peek at their watches.

Traditional	CustomerCentric
Make presentations	Converse situationally
Offer opinions	Ask relevant questions
Focus on relationships	Focus on solution
Gravitate toward users	Target businesspeople
Rely on product	Relate product usage
Compete to stay busy	Compete to win
Close on the seller's time frame	Close on the buyer's time frame
Attempt to sell by	Empower buyers to
• Convincing/persuading	• Achieve goals
• Handling objection	• Solve problems
• Overcoming resistance	• Satisfy needs

Table 1.1 Focus on Solutions

In the same way, when they are making sales calls, how often do sales-people dominate by doing the majority of the talking? The salesperson has his or her own agenda of what they would like to accomplish. Good conversations require both parties to actively participate and exchange ideas. Sellers that do a great deal of telling and sharing opinions to have buyers draw the desired conclusions can be viewed as trying to manipulate buyers.

Here is the issue: *In order to be effective, a salesperson must be able to relate his or her offering to the buyer in a way that will allow the buyer to visualize using it to achieve a goal, solve a problem, or satisfy a need.* This, in turn, requires a conversation. For a variety of reasons, though, only a small percentage of salespeople are able to converse effectively with buyers, especially executives and decision makers.

CustomerCentric Selling has been designed to help you engage in relevant, situation-specific conversations with decision makers, without having to depend on canned slide presentations. In short, we can help you become more effective.

2. Asking Relevant Questions versus Offering Opinions

Traditional salespeople offer their opinions to their buyers, while customercentric salespeople ask relevant questions. It is far more comfortable for buyers if sellers focus on asking versus telling. This allows buyers to steer the direction of sales calls based upon their responses. It also allows them to draw their own conclusions.

Another potential issue occurs when sellers come to a vision of a solution to their buyer's goal or problem before their prospective buyer does. When a traditional seller sees the solution, he or she tends to project that vision onto the buyer, saying things like, "In order to deal with that problem, you will need our seamlessly integrated software solution."

But, meanwhile, what's happening on the other side of the table? Very often, the prospective buyer is thinking something along the lines of, "Oh, yeah? Do we now? Says who?"

People don't like their loved ones telling them what they need, much less a salesperson. Most people, when in the role of a buyer, resent it when sellers try to control or pressure them.

People love to buy but hate feeling sold. We have found that top-performing salespeople use their expertise to frame interesting and helpful questions, rather than to deliver opinions. Asking questions shows respect for the buyer. When buyers come to grips with a series of intelligent questions—questions that are on point and that can be answered, and the answers to which build toward a useful solution—they do not feel that they are being sold.

3. Solution-Focused versus Relationship-Focused

Traditional sellers are relationship-focused, and customercentric sellers are solution-focused.

If the seller does not understand how the buyer will use his or her offering to achieve a goal, solve a problem, or satisfy a need, he or she really has no choice but to fall back on relationships. Why does this happen? In many cases, the answer lies in the training that the salesperson receives. Most sales organizations commission their product marketing department to teach salespeople about their products.

Not surprisingly, the result is a sales force that can tell you all about the esoteric features of their products but can't tell you how the products are used or how buyers can benefit from them. And the rare product marketers who do understand the uses of the products tend to have that understanding at the day-to-day user level, not the decision-maker level.

Salespeople who are not trained to initiate a dialogue with decision makers about product usage tend to gravitate toward focusing on their relationship with their buyers. Many traditional salespeople have convinced themselves over the years that the seller with the strongest relationship will win. And in situations where the seller is selling a product to a repeat buyer—where there are no differentiators other than relationships—we agree. But in situations where the buyer is attempting to achieve a goal, solve a problem, or satisfy a need, we disagree. Under those circumstances, the successful seller has to do far more than simply cultivate relationships. Given a choice of having a buyer like us or respect us, we'd opt for the latter. Certainly the two are not mutually exclusive, and after you earn a buyer's respect, there is a high probability that a strong relationship can be established.

4. Targeting Businesspeople versus Gravitating toward Users

Traditional salespeople gravitate toward the users of their products, while customercentric salespeople target business decision makers.

The strength of traditional salespeople lies in talking about their offerings, and users are the group most likely to be interested in or tolerate this approach. Note that selling to the users is not the same as selling to a decision maker in a way that allows that individual to visualize the usage of the product to achieve a goal, solve a problem, or satisfy a need. In order for salespeople to have the confidence to engage in a conversation with businesspeople, they must be prepared to engage in business conversations. A business conversation should be usage- and results-oriented, rather than feature-oriented. It focuses on why the offering is needed; how it can be used to achieve a goal, solve a problem, or satisfy a need; and how much it costs to use versus the benefits it presents.

Most selling organizations give their salespeople "noun-oriented" product training—that is, a great deal about the product's features but very little about how it is used in day-to-day applications. Not surprisingly, when these organizations hire salespeople, they are most comfortable gravitating toward people who are able to understand the product on that level—that is, as trained users—and then reinforce that perspective. In other words, it's a vicious cycle: a suboptimal selling structure perpetuating itself.

This cycle can be broken. As you will see throughout this book, CustomerCentric Selling maps out how marketing departments can make the transition from product training to product-usage training by creating Sales-Ready Messaging for targeted conversations. This approach enables and empowers traditional sellers to target businesspeople and engage in customercentric conversations.

5. Relating Product Usage versus Relying on Product

Customercentric conversations take place when sellers are able to relate conversationally with their buyers about product usage. Traditional salespeople—working for traditional organizations and using traditional product marketing approaches—have no choice but to rely on their product to create interest. They educate their buyers about products, assuming that the buyers can figure out for themselves how they would use them.

In some special circumstances, this strategy works—but only for a while. Here's a scenario you may recognize: A technology company introduces a hot new product. It finds a guru to endorse the technology, writes a white paper full of snap and sizzle, hires a good PR firm, and wows a couple of technology trade shows. Sales take off.

But how much actual selling took place in this scenario? Were the salespeople helping potential customers visualize how they could achieve a goal, solve a problem, or satisfy a need by using the new technology? Or was this a case where the early-market buyers were sufficiently smart and innovative to figure out their own product usage, through (or even despite) having a traditional product presentation?

So sales take off, and the people at the technology company come to believe that they are superior sellers and marketers. Then, mysteriously, sales plummet. What's happening here? Geoffrey Moore's insightful book *Crossing the Chasm* (2002) and subsequent books highlight the difficulties that technology companies face when they run out of Innovators and Early Adopters. The self-sufficient buyers—those who didn't need effective selling—have come and gone, and there is no one in line behind them.

We are frequently hired by companies that have fallen into this chasm. They have exhausted the supply of Innovators and Early Adopters, and now they have to figure out how to find a new kind of prospect—that is, targeted buyers who don't know that they need the offering and don't have a vision of how they would use it.

Where traditional sellers fall short, sellers who are customercentric succeed. This book will help you and your organization become customercentric. It will give you a framework for creating Sales-Ready Messaging (that is, product-usage messaging) that will enable your traditional salespeople to evolve and become customercentric sellers.

6. Competing to Win versus Competing to Stay Busy

Traditional salespeople and their organizations focus heavily on quantity rather than quality when building pipelines. Salespeople may avoid asking tough qualification questions, fearing that the buyer may decide not to proceed with their evaluation. The challenge lies in failing to ask these questions and as a result, buyers may decide to do business with another vendor or decide to make no decision because they never were qualified.

"Winners never quit and quitters never win" is an expression sales organizations use to justify attempts to hang onto every opportunity in the pipeline. Traditional sellers embrace this expression, yet deep down there is a more valid reason for their approach. If they were to disqualify a sizeable opportunity, they would have to proactively find another opportunity to replace it. If a seller is unable or unwilling to prospect for new opportunities, they will have a hard time deciding to walk.

Superior sellers enjoy two major advantages when it comes to disqualification. By initiating buying cycles at higher levels, they find that those buyers do not want to waste their time nor their staff's time. Therefore, it has to be a mutual decision that allocating resources is worthwhile. Competent salespeople also place a high value on their time and recognize early signs that they don't have a fair chance at winning and decide to withdraw.

Companies focus on their cost of sales, but we suggest taking a slightly different approach to realize the expense of going the distance and losing. If you subtract your average win rate from 100 percent and multiply it by your total cost of sales, you will have a different figure: the cost of competing and losing.

To sum up the difference as it relates to allocating time, consider that an unsolicited RFP (request for proposal) gets delivered to salespeople from two different companies. The first is a "B Player" who anxiously reads it, decides it looks like a good fit (despite the fact that another vendor wired it), and willingly spends hours to respond with a win rate below 5 percent. But when an "A Player" receives the RFP, he asks for access to the buying committee and if denied, he will most likely decide not to submit a bid. The time spent by the B Player responding and losing could be used to find better (more winnable) opportunities.

7. Close on the Buyer's Timeline versus the Seller's Timeline

Suppose you know a salesperson who has been working on a major opportunity for the last three months. You ask when he believes it will close, and he provides a date. Let's also assume you know the buyer or the decision maker and have the ability to ask her when she believes they may be ready to buy, and she provides a date. Whose date do you think will be earlier? Our bet would be that the seller's date would be sooner.

Salespeople and sales organizations are under pressure to not only deliver revenue but to do it on a monthly, quarterly, and annual basis. This often causes close dates to be based upon when the vendor wants or needs the order without regard for when the buyer will be ready. This causes potential issues because when asked for an order before being ready to buy, the decision maker will feel pressured. If the seller pushes too hard, he or she can lose the sale. Often the best result is getting the order, but only after the seller offers a discount to motivate the buyer to order sooner than desired. Frantic quarterly or year-end closes smack of traditional selling. If done on a regular basis, buyers may purposefully delay decisions until the end of a month or quarter.

Wouldn't it make more sense to incorporate how and when the buyer wants to buy? Few A Players have the ability to look at an opportunity as a buy versus a sales cycle; if they did, sellers would see a way to merge the needs of a buyer to make a decision in conjunction with what a seller needs in order to make a detailed recommendation. Those steps can be agreed upon, so that both parties can reach a mutual deadline. This also gives a buyer or buying committee some control over the process.

8. Empowering Buyers versus Attempting to Sell Them

During our workshops geared toward salespeople, we conduct an interesting exercise. We ask participants to take out a blank sheet of paper and pretend that they are the authors of their own dictionaries. Then we ask them to define *selling*.

We're always astounded at the perceptions that salespeople have of their own profession. For example, they define "selling" as convincing, persuading, getting someone else to do what you want, handling or overcoming objections, taking at least five no's before giving up, negotiating to get what you want, and—of course—the big one: closing. ABC—always be closing. Close early! Close often!

Looking at this list and thinking about the mindset behind it, it's no wonder that most people—even salespeople—do not like being approached by salespeople.

We also work with buyers, and when asked to describe salespeople, most buyers use terms like aggressive, insincere, pushy, manipulative, over-familiar, prone to exaggerate, poor listeners, and so on. When asked to boil these negatives down to one word, the number one response we get from buyers is *pressure*. When buyers deal with sellers, they feel pushed, manipulated, and pressured into doing things that they end up wishing they hadn't done.

These preconceptions are traps. If sellers are going to avoid them, they will have to learn to sell differently. Their concept of selling will have to be reframed so that it becomes customercentric (again, empowering buyers to achieve their goals, solve their problems, or satisfy their needs). This is not all that difficult to accomplish. Why do we say that? Because we have taught thousands of self-declared "non-salespeople" how to sell. By non-salespeople, we mean people who do not want to think of themselves as salespeople in the traditional sense—engineers, accountants, lawyers, consultants, scientists.

Think about the engineer, who is a non-salesperson, for example. Engineers love to help people solve problems. By and large, engineers do not want to behave like traditional salespeople, but when the concept of selling is reframed, they are very happy serving as customercentric salespeople. By no means can all engineers be taught to sell, but there are a number of them who have a positive mindset, have few preconceived notions, and are open to the challenge. One of the biggest obstacles with bright, well-intentioned engineers is to break them of the habit of telling buyers what they need (despite the fact they are usually right) and get them to slow down and remember to ask buyers questions so they can arrive at their own conclusions.

We believe a seller's objective, going into a new relationship with a buyer, should be to help the buyer achieve a goal, solve a problem, or satisfy a need—and then be prepared to leave if the seller doesn't believe the prospect can be empowered to accomplish one of those goals. This may sound like only a small shift away from a traditional sales approach, but in fact, it's fundamentally different. Imagine yourself as a buyer. Wouldn't you rather have a meeting with someone who had that customercentric attitude, rather than the mindset of a traditional salesperson?

Even the A Players Can Improve

Over our careers, we have met a number of truly gifted A Players, or natural salespeople. They make it look easy. On a consistent basis, they achieve 200-plus percent of quota, though most of them cannot define what makes them successful. We estimated that only about 10 percent of salespeople were intuitive A Players. A 2008 survey performed by Sales Benchmark Index showed that on average within organizations 13 percent of the salespeople generate 87 percent of the revenue. With a statistical basis we've concluded 13 percent of sellers qualify as A Players.

If you look back at the eight tenets we have just made, these A Players are consistently customercentric, following the first six measures. This is why A Players are successful.

But in our experience, even these A Players have room for improvement for the seventh and eighth tenet. Most A Players believe (like their less skilled peers) that selling is convincing, persuading, and so on. So we believe even the most gifted sellers can become more customercentric. We believe the key to an A Player's success as a sales manager is to first become consciously customercentric. CustomerCentric Selling, as explained in this book, is designed to help all sellers assess where they are and to give them a specific methodology to help them become more successful.

The eighth comparison is one that is more difficult to implement unless organizations embrace the concept. While we would be naïve to say that companies won't have any tight wire acts at the end of a quarter, it shouldn't be the norm. Later in the book, we'll show a way for sales managers to project a buying cycle to get an early warning of a potential shortfall. We'll also show how to negotiate buying cycles with buying committees so that potential closing dates projected become more accurate.

Chapter 2

HUMAN BUYING BEHAVIOR

If vendors or salespeople are going to be customercentric, it is important that they understand how human beings make buying decisions. As with air, water, food, and shelter, humans also have an innate need for control. When buying, people have a sense of control over the process as they set a budget, determine their needs, and take action to satisfy them. In stark contrast, when a person is being sold to, a financially incented salesperson is attempting to convince, persuade, or influence a buying decision from that person. Most buyers at some point have been taken advantage of, manipulated, and pressured while being sold. For that reason, they don't want to allow the seller to be in control. They want to minimize the seller's influence on their requirements and buying decisions.

We would like to share some insights into human buying behavior with you. In 1979 Mike Bosworth, a cofounder of CustomerCentric Selling and author of the 1994 book *Solution Selling: Creating Buyers in Difficult Selling Markets*, was working for Xerox Computer Services (XCS). As a small division of Xerox ($120 million in sales, 100 new business reps, 20 managers), XCS wanted to implement a sales methodology and hired Neil Rackham as a consultant to support those efforts.

Rackham was an experimental psychologist who had been working with companies such as Xerox and IBM to develop new sales models based on research that measured differences in behavior between high performing and average performing salespeople in the way they related to buyers.

At Xerox, Rackham and his team had observed over 1,500 sales calls to identify seller behaviors that resulted in positive reactions from buyers. During this research they developed models of what made individual sales calls successful. Xerox had been using these models to train their divisions that sold copiers, fax machines, training services, and work processors.

Ultimately, XCS struggled to implement the new process. The reason? XCS was selling a disruptive technology—hosted first-generation material requirements planning (MRP) systems. Most buyers in the manufacturing market had no clue about the breakthrough capabilities that XCS was offering. The XCS sale was considerably more complex that the average copier sale.

Shifting Buyer Concerns

Over dinner, Neil and Mike discussed these difficulties. Neil shared what he had learned from his research into long cycle sales in Xerox and other corporations. He shared with Mike the four factors that he had found to be important to buyers during buying cycles. He had discovered that as buyers went through the three phases of a buying cycle that he defined, the importance of those factors varied. This is shown in Figure 2.1, which we'd like to describe in detail for you. Incidentally, at the time of this conversation, neither Rackham nor Bosworth was well known in the selling world. Mike Bosworth went on to develop Solution Selling, incorporating this chart into his work, while Neil Rackham was to become widely known for his books, including *SPIN Selling* and *Major Account Sales Strategy*, both published by McGraw-Hill.

The factors are needs, cost, solution, and risk. Cost is the only one that changes, as price is determined toward the end of the buying cycle. We'll explain why that change occurs when we describe Phase 3. The curves on the y-axis show the relative importance of each of these factors. The x-axis shows the passage of time during buying cycles. The graph is confusing at first glance, so we felt using a common B2C (business-to-consumer) buying example would clarify the concepts for you. After that explanation, we'll relate these buying curves to how B2B (business-to-business) buying decisions are made.

Let's start with an example with which most are familiar: buying a car. For most people, this purchase represents a major expenditure. Let's assume a young couple is about 90 days away from having what they hope will be the first of three children. Both drive older compact cars, and it has become

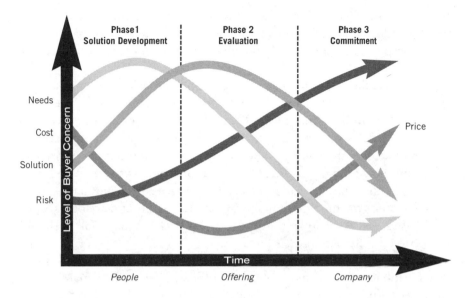

Figure 2.1 Shifting Buyer Concerns*

*Based on the research of Neil Rackham

clear that a larger vehicle is going to be necessary. Let's now walk through the stages that buyers go through.

One of the first decisions is to establish a budget that the couple feels is affordable. While they've enjoyed the benefit of two incomes, that will not be the case for at least two to three months after the child is born, so spending money at this point is an issue. Ultimately, they determine what they can afford, taking into account the value of the car that will be replaced. Cost is one of the first things that is agreed upon, and in the graph, it is a high priority early in Phase 1. After establishing a budget, a couple's needs are discussed, which includes things like number of passengers, safety, fuel economy, reliability, styling, number of cylinders, and so on. These requirements reflect the type of vehicle that can be bought, taking into consideration the amount the couple has budgeted. Phase 1 concludes when the couple has their requirements list and budget. During this phase, "risk" is very low because the buyers are just considering the possibility of buying a new car. The "solution" is ranked low in importance because they can't look for a match until their needs have been established.

Let's assume that early in Phase 2 the couple starts to visit showrooms. A competent salesperson would start by learning what the couple's specifications and budget were. If their expectations were well beyond what their budget was, a conversation would have to take place about either increasing the budget or lowering the requirements. Once those two variables are set, a competent salesperson should only show vehicles that are a relatively good match.

In Phase 2 the solution (match to the couple's needs) is of utmost importance. Virtually every car they look at is being compared to their requirements. It should be noted that in Phase 2, needs might change based on what the buyers see. For example, they might have specified a cloth interior, but then they might see a vehicle with leather and feel it not only looks better but may be more resistant to inevitable spills with small children. The "solutions" they see can influence or change their requirements. Risk is on the rise as the thought of making a financial commitment looms. During Phase 2 cost is the lowest priority, as every vehicle they look at should be approximately within their budget.

After looking at what they feel is a sufficient number of vehicles, the conversations now become comparing to determine the best match given their needs and budget: "What about the minivan?" "I liked it, but. . . ." It is rare for buyers to find everything they're looking for while staying within their budget. Trade-offs become necessary, and after deliberation, Phase 2 ends when the couple agrees on the best option: "You know, honey, the Ford Edge is about 95 percent of what we're looking for and about 110 percent of what we budgeted. I think it is the best vehicle for us." If an agreement is reached, the Edge becomes the vehicle they intend to buy.

Only one vehicle, the one the couple is most positive about, makes it into Phase 3. Before making a final decision, the couple wants to have one more look. At this point their relationship with the salesperson, assuming he or she has been helpful so far, changes. They'd prefer the seller let them see the car another time by themselves. Some people say the reason is that prospective buyers want to talk privately. The primary reason is that once the couple enters Phase 3, the seller has earned the right to close this couple and they don't want to be pressured into such an important decision. They prefer to make their buying decision without being influenced by the seller.

Before making an offer, the couple goes through a risk phase. They suddenly go negative on the vehicle they are most positive about. They worry about resale value, whether they'll get the mileage they'd hoped for, if they can get financing. They may question whether this is the right time to buy a vehicle, as they can just keep driving their current cars, at least for a while. They haven't gone through these concerns with any of the other cars they looked at. If the couple gets through this initial risk, their focus shifts.

For the couple, cost now becomes viewed as price. Cost is what they can afford to pay. Price is what they want to pay. So if the sticker price is $34,595, the couple tries to determine how low they should make their initial offer. At this stage as well, they recognize it is in the salesperson's best interest that the car sells at the highest price possible because that means the highest commission will be earned. The couple offers $30,000, and after going back and forth, the final negotiated price is $31,500.

It is important that risk is overcome before price concessions are made. Let's say the couple expresses concern that a minivan only seats five rather than seven passengers. If the seller's response is a lower price, it would actually validate the buyers' concern. For that reason, negotiation should take place only after buyers overcome risk.

We hope this example helps you validate the buying curves as they relate to how buying decisions on cars are made. The research indicates that people go through this process in making nearly all buying decisions: houses, cars, new computers, and even ordering from a menu. How often are your last two hurdles before ordering filet mignon risk (cholesterol) and, if you pass that hurdle, the price ($34)? We'd like to now apply the buying curves to enterprise sales.

In Phase 1 a buyer's needs are of paramount importance. They rank high to start, and their importance increases through the middle of Phase 1. The advantage of being the first vendor (Column A) is that you have an opportunity to influence the buyer's requirements with a bias toward your offering. Note that the importance of cost lessens as buyer needs are developed. When buyers begin to see potential value as the seller discusses and diagnoses their current situation, concerns about cost lessen.

This supports the psychology behind a major sales blunder. Almost every seller knows or has been told (if not shown how) not to lead with product. Early in Phase 1 if the seller makes the mistake of mentioning product, the buyer's very next question will often be "How much does it cost?" The seller's mistake means he or she faces some unattractive choices, as listed below:

1. Deflect the conversation elsewhere but run the risk of appearing slick.
2. Give a low number so the buyer isn't scared off.
3. Give a best-guess estimate.
4. Explain that it is early and it is necessary to better understand the buyer's requirements. If the buyer persists, give a range or "not to exceed figure" that will likely be higher than the final quote.

In any event, premature price discussion distracts a buyer from determining if the seller's offer is one that should be considered. Without establishing value, almost any figure will seem high to the buyer. The longer a seller can defer pricing and establish value by helping them through a thorough diagnostic process, the less price-sensitive the buyer will be, as shown in the "Cost" curve in Phase 1. Often, the more complex, expensive, or intangible the product or service being offered is, the more it becomes necessary to identify and interview others within the organization who will have a role in making the decision. Research has shown that the average enterprise buying decision now requires approval at least two levels above where it was made only five or six years ago. In other words, a decision that was made at the division controller level in 2004 now likely has to make its way to the chief financial officer (CFO) or, in some cases, the CEO. In a B2B sale, Phase 1 ends when a buyer and the other key players who will be involved in the decision process know their requirements, and have a good idea of the cost. Table 2.1 shows the requirements if there is a seller driving the evaluation, and in many cases, other vendors (B, C, etc.) have not yet been involved. As you can imagine, at this stage Column A enjoys a huge advantage and should win the majority of opportunities at this stage.

Requirements	Column A	Column B	Column C
————	————		
————	————		
————	————		
————	————		
————	————		
————	————		
————	————		
————	————		
————	————		

Table 2.1 Evaluation Driven by the Seller

During Phase 2 the most important issue for buyers is finding a "solution," or a match to their requirements. Proof (demonstrations, reference visits, white papers, etc.) becomes important during this phase because buyers want to verify that the expectations the seller has set for the offering are realistic. As with the couple deciding on a leather versus a cloth interior, things buyers see in offerings can alter what they feel is needed and change the requirements list. This is also a time when the buyer would entertain the need to consider some competitive alternatives. The seller whose offering best matches the buyer requirements is what we refer to as Column A. Risk starts to increase as a buyer evaluates alternatives, cost is not an issue provided there is potential value, and other vendors are in the ballpark. If price had been a showstopper, the buying cycle should not have progressed to this point.

Phase 2 ends when the buyer (or buying committee) chooses what is believed to be the best alternative. If you're fortunate to be their choice (Column A), you may encounter a buyer behaving differently than before. A buyer may raise risk items (resale, actual mileage, etc.) and go negative on the offering and vendor they feel is the best alternative. Risk is typically only seen by Column A and is a positive sign that indicates the buyer is seriously considering buying your offering.

Sellers often misinterpret this change in behavior and panic. They see a buyer who has been very positive throughout the buying process who suddenly starts challenging what has been proposed. Sellers could assume these sudden concerns indicate that another vendor has gained favor. This can cause sellers to react in ways that can cost them a sale that was theirs to win. Some sellers try to address risk objections that they can't control (concerns about the economy, whether this is the right time, etc.). These efforts can compromise the seller's credibility and actually heighten risk. The absolute worst thing a seller can do is to start discounting. At this stage, buyers aren't concerned about cost; they are concerned about whether they will achieve what they want with the offering. Discounting actually validates a buyer's risk and is analogous to throwing gasoline on a smoldering fire. The sad thing is that buyers only show risk to Column A (the only vendor they are about to buy from), and at that point misbehaving can cause a seller to lose a sale.

A strange thing happens if the buyer successfully overcomes risk and becomes ready to buy. At this point, the person the seller saw that was confused and undecided about pulling the trigger has a sudden personality change. Once past risk, price now becomes the issue, and they will beat the seller like a rented mule to get the best possible deal.

As shown in Table 2.1, during Phase 1, people (sales and support staff) are the most important influencers. During Phase 2, the offering, your "solution," is the star of the show, as the buyer has to verify in some fashion that the capabilities discussed can be delivered. In Phase 3 the company becomes important. Buyers are more comfortable doing business with companies that have a strong track record and balance sheet. Smaller companies or start-ups need a significant price/performance advantage when competing with perceived industry leaders, especially for mainstream market buyers.

By understanding this behavior, sellers can better align with buyers and be more customercentric. Let's see how this can put an objection in clearer perspective. First, try to determine where the buyer is in the buying phases. An objection means different things depending on where the buyer is:

- A Phase 1 objection means the buyer is trying to determine if a feature is needed.
- A Phase 2 objection means the buyer is wondering if that feature will work in his or her environment.
- In Phase 3 an objection can be used as a negotiating ploy. The buyer could highlight a competitor's feature to highlight an area where your offering is not as strong.

Please note in Table 2.2 that the buyer's requirements are oversimplified in that it may not represent a committee's view. It is likely that different committee members may have different Columns A's for different reasons. In these cases the best strategy is to own the requirements list for the higher levels in the committee, as often subordinates find a way to support the choice of the senior executive.

Committee sales (whenever more than one person is involved) are also challenging. If you have a three-person committee of equals with one buyer wondering what he or she needs (Phase 1), another wondering which vendor is the best choice (Phase 2), and the third concerned about what can go wrong if they choose Column A (Phase 3), that opportunity may not be closeable at that point. It is important to take committee members through the buying phases together if at all possible, and we'll discuss an approach to doing that in a later chapter.

Vendors Are Part of the Problem

Companies seem to be unaware of human buying behavior. It may be that their main focus is selling and closing deals. Such companies fail to step back and realize that their selling process doesn't provide a positive buying experience. There are specific places where companies start to steer salespeople down the wrong path:

- By failing to redefine and view the role of a salesperson as a buying facilitator rather than a pushy seller, they perpetuate the tension between buyers and sellers.
- Toward the end of a month, a quarter, or a year, tremendous pressure is exerted on salespeople to deliver top-line revenue. Sellers who are asked to do whatever they have to do to close orders before a dead-

line have a good chance of misbehaving. How do you think the buyer is going to feel with high-pressure closing and a sudden barrage of discounting?

- Executive buyers despise "spray and pray" sales calls, and yet the product training that is provided to salespeople leads them in that direction.
- Companies offering traditional sales training are in conflict with how buyers buy.

In implementing customer relationship management (CRM), one of the first steps is defining the milestones in a vendor's selling process. Companies that fail to align these steps with how their buyers want to buy are attempting to impose their sales process on every opportunity. The Buyer's Curve defined human behavior that slowly evolves over time. It assumed in B2B selling situations that sellers were able to talk or meet with buyers during Phase 1 before requirements had been established. The research is still valid, but given the technology available, it is necessary to understand that buyers leverage the Internet on an ever-increasing basis. The result is that in many initial encounters, buyers have navigated Phase 1 without talking with any salespeople. These buyers are already in Phase 2 and want to be treated as knowledgeable buyers, as we'll discuss in the next chapter.

Chapter 3

POWER TO THE BUYERS

Since the publication of the first edition of *CustomerCentric Selling*, significant changes in buying approaches and behaviors have evolved. As people who believe selling can and should be an honorable profession, it is discouraging to realize that the perceptions of salespeople haven't improved much over the last 50 years. Perhaps this explains why recent changes in the selling landscape are in response to new buying behaviors. This presents a challenge to sales organizations. Those that can better align with these new buying approaches will enjoy a sustainable, competitive advantage.

The primary reason the perception of salespeople has not improved is because B2B vendors have refused or failed to abandon their traditional beliefs—the belief that selling involves convincing and persuading buyers. As early as children can talk, they resist being convinced, and even resent being persuaded about almost anything. What makes vendors believe adult buyers will be receptive to this approach? This traditional view of selling lays the foundation for confrontation, rather than collaboration when buyers and sellers interact.

Traditional sales training reinforces the negative stereotype by teaching sellers the approach to manipulate buyers. Salespeople see posters and hear phrases that support this notion:

- Selling begins when the buyer says no.
- Every buyer objection is a selling opportunity.

- Overcome or handle buyer objections.
- Assume the buyer is going to buy.

The ABCs of selling: Always Be Closing Sellers are led to believe they can talk buyers into (or out of) almost anything. That summarizes the essence of what is wrong with the traditional view of selling.

This attitude directly conflicts with the fact that human beings prefer to buy. Buyers view selling as something that is done to them, rather than done with or for them. In fact, most salespeople approach their initial meeting or meetings with the buyer with a focus on "what I want to tell them" rather than "what do I want to learn about them." As we outlined in Chapter 1, salespeople who offer opinions by showing up with and delivering canned presentations create an immediate disconnect, establishing a one-way street to the relationship, which may never go away.

Everyone has had unpleasant interactions with salespeople when they felt oversold, felt pressured into making decisions, or experienced buyer's remorse after the sale was made. It is almost in a buyer's DNA to be distrustful of a salesperson they meet for the first time, unless or until sellers can avoid conducting themselves in a way that reinforces the negative stereotype.

While teaching a workshop a few years back in the Czech Republic, we verified a suspicion we had about the negative stereotyping of salespeople. Before our workshop, we had dinner with the director of sales of a language localization company and we were surprised to learn that selling is a profession held in high esteem in Eastern Bloc countries. Under communist rule, there were no salespeople, meaning that buyers had none of the baggage from unpleasant buying experiences. Until proving they are different than the stereotype, sellers are held responsible for past missteps committed by other salespeople in most parts of the world.

Vendors had high expectations for leveraging technology to improve buyer-seller relationships. Without question, sales has been the business application most resistant to improvement through the use of technology. Significant increases in productivity have been realized in many other applications: accounting, engineering, manufacturing, and supply chain, to name a few.

Returns on B2B company investments in sales force automation (SFA) and customer relationship management (CRM) software have been disappointing. The primary reason is shockingly simple: Technology without a defined and repeatable process merely speeds up the mess. As we'll discuss further in the next chapter, input to CRM systems can be netted by salespeople's subjective opinions of the outcomes of their sales calls. Whether using spreadsheets or CRM software, the quality of the pipeline and ultimate win rates won't vary too much. The primary variable in an opportunity comes down to the salesperson, and is not contingent on whether he or she is using sales automation software.

Executives buying CRM viewed it as a way to have their organizations become more customercentric. We believe the opposite to be true. One of the initial steps in implementing CRM is for vendors to define milestones describing how they want to sell to their customers. According to Robert Schmonsees, over 90 percent of these companies never researched and incorporated their customers' buying processes into their milestones. This means that CRM institutionalizes the way an entire sales force is going to sell to their customers (and make them buy). Ninety-plus percent of CRM implementations look internally and are only concerned with sales cycles, while completely neglecting buying cycles. Organizations that operate in this manner run the risk of being out of alignment with peoples' desire to be empowered to buy. They try to impose their selling approach company-wide with every transaction.

Having been victimized by being oversold for years, buyers may be paying attention to a vendor's disappointment with CRM, experiencing a degree of satisfaction. Sales organizations that try to automate their pipelines bought products that were hyped and oversold to them by salespeople working for sales automation companies. For buyers it is analogous to having the experience of watching a state trooper get a speeding ticket—it's quite ironic.

As SFA began to lose favor with the market based upon a lack of tangible results, a tactic used for manufacturing software was employed: Change the name, add functionality, and increase the hype. Initially launched as MRP (materials requirements planning), this software for manufacturing applications was renamed MRP II and currently is called ERP (enterprise resource planning). Borrowing a page from that precedent, SFA was rechristened as CRM. To be fair, there were extended capabilities that were missing from SFA, but look no further than the name to get a sense of the hype. How in the world is software going to manage relationships? Even if it could, would you want it to?

Speaking of hype, there has been an emerging movement to raise the stakes and hype for CRM software. There are many people that believe the next generation should be named CEM (customer experience management). It is hard to imagine how software is going to help accomplish that goal without capturing and sharing best practices because the buyer experience is so highly dependent upon each salesperson.

The advent of "Software as a Service" (SaaS), pioneered by salesforce.com, made CRM affordable to any organization and greatly reduced both the cost and implementation effort. This contributed to the buying frenzy that lasted for a number of years. Yet, ultimately, the expectations were far beyond what could be achieved. CRM can capture customer inter-actions, capture historical close rates, and make intelligent cross-sell/up-sell suggestions, but it doesn't help salespeople do a better job of selling. A mediocre salesperson supported by CRM will provide results similar to a golfer with a 30 handicap using the most expensive custom golf clubs money can buy.

Vendors have moved their lips but not their feet in wanting to improve the customer buying experience by failing to make the organizational changes necessary to back up that commitment. Many companies just don't know how to go about it. A step in the right direction would be to rede-fine the seller's role to help buyers buy. Another would be to do a mental search and replace. The term "buying cycle" should be used instead of "sell cycle." At least their focus would shift outward toward the buyer.

Buyer-Seller Dynamics

To better understand a buyer's view of selling, imagine a buyer visiting a retail store to buy a new television but having limited knowledge about what's available. A clerk approaches and asks, "May I help you?" Despite desperately needing assistance, the buyer gives the most common answer: "No. I'm just looking." Why do buyers respond this way? They distrust salespeople who haven't demonstrated they are different from the negative stereotype. They don't want their decision influenced by someone who may not have their best interests at heart, though this may be completely untrue in that many sellers make an earnest effort to help you determine what you need. Having said that, everyone who has been burned before carries that experience into each encounter with a new salesperson.

After a frustrating 15 minutes of wandering through the store looking at TVs, you leave more confused and with more questions. How big? LCD? Plasma? DLP? How do I decide which TV to buy? When you return home, a neighbor hears about your experience and gives you a copy of the latest *Consumer Reports* with evaluations and recommendations of new televi-sions. You read the entire article and determine that a 46-inch, LCD, 1080p, JVC television is the best option available for what you want to spend. You are comfortable with your decision because you believe that *Consumer Reports* is a reliable and unbiased source, having no financial stake in whatever decision you make.

Armed with this knowledge, you revisit the same store and are approached by another clerk, who asks, "May I help you?" This time you respond, "Yes. I want to buy a 46-inch, LCD, 1080p, JVC television." Why is your response different from your initial visit? You know what you want and will not have to be subjected to a salesperson's efforts to influence your search. With this knowledge, you view the seller's role as that of a buying facilitator—someone who is going to help you buy what you have already determined best fits your needs. Potential buyer-seller tension is minimized unless the seller tries to talk you out of the decision you've made. Having said that, despite the seller championing your decision for which TV you want to buy, be prepared for the attempted up-sell of an extended warranty.

As with any need, like air, water, food, and shelter, humans have an innate need for control. When buying, people are in control. They set a budget, decide what their needs are, and take action to satisfy them. Buying feels good! Being sold means a financially motivated salesperson is attempting to convince, persuade, or influence your decision. Buyers who have been taken advantage of, manipulated, and pressured in the past don't want the seller to be in control.

Handing Over the Keys

During the early 1990s, if someone wanted to learn about a vendor's offerings or how he or she could improve an aspect of his or her business, the only option was to contact a vendor and schedule a sales call or a presentation to learn about the latest industry trends and offerings. Interaction with a salesperson was a mandatory step to becoming an informed buyer. During the first encounter, the buyer had no predetermined requirements, so the seller had an opportunity to strongly influence the buyer's "solution." Salespeople sometimes made calls with the objective of educating buyers.

That began to change in the late 1990s as the Internet evolved from a scientific resource linking universities and research labs into a commercial communication platform populated by vendor Web sites that made a tremendous volume of information available electronically and, nearly as importantly, anonymously. Increasing Internet speeds allowed downloading of material and, in some cases, full working "trial" versions of their offering that could be reviewed at the buyer's convenience. By visiting a company's Web site, buyers could get a sense of their offerings, markets, and organization. Two issues remained, however:

1. You had to know the names of the vendors you wanted to research.
2. Every vendor made it sound as though they provided great offerings, high quality, and impeccable service. When visiting Web sites, buyers were skeptical about nonfactual information that was being "pushed" to them by vendors.

Search engines led by companies like Google, Yahoo, and Lycos addressed the first issue. Depending on the search terms you enter, in a frac-tion of a second, you had hundreds, thousands, or even millions of potential links to explore, ranked in order of relevance based on your specific needs (i.e., the search terms you entered). The problem now became that of how many of these links should/could be reviewed. You could quickly identify which companies were players in the space you were researching. You could then visit the sites for the vendors you felt were viable. The good news was you didn't have to speak with a salesperson. The bad news is that every vendor's Web site provided opinions of why they were the best choice. Buyers were also aware that vendors were bidding for position with every search engine company.

Blogs and social networking sites are now starting to address the second issue. They have become the electronic equivalent of a B2B *Consumer Reports,* and our experience at CustomerCentric Selling illustrates how they can be leveraged. In 2008, CustomerCentric Selling needed to hire an adult-learning specialist for a project. Rather than use a search engine and then visit multiple Web sites where every consulting group was trying to put their best foot forward, we took a different approach. We described our situation, the scope of the engagement, and the type of consultant we were looking for, and we electronically polled our social networks of trusted people for suggestions and recommendations. We used tools such as LinkedIn and searched public profiles of candidates that may have met our criteria and had the experience we were looking for. We were able to cross-reference their backgrounds with other searches to verify the credibility of their claims.

Within a week, three candidates emerged that seemed to have the background and skills that we required. We had developed our short list of vendors without talking to any of the consultants. Between the references from our network and the descriptions on their Web sites, one candidate appeared to be the best choice. That consultant was called and handled our questions in a professional manner. We asked for three references for work that was done for engagements that were similar in scope to ours. The references checked out, and within two weeks, we had finalized an agreement.

We, the buyer, were in complete control the entire time. The consultants who weren't selected, those who lost, never even knew they were in the game. They would have been contacted if our interaction with our first vendor choice hadn't gone well. In our case, we decided that it didn't make sense to "run a contest" by inviting the others to bid in order to get quotes. Our rationale was that consulting rates didn't vary greatly and time was of the essence. You can see, however, how we could have leveraged the other two consultants who would not have had much chance of getting the business to try to negotiate a better price with our vendor of choice.

Imagine the implications for B2B vendors today. Prospects can visit your Web site, gain insight into your offerings and reputation by leveraging media, including social networking, and even get an idea of how you price your offerings. At that point, the following things can happen:

- You don't make the short list based upon the buyer's perception of your offering, reputation, pricing, support, and so on.
- You are invited to compete, but there is a clear "Column A" that owns the requirements list. Unless your seller can alter the list of buyers' needs, you are merely being brought in for pricing leverage with the vendor of choice.
- You are invited to compete along with some other competitors, where there is no favored vendor.

It is becoming commonplace for potential buyers to electronically poll their trusted communities for input about companies and their offerings. In doing so, they receive firsthand input from buyers relating their buying experience with the salesperson, functionality of the offering, support, reliability, usability, and so on. When salespeople are finally contacted, buyers are already informed about their requirements and available offerings from several vendors. The chances they will be manipulated or oversold are dramatically reduced. Knowledge is power. It has shifted from sellers and into the hands of savvy buyers.

As buying behaviors change, enlightened vendors will take measures to react by adjusting their sales processes. According to Sales Benchmark Index research, World Class Sales Organizations realize significantly higher revenues by shifting their focus from improving their sales processes to empowering buyers. It is necessary to rethink the salesperson's mission during initial meetings, so that they are better aligned with buyers. Because seller involvement comes later in the buying process (no selling has yet taken place), buyers are no longer the blank canvases that they once were with respect to determining their needs or requirements.

While traditional selling was tolerated in the mid-1990s, trying the same approach for knowledgeable buyers is a recipe for disaster. If a seller mentions (tries to sell) features that aren't on a buyer's list of requirements, the buyer senses that he or she is being manipulated. Objections and resistance won't be far behind. The ultimate result is likely to be a poor buyer experience, causing the vendor to be deleted from the short list.

While the research done on Buying Curves (buying behavior and phases) remains valid, the sequencing of the seller's involvement means that initial seller contacts with buyers are different from those that were pre-Internet. Most salespeople are ill prepared to make an initial call to a knowledgeable buyer. Failing to align with these buyers can compromise the buying experience. Now let's apply the Buying Curve to the new way buyers buy. We refer to this as "empowered buying" or "empowered buyers." The major takeaway for you is an awareness of how to better align with this new type of buyer.

Buying: Ten Years Later

The major difference now as opposed to the mid- to late 1990s is that empowered buyers are now able to define their requirements by utilizing technology and most importantly, without speaking with salespeople. Now sellers are denied the luxury of participating during Phase 1; there isn't necessarily any "Column A" salesperson or vendor. The buyer requirements are an aggregate of all the research that the buyer has done on vendors. The buyer requirements table that you saw earlier has now changed to that shown in Table 3.1.

Requirements[1]	Vendor 1[2]	Vendor 2[2]	Vendor 3[2]
————			
————			
————			
————			
————			
————			
————			
————			

[1] An aggregate of capabilities discovered during the buyer's research.
[2] Vendors chosen through social networking and other research.

Table 3.1 Determining Buyer Requirements Using the Internet

The reality today is that the buying experience begins for a particular vendor when a potential buyer accesses that company's Web site or logs into a Webinar hosted by the vendor. The "requirements" list created before talking with a salesperson represents the aggregate of visiting multiple vendor Web sites, looking at blogs, and checking out social networking sites. The buyer can readily get a ballpark figure of what an offering will cost. This means that the buyer has entered Phase 2 of the buying cycle through self-service and is now starting to evaluate vendors to determine which one represents the best buying decision.

Now more than ever, it is important for sellers to engage initial interactions by doing interest qualification to uncover a buyer's self-generated requirements. This validates and respects the research about the vendor that the buyer has already done. It can earn the right for the seller to take the buyer back to Phase 1 and have the buyer modify his or her requirements, but only by establishing competence and then asking questions to help buyers understand why that particular vendor may be needed. Failing to extend the courtesy of learning buyers' self-discovered requirement trivializes their research and reinforces all the negative stereotypes of traditional selling. Later, we'll discuss our approach to interest qualification.

Chapter 4

OPINIONS — THE FUEL THAT DRIVES CORPORATIONS

This is a chapter about opinions: how they are shaped, and how they could be shaped.

Opinions play an all-important role in our personal and professional lives. When you think about it, we rarely make significant decisions without soliciting other people's opinions. At the same time, when we want help in making important decisions, most of us are selective about the people we're going to listen to.

When organizations need to make important decisions, most hire experts to become familiar with their situation and make recommendations. A case can be made that CEOs receive huge compensation packages because of their ability to evaluate situations and formulate opinions—informed guesses that ultimately shape the strategic direction of their companies.

Not everyone's opinion is valued equally, of course. As we proceed down an organization chart, the power of individual opinions to shape company policy decisions sharply drops off. In fact, most organizations have structures in place to ensure that decisions will be made based *only* on opinions that have trickled down (or at least have been signed off) by higher-level people. In a manufacturing company, for example, employees on the shop floor execute procedures and act on decisions shaped by opinions that have been developed by others. Few, if any, decisions about policy are made on the shop floor.

But there is a major exception to this rule: the sales function. Yes, in most cases a business plan is finalized, and specific marketing plans are put into place to execute it. And, yes, for most companies with a sales organization, the revenue plan is broken down into revenue objectives (quotas) for each territory. Yet while salespeople may be given very specific targets to achieve, they are also given enormous latitude when it comes to arriving at opinions, and making decisions, that not only affect the organization's performance but also ultimately shape the customer's experience. How many organizations are salespeople given the latitude to decide the following:

1. How to position their offerings to buyers?
2. Which accounts and titles to call on?
3. Which accounts to include in their pipelines?
4. Which accounts to close and when?
5. How to interpret lost opportunities?
6. Which changes in offerings are needed to improve competitive positioning?

Without realizing it, companies rely on the opinions of traditional salespeople to build a pipeline, create a forecast, and deliver top-line revenue. As it relates to forecasting, imagine how seller estimates of close dates may vary from when the buyers will be ready to buy.

Depending on the specific circumstances, relying upon seller opinions may be exactly the right thing to do—or it may be a complete disaster. The most common reason that new companies fail is because sales does not deliver according to plan (although, of course, the reasons for that failure to deliver may be more complicated). So let's peel the onion and take a closer look at how salespeople form opinions, and how those opinions affect their company's successes or failures.

Who's Responsible for What?

When we ask CEOs a critical question—"Who positions your company's offerings?"—we often hear the same response: "Marketing." This is true in most cases, whether having a direct or an indirect sales organization. In our experience, though, this is a gross oversimplification—to the extent that this isn't a response at all. As a follow-up question, we ask the CEO to consider the following scenario:

Your company makes a major new product or service announcement and trains the entire sales organization on the offering in regional meetings for two days. The following week, your salespeople begin calling on buyers and customers. Let's assume that calls are made by three different salespeople attempting to sell the new offering to the same title and vertical industry, and let's assume that these calls are videotaped. Would someone reviewing those tapes be able to determine whether

1. The same offering was being sold?
2. The salespeople worked for the same company?

At this point, most executives—especially those who have come up through the sales ranks—face a sobering reality that they don't like to dwell on. The burden of positioning offerings, by default, is placed on the shoulders of individual salespeople. This is true no matter how many hours the human resources (HR) department has devoted to carefully creating job descriptions and detailing responsibilities across the entire marketing segment. In the final analysis, many CEOs simply shirk responsibility for their customers' experience—as well as the responsibility to attain top-line revenue targets—and delegate to individual salespeople.

A CEO can safely assume that tactical marketing has responsibility and exerts control over literature, brochures, advertising, Web site content, trade shows, seminars, and so on. But marketing support and the control of the selling process are far more tenuous. At the end of the day, the positioning of offerings boils down to the words and phrases salespeople use when they communicate with potential buyers. So how consistent is the message that is being delivered? Most CEOs, when answering truthfully, have to say, "Not very consistent."

Who's to blame? We now hear from many senior sales executives that marketing has become irrelevant in terms of supporting their selling efforts. According to the American Marketing Association's Customer Message Management Forums held in 2002, between 50 and 90 percent of the material created by marketing to support sales is never used by salespeople. Of course, marketing should not shoulder all the blame for this situation. Part of the problem results from the fact that in many cases, no effective interface between marketing and sales has been defined. In addition, it is virtually impossible to provide effective support if a standard sales process has not been established. Sales is inundated with colorful brochures and glossy case studies, but they are never told where and when to most effectively use them.

We have already discussed how most PowerPoint presentations and glossy brochures provide minimal benefit to salespeople in their efforts to structure conversations with buyers or close business transactions. Much of today's marketing collateral is simply not designed to be used by salespeople while making calls.

Similarly, much of the training provided to salespeople also misses the mark. It is, for the most part, product-centric, not customercentric. We've already seen how traditional salespeople tend to launch almost immediately into a product pitch, without regard for what the buyer may either want or need. Well, cramming a newly hired salesperson's head full of product information points that salesperson down this same exact path—the *wrong* path if the goal is to engage in a customercentric conversation with a buyer. Yes, there is a need for product training, but we believe it should be distinguished from sales training.

Companies that are unable to bridge the gap between tactical marketing and sales have no alternative but to rely on—and be at the mercy of—the opinions of their salespeople. Is that such a bad thing? Well, salespeople are just like doctors, lawyers, electricians, or the members of any other profession:

- 10 percent are exceptional.
- 70 percent are average.
- 20 percent should probably be doing something else.

The small percentage of salespeople that are naturally customercentric are capable of overcoming the lack of marketing support. They are able to resist the temptation to recite verbatim what they have learned during product training. On sales calls, they listen, respond, and ask smart questions to properly position offerings during conversations with their buyers. The question or challenge then becomes, "How is your bottom line affected by traditional salespeople?"

Hiring and Training: Where Selling Begins

Let's examine the hiring and training of new salespeople, explore how offerings get positioned, and see how a series of opinions ultimately rolls up into the CEO's revenue forecast.

Some large organizations have established hiring profiles designed to help them select candidates who possess the skills, intelligence, and personal characteristics to become successful revenue-producing salespeople. Other large organizations prefer to start with a blank canvas; they favor hiring recent college graduates, with the intent of teaching them everything they need to know about the company's offerings, about vertical markets, and about how to sell.

For the companies that hire "smart, experienced salespeople" with proven track records, the investment in training, whether it is time or money, is typically minimal. The assumption is that if we've hired someone with 10, 15, or 20 years of experience, these are "professional" salespeople. Give them a user ID and password for the CRM system and some high-level "training" on the product (usually a PowerPoint overview of technical capabilities delivered by either someone in training or sales support), and cut them loose to go start selling. After all, they've always been successful before, right? Even though they've changed companies every two or three years, that's probably just the result of an unrealistic compensation plan or a change in management. It couldn't possibly be that, after 18 months of either closing or torching every prospect in their territory, they figured out it was easier to start over somewhere else than try to repair the damage that had already been done. Could it?

In the case of the "blank canvas" hire, after an orientation period in the branch office where they will be working, these new hires are often sent to a central location for indoctrination. The length of these sessions can range from a few days to several months, depending on the complexity and number of product offerings. Classroom sessions often run all day, with evening assignments or after-hours case study work also being fairly common. In addition to product training and immersion in their company's sales culture, sales trainees are introduced to corporate policies and procedures, headquarters staff, administrative reporting, and so on.

The primary objective of these sessions, however, is to teach new hires about the company's product and service offerings. Frequently, these corporate training sessions are designed and delivered by a product marketing staff member having limited direct experience with, or even exposure to, customers and salespeople in the field. The focus is more inward ("These are our offerings"), rather than outward ("Here are some ways your customers and prospects could use our offerings to achieve their goals, solve their problems, or satisfy their needs"). Attendees are asked to memorize specifications of different offerings. They learn to deliver canned presentations, perform demonstrations, handle objections, and recite competitors' strengths and weaknesses.

As suggested earlier, such training presents the company's offerings as *nouns*, with a relentless focus on what it is and what it will do. This rarely works. A few years ago, we ran into a salesperson working for a company that sold adhesives. Asking him about his offerings prompted an astounding "core dump" about viscosity, drying properties, resiliency, and so on.

Within the first few seconds of this onslaught, the salesperson had lost our interest, and he didn't seem to be aware of that. He droned on for many more minutes, telling us far more than we ever wanted to know. Finally, he paused to take a breath. Leaping through this narrow window of opportunity, we commented that he had described his products as if they were nouns. We then suggested that he try to discuss his adhesives as if they were verbs.

Give him credit: He gave it a shot. He stepped away from his normal presentation mode (inward focus) and came up with applications of his products (outward focus). He described how some of his customers were using his company's adhesives, which was far more interesting and easier to understand than listening to him drone his way through a laundry list of properties, attributes, and features. And something else interesting happened, too: we had a conversation. No, that conversation could not have been described as scintillating, but as a sales approach, it represented an enormous improvement over his feature-dump approach.

Perhaps because they are aware of (and maybe even feel a little guilty about) the intensely inward focus of their new-hire training, some companies attempt to provide their new salespeople with industry knowledge. These studies of industry segments typically represent a small percentage of the total class time. They often appear to be an afterthought, or filler— a kind of cultural time-out.

During this small percentage of the overall sessions, attendees are exposed to the functions and responsibilities associated with the various job titles within vertical markets. They may be introduced to industry buzzwords and potential buyer hot buttons, both of which they are encouraged to work into their sales calls. Hope springs eternal. The hope is that by using these terms, salespeople will appear to possess industry knowledge— perhaps even expertise—which, of course, should prove useful when the salesperson attempts to relate to the person on the other side of a desk or on the other end of a telephone line.

In our experience, it's a forlorn hope. The new salespeople rarely gain expertise through these truncated, but often intense, industry segments. For them, it's information overload—the equivalent of trying to drink from a fire hose. And even if they're successful at ingesting and regurgitating buzzwords, the potential buyer is rarely impressed. The seller may just be one question away from exposing an underlying lack of understanding of the buyer's business environment. The buyer lives this industry every day. When a salesperson misses by an inch, he or she misses by a mile.

Another difficulty with this overall sales-training approach is that it is not integrated. It presents product, sales, and industry information separately, and leaves all three in separate "silos" of information. Salespeople are thus required to do the integration themselves, and to create a coherent message that they can deliver during sales calls. This is a huge challenge. Even customercentric salespeople can require months in the field to accomplish this integration and convert product knowledge into product-usage knowledge. Think about how wasteful it is for salespeople to learn to achieve this integration and conversion individually and how unreasonable it is to expect traditional sellers to ever get there.

Positioning: The Next Challenge

A product is positioned in the market by how the product is described to potential buyers. Positioning is critical when it comes to the sales process. Although many people harbor a negative stereotype of salespeople, that may be in part because they don't fully appreciate the skills needed to successfully position a product in the mind of the buyer—or the training that lies behind that success.

In the mid-1970s, one of us—fresh out of college—was hired by IBM's General Systems Division. The assignment: to sell first-time computer users on the benefits of migrating from their manual accounting systems to a computerized setup. Most trainees fell into the trap of believing that they were selling hardware and software. It took us a frustrating couple of months to make the leap—to understand that the decision makers we were pitching had little or no interest in learning about computer hardware and software. In fact, the product approach actually frightened some of them. It reinforced all their worst notions about the complexity and general scariness of computers.

On the other hand, if the business owner could be shown reports generated by our systems, and if these reports could be shown to be useful tools for making real-life business decisions, we were home free. For example, seeing an inventory report with items sorted by date of last usage would enable buyers to visualize reducing inventory. Who cared about CPU (central processing unit) processing speeds and disk capacities? The hardware and software needed to be described only as the means to a desired end. Remember that this was IBM, which at that time was considered to be the gold standard in most aspects of business, the company that all the others were imitating. IBM, with all of its vaunted staff, expertise, and experience, was leading its new hires down the wrong path. It was teaching them to position products as nouns rather than verbs.

The problem of effectively positioning products is not limited to new hires. For companies with multiple offerings that are selling into multiple vertical industries, the challenge of positioning offerings becomes formidable, even for the most talented and experienced salespeople.

For example, think about the wide range of people with different job functions a salesperson must communicate with in order to get an enterprise productivity-improvement offering sold, funded, and implemented. In the case of some organizations, this cast of characters can range from technical staff within the information technology (IT) department, through middle management, vice presidents, and all the way up to the CFO and the CEO. Think how different each of these calls should be. Consider, too, how the length of the sell cycle can vary depending on whether the salesperson's point of entry into the buyer's organization is low, middle, or high.

Let's go back to the less experienced salesperson. Imagine that a new hire has completed his or her company's six-month training program and that you have the distinction of being the first buyer (victim?) that he or she is calling on. Picture where this call is likely to head, right after the introductions. Unless the salesperson has rare, innate customercentric sales talent, he or she is likely to jump right into the pitch, regardless of the interests of the buyer sitting across the desk. Most likely, the salesperson is thinking, "Hey, if my company thought it was so important for *me* to understand our offerings, then it must be important for the buyer to understand them as well."

When was the last time a salesperson called on you and took a while before discussing the offerings? Before the salesperson began his pitch, did you indicate any need for the offerings or any reason that you would be a potential buyer? When the salesperson was reciting the features of the offerings, what percentage of them were you actually interested in, or felt could be useful to you?

The answer in most cases, of course, is "a very low percentage." So why do traditional salespeople go this route? Talking about their offerings represents their comfort zone, partly because it was what their company trained them to do. It allows them to feel like experts, and to control the meeting. But leading with features is, in most cases, like driving a car off a cliff. Sure, you're in charge. But do you really want to be in charge of a car crash, or a failed sales effort? Wouldn't it be better to succeed?

Why *Not* to Lead with Features

The irony is that leading with features—operating in the comfort zone, as described earlier—can also cause a salesperson to lose control.

How? Once a specific offering is mentioned, many buyers ask a very logical question: "How much does it cost?" But it's often too early in the conversation to discuss pricing, because goals, problems, potential usage, or value have not been established in the buyer's mind. A stick of gum costs too much, no matter what it costs, if you haven't decided that you want or need a stick of gum.

The traditional sales technique at this point—when price comes up too early—is to attempt to provide waffling kinds of responses ("Your mileage may vary") in an attempt to dodge the question. This can create a negative impression and sometimes causes the seller to conform to the pervasive, unflattering stereotype of a "slippery salesperson." But there's an even worse scenario. Particularly among traditional sellers, there is also a powerful desire to hang onto this buyer at all costs, which can prompt the salesperson to quote unrealistically low numbers. If the sale progresses, the buyer will remember the unrealistically low figure quoted in the initial meeting. Eventually, it can become a barrier to moving toward a buying decision.

Yes, price is a qualifier, and it should be shared with buyers relatively early in the sales cycle. But until the buyer begins to understand the potential usefulness of the product, he or she is very likely to think, "Hey, that seems expensive." And once that conclusion is drawn, the seller faces an uphill battle to regain mind share. While there is no easy way to prevent buyers from requesting information on pricing earlier than the salesperson would like to divulge, discussing the potential use of the product can defer these discussions until later in the sales cycle. If a buyer finds the offering valuable *before* cost is shared or discussed, that price is likely to sound more reasonable when it finally is disclosed.

So again, this makes a case for discussing uses rather than features. But that's rarely what gets discussed in traditional sales calls. Given their training, their enthusiasm, and their formidable quotas, traditional salespeople feel compelled to present each buyer with every possible feature.

Assume a buyer is exposed to 25 product features but needs only five of them. The buyer is very likely to draw the conclusion that the product must be too complicated and too expensive. In other words, it looks like overkill for the buyer's requirements. Buyers will object to having to pay for features that they believe they won't ever use. (No matter that they may be wrong in this; it's what they believe that counts.) Some traditional salespeople have been trained to believe that selling begins after the buyer says no, but the fact is that it's extremely difficult to turn someone around after he or she has voiced an objection about a feature. The traditional school of selling holds that an objection is a selling opportunity. We strongly disagree. Once a buyer has voiced an objection, the salesperson has to get the buyer to change his or her mind, and this is something that most buyers are reluctant to do.

Although traditional salespeople lead with their product features to head off potential objections, they are far more likely to generate these kinds of objections when they take this approach. Part of the problem is a control issue. Who is controlling the conversation? The salesperson? He or she is doing all the talking, and the buyer is in the unenviable position of passively listening. Most human beings like to be in control, and buyers are no exception. In fact, they may be fully accustomed to being in control of most of the conversations they have in the workplace. So they may feel a strong need to seize control of this conversation—and the easiest way to do so is by offering objections. This job is made far easier if a seller generates a tidal wave of features. All the buyer has to do is wait for a bad feature and then pounce with an objection.

Opinions: Right and Wrong

Let's go back to the scenario introduced earlier in this chapter. Let's assume that a new offering is announced and that traditional salespeople from New York, Chicago, and Los Angeles who have been with the company for an average of five years attend two days of training. Their first post-training calls are scheduled for Monday. Each trainee will be calling on the CFO of a manufacturing company.

If these calls were videotaped, would an outside observer realize that all three were selling the same product? Would the observer conclude that the salespeople worked for the same company? What might be the range of expectations in the minds of the three CFOs? Which of these three accounts should become part of the company's pipeline? In whose opinion?

Does it look as though all three are selling the same product? In most cases, as noted, the answer is no. Most likely, the presentation of the company's offerings and the shaping of the discussion with the buyer have been left to the salesperson to figure out. The result is a wide variety of sales approaches (although most will tend to be in the traditional vein).

After training, in many cases misdirected and all too brief, newly hired salespeople are asked to begin volunteering opinions. First, they must condense their understanding of the company's offerings into some format with which they can communicate a coherent message to buyers. This is an opinion. Once that task is completed, they have to analyze their territory—to decide what their target markets are and what titles to call on—and then start filling their pipelines. Again, these steps begin with opinions.

Meanwhile, new hires understand that their honeymoon period is likely to last about 60 days, after which their pipelines must grow. Again, opinions come into play as the salesperson decides what approach to employ: go for quantity of buyers or quality of buyers? Remember, traditional salespeople think quantity; customercentric salespeople think quality. Even if they try to focus on what they feel are qualified opportunities, their judgment may be clouded, and their opinions shaped, by the pressure to show activity.

Within a few more months, they will be required to provide their opinion as to which opportunities in the forecast will close, why they will close, and when. Opinion, opinion, opinion. Is it any wonder that many CRM systems are flawed, at best? Many companies gather information for their CRM system by asking their salespeople to interpret the outcome of their calls. But in many cases, the weakest link in the chain is a salesperson's opinion of what constitutes a qualified opportunity.

Salespeople are also asked to give reasons—opinions—when fading prospects finally must be removed from their pipelines. The most common reasons given are product and price. In most cases, we believe, neither is valid. If "product" is cited as a reason for the loss after a six-month selling effort—for example, "we can't run under Linux "—the salesperson should be asked: "How long did it take you to discover that the buyer needed Linux support? How long did it take you to realize that we don't provide that support?" The hard fact remains that if the product is not a good fit, the opportunity was never properly qualified, and those six months of work were wasted.

And, yes, unless you are selling a commodity like pork bellies, wheat, or gold, price is likely to be a factor in your success (or lack thereof). But we believe it's not always—or even often—the *determining* factor. Buyers tend to use price as an excuse when delivering bad news to salespeople. Think about it. Often, when a salesperson learns that a sale has been lost on the basis of price, he or she asks, "Where do we have to be?" In most cases, the buyer declines to give an answer. Sometimes, this is because the buyer has psychologically closed the door and doesn't want to reopen it. But many times, as noted, price is used as an excuse for turning down a sale, but it was only one of many factors that went into the purchasing decision.

Conversely, if price were the be-all and end-all, vendors could post their prices on the Web and do away with salespeople. Purchasers could make all their buying decisions based solely on price. But they don't—so clearly, other factors are involved.

After a salesperson has competed for months and then lost, the buyer tends to let him or her down easily. One of the easiest ways out is to blame price or product, and most traditional salespeople are happy to take these reasons back to their managers. How many professions have situations where there is one winner and a four-way tie for the silver medal? The real reason most opportunities are lost, however, is that the losing salesperson got outsold.

The odds are high that "I got outsold" or "I should have walked away months ago" will never appear on a loss report (that is, the write-up of a lost prospect). This, in turn, is one of the reasons why most loss reports are exercises in futility. Companies that attempt to direct product development based on loss reports, therefore, are doing the equivalent of driving down the highway by looking through rearview mirrors distorted by the opinions of salespeople.

A while back, we worked with a company that sold software to help manufacturers schedule preventive maintenance on their production equipment. They were one of three or four major players in this particular niche. About a year before we began working with them, they offered only a disk operating system (DOS) version of their product, while two of their competitors had developed Windows support. Predictably, the most common reason cited by the salespeople to explain the loss of sale was because of the product not having the Windows version. In fact, the salespeople complained to the point where the company made the investment, developed the new offering, and withdrew support for the DOS version.

What happened next? The next round of loss reports highlighted the fact that many buyers were still running DOS and couldn't use the new Windows product!

We did an analysis of the pipeline and found two major problems. First, reps were filling their funnels with unqualified opportunities. Second, their opinions about which transactions were winnable, and how they could be won, were simply wrong. The company's strategic direction—to develop a Windows product and to stop supporting the DOS version—was misled by the opinions or the excuses of their salespeople.

Turning Opinions into a Forecast

As you may have surmised by now, opinions permeate throughout most sales organizations. Their importance is magnified when people are asked to predict the future. This barbaric ritual is euphemistically referred to as *forecasting*.

If a salesperson is under the gun—in other words, if he or she is busy and hasn't made much progress with the pipeline—then forecasting is likely to mean spending a few minutes massaging dates, amounts, and percentages from the previous month's report, most likely late in the afternoon on the day the report is due. The poorer a person's year-to-date position against quota, the greater the temptation to inflate the forecast. In such cases, the report should carry a disclaimer patterned after the one on side-view mirrors: "Warning! Objects in forecast may be further away and smaller than they appear."

Salespeople quickly learn that monthly review meetings with their managers go much better when they have lots of accounts listed in their pipelines, making activity look like accomplishment. Because there is no standard way to position offerings, it is up to each salesperson to list the accounts he or she feels are viable. First they persuade themselves of that viability, and then they persuade their managers. By the time they get to this second round of persuasion, they may be quite eloquent in arguing for an opportunity's viability. In fact, if these salespeople could sell to buyers and customers as well as they do to their managers, they would be 200 percent of quota every year!

Sales managers are required to give their opinions of their salespeople's opinions. They are measured in the short term by the aggregate of the pipelines of the salespeople reporting to them. Inevitably, their opinions are influenced by what they want to believe. They want to believe that the opportunities in the pipeline are winnable and that all the salespeople will make their numbers.

The job of sales manager is a very difficult one, and most are subjected to a great deal of pressure to deliver revenue objectives. Salespeople's lives are better if they can either (1) show a strong pipeline or (2) defend a weak pipeline. First-level managers have exactly the same challenge when doing a pipeline review with their managers. For this reason, first-line managers want to believe the yarns being spun by their salespeople.

There's another reason not to stir the pot. If the sales manager is able to poke holes in a rep's funnel for several months in a row, his or her "reward" is to put the salesperson on a performance improvement plan, which in many cases must be overseen by the HR department. Writing and monitoring this plan requires a huge commitment of time and serves as a distraction from the task of achieving branch or district quotas. It is also an unpleasant task to finally realize that a potential hiring error was made.

Ultimately, if the salesperson is unable to achieve the established objectives, he or she will be terminated. Now the manager is faced with the daunting, expensive, and tedious task of recruiting, hiring, and training a new salesperson. Does all of this influence how hard a manager drills down into a given rep's pipeline? We think so. All things considered, it is far easier for managers to believe their salesperson's overoptimistic assessment of the opportunities that are out there, soon to be closed.

The barbaric ritual continues all the way up the chain—from district, to region, to the vice president (VP) of sales. Each level puts its happy spin on the figures and then passes them along. The accuracy of the forecast usually improves over this long journey; the major reason it does so, though, is that the statistical base behind the forecast is getting larger, and this generally leads to a more reliable final result. This forecasting activity happens either weekly (weakly?) or monthly, and culminates with the forecast from the senior sales executive that arrives on the desk of the CFO, who must project earnings for the quarter.

Virtually all companies have become skilled at controlling their expenses, so the largest variable in projecting profitability is top-line revenue. But CFOs have learned from experience not to take revenue projections from sales at face value. In fact, not believing the projected total for a moment, CFOs multiply the gross forecast by a heuristic factor—always less than 1, often written on a scrap of paper and then stuck in their top right-hand drawer—to take some of the sunshine out of the forecast. After making this adjustment, they tell the CEO what the results for the quarter will be, so that he or she can set earnings expectations for analysts and investors.

So, as we've seen, senior executives have good reason to doubt the accuracy of the forecasts they receive. On the occasions where they are accurate, it may be due to offsetting errors. For example, the ABC Company (95 percent probability) did not close, but the DEF Company unexpectedly placed a huge order for add-on business that was never factored into the forecast. The most important revenue number at so many companies turns out to be little more than a piling up of opinions, many of them extracted from people under pressure to protect their jobs. Unless organizations take responsibility for forecasting out of the reps' hands, this key number will continue to be unreliable.

In reality, monthly forecasts can be most useful in serving as potential wakeup calls, alerting salespeople that their pipelines are thin and warning them that they've got to ramp up their business development activities. When the revenue forecast starts looking overly optimistic and it appears that there could be a shortfall late in a quarter, the pressure (internal and external) intensifies. Salespeople are encouraged to close business, often by offering "Hail Mary" discounts. Even if the current quarter is salvaged, though, this can become a vicious cycle, with the pipeline being flushed at every quarter end and then having to be filled from scratch the next quarter.

One of the most difficult aspects of forecasting is projecting when opportunities will close. If a salesperson forecasts the Acme Company to close in September, then in October, and then in November, and it finally closes in December, the forecasting accuracy is 25 percent, even though they got the business. Estimated dates in forecasts reflect when the seller wants or needs the order to close.

Too often, close dates have nothing to do with buyers' agendas, but correspond to sellers' agendas. Under the best of circumstances, closing before buyers are ready is a costly proposition. Pressuring buyers prematurely can cause the seller's organization to either (1) lose the sale or (2) have to offer discounts as an incentive for the buyer to commit before the buyer is ready. In the latter case, if the order doesn't close, the seller can anticipate either having to honor the discount at a later time or having to talk his or her way around it. In fact, according to an article published in *Forbes* magazine in 2001, in the quarter ended September 30, 2000, Computer Associates closed $1 billion of its total $1.6 billion in total quarterly revenue in the last week of the quarter with an average discount of 55 percent.

Organizations spend a significant amount of time forecasting. A great deal of time and effort is spent to create the forecast, and—in months where there is a shortfall—more time and energy may be expended defending the bad numbers and explaining how they were generated in the first place. (These resources should, of course, be devoted to selling, rather than finger-pointing.) And in many cases, after the last dust settles, things return to normal, dates are shifted back, and the process is repeated. The quality of the pipeline remains fairly consistent, still reflecting the (optimistic, undisciplined) opinion of each salesperson.

Many libraries offer amnesty programs to their borrowers, whereby fines on overdue books are forgiven. The books come back, their borrowers are reinstated, and everyone starts with a clean slate. Sales organizations would benefit from the same strategy. They would benefit from getting rid of all the dead wood contained in the pipeline and starting from scratch, without unduly penalizing those who come clean.

One of the most extreme examples of dead wood in a sales funnel emerged during a workshop we taught for a company in Cleveland. We asked what was the longest sales cycle that the company had ever encountered. Without hesitation, the VP of sales answered, "Seven years." Knowing that their average sale was about $50,000, this seemed to be impossible, so we asked a number of follow-up questions. As it turned out, the company had indeed competed for a particular account for seven years. During that period, they actually wrote four separate proposals.

The business was initially awarded to one of their competitors by a decision maker who was comfortable doing business with that vendor. After seven years, that decision maker left to join another company. At that point, in response to a fifth proposal, the buyer switched vendors.

Amazingly enough, during the entire 84 months, this "opportunity" was never removed from the pipeline. We've already suggested the reasons for this. Salespeople take comfort in having a long list of buyers as they set out to convince their manager that things are going to be great and that removing a dead opportunity would create more problems than it would solve. A new prospect would have to be found to replace it. Embarrassing questions would have to be answered. Better to sell your manager on being unrealistically optimistic.

Aiming for Best Practices

As long as there is a system, there will be people who abuse it. This is as true in sales as in any other walk of life. In this book, we want to propose ways to make the scenarios described earlier the exception, rather than the normal course of business.

The concept of "best practices" has been associated with virtually all aspects of business. Sales has been, and remains, the most notable exception. Most senior executives and investment analysts believe that sales is more of an art than a science, and therefore not amenable to a best-practices approach.

We believe this view of selling can be changed—but only after companies provide direction to all their salespeople about how to have conversations with buyers about how to use offerings to achieve a goal, solve a problem, or satisfy a need. Until this happens, companies will continue to be dependent on the opinions of their salespeople in the following areas:

1. How their offerings are positioned to buyers
2. What accounts and titles to call on once given a territory
3. What accounts should be included in their pipelines
4. What accounts will close, why and when
5. What the reasons are for losses
6. What enhancements to offerings are necessary to improve win rates

We have learned from our years of experience in this business that reports are only as good as the quality of the information that goes into them. Consider again the disappointing results that most SFA and CRM systems have delivered with respect to pipeline management. Why? Because the information funneled into these systems consists largely of salespersons' opinions of the outcomes of sales calls they have made. When you factor in the notion that product positioning is left up to individual salespeople, and that they often are under enormous pressure to justify their positioning, you can see how problems are caused and perpetuated.

Automation without improving the process quickly deteriorates the system. In the following chapters, we focus on the kinds of improvements that are necessary to make the sales process more effective.

In closing, consider the misnomer of the term *forecasting*. If that were the objective, CFOs would just take the number they receive from their VP of sales and run with it. We believe that senior executives crave control and preparing weekly or monthly forecasts is a flawed attempt to give them an illusion of control. The fact is that allowing salespeople to forecast gives control to people whose mission is to justify their jobs, not to predict what sales will actually close. Without process, opinions rule and revenue shortfalls are inevitable.

Chapter 5

SUCCESS WITHOUT SALES-READY MESSAGING

After reading the previous chapter, you might be asking, "Aren't some companies successful despite their reliance on the opinions of their salespeople?" The answer, of course, is yes. We learned a long time ago that using the words *always* and *never* in the context of selling techniques is (usually) a bad idea.

Throughout this book, we extol the virtues of what we call Sales-Ready Messaging. Some companies were already succeeding long before this book, and we think there are at least two explanations. The first is that a small number—roughly 13 percent of all salespeople—use a customer-centric approach intuitively. The second is that there are certain market conditions that make success without Sales-Ready Messaging possible. This chapter describes those conditions—and also explains why it is important for almost all companies to migrate toward supporting their salespeople in positioning their offerings. Without doing so, it is difficult to provide a consistent buying experience.

Understanding the Early-Market Buyers

The early success of start-up companies or new offerings can often be attributed to the existence of one or more of the following conditions:

- High percentage of early-market buyers
- Significant price/performance advantage in established markets
- Early successes with recognized industry leaders
- Entry into a hot market space
- A disproportionate percentage of customercentric salespeople (attracted by stock options in start-up situations)
- Strong external factors (Y2K, government regulation, and so on)
- Offerings whose applications are obvious to buyers

Looks like a good list, right? But look again. With the exception of the last item, all of these factors are fleeting. The first condition is a good illustration. What happens when the supply of early-market buyers is exhausted? Because of the "opinions problem" described in the previous chapter, companies may be ill prepared to sell their offerings to mainstream-market buyers, who over the long run buy the lion's share of an offering and ultimately determine if revenue objectives and profitability will be realized.

Geoffrey Moore has authored several books describing stages of market acceptance of offerings, and especially of new technologies. He offers an approach to changing marketing's message as offerings mature. See Figure 5.1. The premise for much of Moore's work is that there are different types of likely buyers at different phases of an offering's life cycle. This may sound obvious and easy to act on, but it isn't. Even if marketing recognizes the need to change its approach and is capable of doing so—two big ifs— how is the message conveyed to the field sales reps?

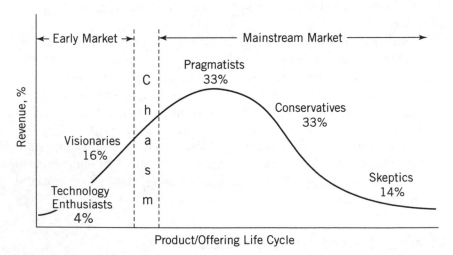

Figure 5.1 Market Acceptance of New Offerings (Geoffrey Moore, *Inside the Tornado*)

We'd like to provide our views of the life cycle of an offering from a *sales* perspective.

The early-market Innovators and Early Adopters are composed of savvy people who are willing and able to buy from companies with a limited track record and/or offerings that few organizations have implemented. In terms of technology, early-market buyers have the ability to visualize usages and view new offerings as potential competitive advantages, if they can implement them early enough in the offering's life cycle.

Why is this interesting to us? Because early-market buyers excel at determining applications for technologies that can give them a return on their investment in those technologies. In other words, they're doing what we contend traditional salespeople don't do. They can see features of an offering and understand how they can be used to their organization's benefit. This is a talent that is in short supply in most selling organizations. Early-market buyers have defined and will continue to define start-up organizations' niches.

A few years ago, we were hired as consultants to a venture capital (VC) firm that had identified specific market segments for potential investments. One of their criteria was that companies had to have shipped to at least two customers; another was that the management team (and especially the CEO) had to have a strong track record. The VC team felt comfortable in assessing these areas but also felt that there was a missing piece in most business plans. That missing piece was a clear statement of how prospective portfolio companies were going to achieve their top-line revenue projections.

Why? In our experience, people with the ability to develop new technologies and build companies around those technologies are truly gifted individuals—but those gifts are in specific areas. The habits that make them great innovators are not necessarily those that will serve them well in the marketplace. Many are so enamored of their offering—their "child"—that they have what we call the *Field of Dreams* mindset: "If we build it, they will buy." When challenged to talk about vertical industries, applications, and potential business uses—as opposed to technical artistry—some of these brilliant innovators get defensive, or even feel insulted. Converting their creation into a business offering somehow seems beneath them.

In many of the business plans we reviewed at the request of the VC team, little thought had been given to which industries could use this new offering, which titles would be involved in making the decision to buy, how the offering would be used to achieve goals or solve problems, what business objectives could be achieved through its use—and so on and so on. In other words, very little thought had been given to how the offering was actually going to be sold. A more customercentric perspective is asking who would buy it and how they would realize value for their expenditure.

Typically, the revenue plans assumed the acquisition of a few customers in the first year. Future revenue projections consisted of pie charts showing growth in that market segment and assumed that the company would attain an increasing percentage of that market and the associated revenue over the next several years. But the mechanics of getting there, from a sales standpoint, were sorely lacking.

Companies going down this track may wind up creating technologies in search of markets. And unfortunately, brilliance alone is not enough. Xerox provides a powerful and sad example of a brilliant research-and-development operation that failed to find the applications for many of its creations. The mouse, icons, and desktop that are now used on every PC were all developed by Xerox. And yet Xerox reaped few financial rewards for all its innovations. If you build it, they may not buy from *you*. They may go to the company that figures out how to show buyers how to use it and sells based on that application.

Let's take a closer look at these early-market buyers, who have the rare ability to (1) grasp new capabilities and (2) visualize how those capabilities can be used for business applications at an acceptable cost. How do they work their magic?

In most cases, it's not easy. Within larger companies, early-market visionaries face a series of challenges, even after they have identified a new technology that they feel should be implemented. If they are unable to allocate unbudgeted funds, for example, they must have the ability to champion a new approach and sell one or more people within their organization on the potential benefits of this new offering.

To succeed at this, they have to know the right person to approach and the right way to make the case. Most decision makers up the ladder are likely to be risk-averse and therefore ask the question, "Why don't we wait until some other companies in our industry validate the approach?"

Our experience suggests, however, that early-market visionaries control (or can get access to) adequate funds. As a result, most early purchases are made impulsively, without extensive debate. In other words, gut instincts play a much larger role than formal cost-benefit analyses.

Early-market buyers are willing to endure the inconveniences and disruptions that always come as a result of being first-generation customers. Problem areas include poor product reliability, inadequate training, limited documentation, missing functionalities, and so on. Early-market buyers often participate in identifying these problems and make suggestions about possible improvements. In fact, these customers sometimes use their position to drive product development in directions that will be most advantageous to their own agenda. In such cases, they're unlikely to be worrying about what the requirements of mainstream-market buyers may be.

Assuming you want early-market buyers—and in most cases, you should—how do you find them? The best approach we've seen is to try to get exposure for new offerings by asking marketing to create "buzz," and then to wait for the early-market buyers to find you. If your product is good and the buzz is adequate, they will find you. And when they do, you'll be in good shape, because early-market buyers tend to buy. They don't need to be sold. This is one of the only times that we believe leading with product is the right approach.

Early-market buyers are often found at small to mid-size companies (or divisions of large companies) that (1) have minimal red tape and (2) aren't burdened by the need to get a consensus when making an adventurous buying decision. Like venture capitalists, these buyers understand and accept that some decisions will not achieve the desired results. Let's say that they make 10 buying decisions. If two exceed expectations and six are moderately successful, they can easily tolerate and ultimately write off two mistakes. They can be confident that the advantages accruing from those two good decisions will outweigh the bad ones.

When implementing new offerings, early-market buyers generally have the expertise to integrate the new technology into their current environment. Let's take a humble example at the retail level. An early-market audiophile assembling a sound system would research all options, focusing on recently announced offerings and also considering lesser-known companies. The best individual components would be chosen, and the task of integrating them would begin. The early-market audiophile would buy (or make) the necessary interface cables and might even make a custom cabinet to house the system.

Understanding Mainstream-Market Buyers

In contrast to early-market buyers, mainstream-market buyers would buy a consumers' guide, go to a national electronics chain store, and buy a standard package, complete with mounting brackets for the speakers, cables, prebuilt cabinet, instructions, and so on. The mainstream-market buyer is willing to pay extra to have the system delivered and installed. He or she may take out an extended warranty for extra peace of mind.

Few of them will admit it, but mainstream-market buyers don't want the latest technology. The concept of being first, or even early, is an unpleasant one. Their comfort zone lies in being in the middle of the pack—

following, not leading. They focus on issues that the early-market buyer either doesn't consider or minimizes. For example:

- Is this a proven offering?
- What is the track record of this company?
- Who are the more established competitors playing in this space?
- Will this offering become a de facto standard for my industry?
- Who else in my industry is using it?
- What business results have others achieved?
- What will the return on investment (ROI) on this project be?
- What do industry experts think about this offering?
- Can we get consensus from an evaluation committee?
- What type of support will we get during implementation?
- Is my career at risk by committing too early in the product life cycle?
- Is making no decision better than making the wrong decision?

Prior to making decisions, mainstream-market buyers need to make comparisons. Getting a minimum of three bids, for example, may be corporate policy. If your offering is so unique that there are no vendors to compare it to, the evaluation may come to a grinding halt, because the mainstream-market buyers cannot validate that they are making the right decision.

If other vendors can be assembled, they may be more established than you are. If they don't have an offering ready, they may sow seeds of doubt with the buyer about committing early to a little-known company (i.e., yours) and a technology that has not been accepted as a de facto standard. Larger companies refer to this strategy as "sowing FUD" (fear, uncertainty, and doubt) and employ it to scare mainstream-market buyers into a "no decision" posture—giving them time to come up with their own offerings.

Prior to signing, mainstream-market buyers may want a cost-benefit analysis of a potentially risky expenditure. In most cases, it will be incumbent on the vendor to help facilitate these calculations. Salespeople who don't fully understand how buyers can use their offering will have difficulty facilitating this analysis.

Finally, mainstream-market buyers often require references and reassurances that the early market doesn't ask for. Typical requests made by mainstream-market buyers prior to making a buying decision include:

- Contractual vendor guarantees
- Your entire reference list to perform their due diligence
- Delayed payment contingent on performance

- Meetings with your senior executives
- Prototypes or free evaluations
- Headquarters visits

Crossing the Chasm

While early-market buyers can serve as a start-up's lifeblood for the first several months, longer-term revenue objectives (a much larger piece of the revenue pie chart) cannot be realized within this segment, which makes up only a small percentage (5 to 20 percent) of the overall market.

Companies remain in the early-market stage for offerings within vertical markets until they establish a beachhead consisting of a critical mass of customers who can provide credible references. These are invaluable in emboldening the initial mainstream-market buyers—the "early majority"—to evaluate and consider making a buying decision. Eventually, if all goes well, these buyers are followed by other groups of mainstream-market buyers: the "late majority" and—very late in the cycle—the "laggards."

Even in the case of horizontal offerings—that is, products that are applicable universally, rather than to a particular vertical segment—mainstream-market buyers respond best when selling organizations appear focused on their particular vertical segment. An example of a horizontal offering would be e-commerce software that applies to a wide range of businesses. If you are selling this product to a mainstream-market catalog retailer of clothing, for example, the retailer is likely to be most comfortable with you if your company has already sold to other customers in its market segment. The fact that you've sold successfully to, say, a tire manufacturer isn't likely to carry much weight with the retailer—even if the product is equally as applicable to selling tires as to selling clothes.

After the initial missionary sales effort—often accomplished through heavy involvement by the founders and intensive product redevelopment—the following months can be heady ones. Sales come more easily, and momentum is established. Customers are providing validation with their checkbooks, and this feels good. The sales team now begins a round of recruiting to handle what they perceive to be increasing demand.

The company is now approaching the chasm between the early and mainstream markets. To get across this chasm, the company needs to be sure that at least two fundamentals are in place: (1) the new offering has been proven functional and reliable, and (2) there have been quantifiable results. With these two criteria met, and with a sales force that is up to the new challenge—a subject to which we'll return later in the chapter—the company is ready to attempt to penetrate the mainstream market, which usually represents a minimum of 80 percent of the market potential.

An example of the chasm is the artificial intelligence (AI) industry during the early 1980s. This industry had developed a disruptive technology that could be used in all sorts of applications. The early market (think tanks, universities, and so on) saw this potential and bought the products. Purchases were not usually based on near-term business applications; rather, they were made to allow organizations to explore. Many traditional salespeople who represented companies with a competitive product killed their quotas and cashed huge commission checks.

This wave of buying and euphoria lasted about 18 months. Then suddenly the superstars couldn't achieve 50 percent of their numbers. While there certainly were other factors at work, one underlying problem was that the artificial intelligence companies failed to cross the chasm. They never showed the mainstream market why the offerings were needed and how they could be used to achieve improved business results. Artificial intelligence has been recovering from this debacle ever since. Decades later, AI has made a modest reentry into the marketplace.

Unfortunately, getting across the chasm is not an optional exercise, nor can it be done at a casual pace. Failure to execute this phase of the larger business plan will adversely affect revenue. Delays may afford competitors an opportunity to catch up and may fritter away whatever first-mover advantage the company had.

Post-Chasm Sellers

Mainstream-market buyers, as suggested earlier, prefer to follow rather than lead. In adopting that attitude, of course, they're simply being human. Mainstream humans crave predictability. We want to know what we're getting into. How often do you go to see a play, try a new restaurant, or read a book that you know absolutely nothing about? An enthusiastic recommendation from a personal acquaintance, or a trusted reviewer in a newspaper, dramatically increases the probability that you'll try something new and different.

In fact, there are whole industries devoted to providing these kinds of recommendations and assurances. Think of all the movie critics, travel guides, consumer magazines, and so on that are alive and prospering.

We've already alluded that a sales force should be prepared to align offerings with the needs of a more cautious buyer. What might hinder a company's development in this area is their success in selling to early-market buyers—closing sales by evangelizing a leading-edge offering and by metaphorically challenging buyers to "be the first one on the block" to have it. But as they say of generals, the great temptation is always to fight the last war. Early-market buyers can make traditional sellers seem brilliant—that is, make sellers look customercentric—because they buy. But in many cases, they buy despite the product pitches. For the mainstream-market buyer, the leading edge sounds too much like the bleeding edge—in other words, something to stay away from.

What of the sellers? In many cases, a high percentage of the initial salespeople hired were naturally customercentric. They may have been recruited by the founders themselves, and given incentives (through the use of lucrative stock options) to take a high-risk, high-reward gamble. But as revenues grow and some of these top performers accept promotions to sales manager positions, a shift begins to take place within the organization.

As the company begins to migrate from start-up mindset to a more conservative mindset, stock options for new salespeople become less generous. An initial public offering (IPO) can be great for those salespeople with founding stock; it does little for those who join the company after the IPO. Compensation similarly becomes more bureaucratized and less lucrative. Senior executives, meanwhile, are preoccupied with building and running the business, and perhaps with keeping Wall Street happy. They are less likely to personally recruit salespeople and make sales calls.

What is the outcome of all these changes? The sales talent that the company was able to initially attract and hire begins to fade.

Newly promoted managers—that is, those who were responsible for early sales results—now are responsible for hiring new salespeople. In many cases, this is a task for which sales managers are ill prepared and temperamentally unsuited to execute. Even if they were customercentric salespeople in their former incarnations, how do they evaluate the skill sets of new sales candidates and how do they gauge the chances of success during an interview? Will insecurity in their new positions tempt them to hire less talented people who won't be a threat? In our experience, the answer is often yes. Many 10s (highly talented people) hire 9s, who hire 8s, and so on.

Ultimately the title "sales manager" at many companies is an oxymoron. Most are 98 percent sales and 2 percent manager. They have a group of five to seven direct reports who can only "cook" a deal to a certain point and then the manager has to come in and close the deal. The manager is frustrated because he or she doesn't understand why their salespeople "don't get it." The salespeople are frustrated because they feel they are being babysat or micromanaged. It's not a pleasant environment for anyone.

Winging It

The major difficulty with the selling environment we've described so far is that few companies develop a repeatable way for traditional salespeople to navigate buying cycles with mainstream-market buyers. Instead, they offer disparate silos of product and industry knowledge, backed up by largely irrelevant sales collateral. Ultimately, in the absence of a workable structure, salespeople have no choice but to wing it. Revenue growth stagnates, and no one can explain how or why.

Contrast this with other professions. For example, you won't find plumbers or electricians winging it. They are required to take courses and get certified. Most serve an apprenticeship, working under someone who is experienced. Finally, jobs have specifications showing which materials will be used, drawings that define how the work will be done, on-site supervisors or post-job building inspectors who monitor quality, and so on. All these factors combine to create a structure designed to ensure that (1) the worker is competent and (2) the outcome is predictable and satisfactory.

Why do so many salespeople wing it? We believe it is due to the lack of a clearly defined structure within which salespeople can operate. Expectations (beyond achieving quota) are vague; a definition of a standard sales process is almost nonexistent.

Don't believe us? Based on your own experience in sales, try this experiment: Get out your laptop, and take a moment to write down the steps you follow in selling to a prospect. (If you aren't in sales, ask someone who you believe is a competent salesperson to perform this exercise for you.)

Now look at that document. If your son or daughter were just starting a sales career, how helpful would this description of selling be? Does it give specific direction about *how* to sell? If your son and your daughter went off to sell the same product based on your document, how similar would those two sales efforts be?

The underlying reason most traditional salespeople wing it is that their sponsoring organizations haven't codified the selling process. So—as discussed earlier—the positioning of offerings is entirely up to salespeople, even though it never appears (and doesn't belong) in their job descriptions.

What about the A Players?

As we've already pointed out, some salespeople are exceptionally talented, in the sense of being naturally customercentric. Based upon the Sales Benchmark Index survey, they represent about 13 percent of the sales population. These are gifted, intuitive salespeople, with the remarkable ability to transform (mostly irrelevant) product training into a coherent message—one that is tailored to the title and function of the person they are calling on.

Remember, calls made by customercentric sellers are conversational. These salespeople relate to buyers, establishing their credibility by asking intelligent questions. Rather than opening with a product pitch, customercentric salespeople ask questions. They seek to understand a buyer's needs, so that they can focus on the parts of their offerings that provide a fit. By so doing, they are preparing buyers to want what they are going to offer, later in the conversation.

Naturally, customercentric sellers are the only salespeople who are capable of doing an adequate job of positioning offerings without Sales-Ready Messaging. Their opinions of what is qualified and what will close can be taken to the bank. (Even customercentric sellers, we should note, may have trouble forecasting when opportunities will close.) They rarely waste time—the buyer's or their own—on unqualified opportunities.

Customercentric salespeople need minimal coaching. After completing new-hire training, they find the best product and support people, and pick their brains to understand what this offering allows the buyer to do. Customercentric sellers make their first sale quickly, and most make their numbers the first year. In subsequent years, they almost always exceed whatever quota they are assigned.

Some organizations, having spotted this pattern, conclude that the best approach is to recruit and hire only naturally customercentric salespeople. There are two problems with this approach: (1) There are not enough to go around, and (2) customercentric sellers are selective about the types of companies they join. They know how good they are. As a rule, they seek smaller companies. They like to be recruited and interviewed by senior executives. They want opportunities that offer equity and highly leveraged compensation plans, reflecting the difficulty of selling the first several accounts. They do not want to be managed, they hate red tape, and they like to have the freedom to do whatever it takes to get the business—even if that sometimes means stepping on toes internally. Therefore, companies that don't fit this description have to either develop their own customercentric salespeople or do without.

When asked to summarize the difference between customercentric and traditional sellers in a single word, we respond, "Patience." Customercentric salespeople are patient; traditional sellers are not. Once a buyer shares a goal or reveals an organizational problem, traditional salespeople launch into a "here's what you need" product pitch. This creates problems at several levels:

1. Most people don't like to be told what to do or think. This is especially true when the person telling you what to do is a salesperson—a person that has a quota to meet and therefore can't be seen as an objective party.
2. When assaulted by a "spray and pray" pitch, buyers may realize that there are features in this offering that they don't need. The conclusion that the offering is too complicated, and therefore too expensive, may not be far behind.

3. By failing to ask relevant questions and listen to the answers, the traditional salesperson fails to understand the buyer's current environment and the reasons he or she cannot accomplish the goal or solve the problem being discussed.
4. Similarly, the traditional salesperson has no way of discovering if the offering is a good fit with the buyer's needs. The buyer hasn't been allowed to describe his or her current situation. Failure to understand the customer environment leaves the door to misaligned expectations wide open.

Customercentric sellers are patient. They intuitively understand that the one thing that everyone loves to talk about is themselves. They ask buyers what their business goals and objectives are. Then they ask buyers *why* they are having trouble accomplishing their goal. They dig into the barriers that are standing in the way of a solution. By so doing, they can hone in on the capabilities of their offering that may actually benefit the buyer.

Punished for Success

Imagine that a company has grown to the point where it is time to open a new branch office. The decision has been made to promote a salesperson from within the company to be a sales manager. Whom do you think the company will turn to? Do you think it will promote a salesperson who has struggled to hit 100 percent of quota, year in and year out? Or do you think it will promote someone who has consistently exceeded quota?

Companies almost always promote their top-performing sellers. This may seem like the right thing to do, but in fact, it often creates a whole new set of problems:

1. When a top-producing salesperson is removed from a territory, his or her replacement will not achieve at the same levels.
2. In the absence of a sales structure, as described previously, a top-producing salesperson is likely to make a poor sales manager, and may make life miserable for the less talented sellers reporting to him or her.
3. This may be the first job in which the top-producing seller fails. Many first-year sales managers go from a hero (top-performing salesperson) to a zero (bottom-third performance as a manager). As a result, he or she may ultimately leave the company.

The skill set needed to teach traditional salespeople to be customer-centric is vastly different from the skill set needed to perform as a top-producing salesperson in a territory. Customercentric salespeople have an Achilles heel, which rarely shows up until they are promoted to sales manager: they are unaware of what made them successful in the first place. They were intuitive; it "just happened" for them. They have never broken down their successful sales process into understandable (teachable) components.

For that reason, they will tell their direct reports what to do but fail to share an adequate explanation of how to do it—they don't pass along the knowledge for how to be a successful salesperson. They've never been asked to be articulate about their work; now they're expected to be. Imagine former NBA star Michael Jordan becoming a coach. He tries to explain to an average basketball player how to do a 360-degree turn while hanging in the air, switch the ball from the right to the left hand, go under the basket, and put reverse spin on the ball so that it will rebound off the backboard and drop into the hoop. Unlikely! As an individual performer, Jordan did his thing, and the rest of us admire his artistry and athleticism.

Think about the athletes who become outstanding coaches. Many of them were average players, at best. It didn't come naturally for them. Because they lacked the talent of a Michael Jordan, they had to plod along and learn all aspects of the game. As a direct result, they prepared themselves to be better teachers. Average performers are process-friendly. They are more likely to be patient with other average people, and therefore, they are more likely to help them improve.

The newly promoted top producer, as described previously, has always hated the administrative aspects of selling. Now, thanks to this promotion, he or she is expected to spend 20 to 30 percent of his or her time performing these tasks. Promoting a top-performing salesperson to sales manager is analogous to "promoting" a top gun pilot to air traffic controller. It's taking them out of a realm in which they are almost certain to succeed and putting them into a realm in which they are almost certain to fail. In effect, it's punishing them for their past successes.

A Changing Context

Meanwhile, our former top guns find themselves in a changing context. As the ranks of salespeople swell, the percentage of top performers declines. The company begins the task of creating and implementing policies, procedures, and structure.

As the landscape shifts to the mainstream market, new sales managers may start to find that they no longer have the same flexibility in pricing and terms that they enjoyed when they were enticing early customers to sign. The customer base is changing, too. As we've seen, early-market buying behavior is driven by a small number of participants, sometimes even by one primary supporter. A high percentage of early customers was small to mid-size companies.

Now, senior management is determined to pursue larger transactions at larger companies. These are very different beasts, with multiple layers of management, infrastructure, and so on. Mainstream-market buying involves a larger number of people, often through a committee structure, and requires the need to gain consensus (usually a majority prevails, but in the worst case, decisions must be unanimous). Even in cases where committees conclude that an offering is viable, there may be delays until other options are considered—for example, an RFP that is distributed to multiple vendors. Mainstream-market buyers are pragmatists. They believe in due diligence. As a seller, you may even be punished for your uniqueness: Mainstream-market buyers sometimes defer a decision indefinitely because they are unable to evaluate alternatives.

Meanwhile, as the sales organization grows, the marketing department expands (or is organized for the first time). There is an attempt to codify how offerings are sold with standardized product presentations and brochures. What began as handwritten notes on a cocktail napkin by the founder early in the company's history has now transformed into a glossy six-color brochure, bursting with high-end graphics and riddled with ambiguous terms like *leading edge, robust, synergistic, scalable, seamless, state of the art*, and so on.

These marketing efforts may be flawed because they are based upon successes with early-market buyers who didn't need to be sold. The deliverables to the field are product-intense, treating offerings as nouns rather than verbs. But the strengths embraced by the early market—and now highlighted in the newly created collateral materials—may be out of alignment with the concerns of pragmatic buyers. In fact, they may raise issues that will be barriers to getting buying decisions made.

In this changing context, the danger lies in not knowing when or how to change the selling approach. Leading with features was (sometimes) acceptable with the early-market buyers, but leading with features when approaching mainstream-market buyers is deadly poison. Telling them that this is the latest technology, and that they'll be the first on their block to have it, is simply too scary for them.

The 69 Percent Zone

Now let's look at Figure 5.2. If you create a standard two-by-two grid, segmenting salespeople and buyers into two categories, you come up with four possible buyer/seller combinations.

	Customer- Centric Sellers (10%)	Traditional Sellers (90%)
Early-Market Buyers (20%)	2.6%	17.4%
Mainstream- Market Buyers (80%)	10.4%	69.6%

Figure 5.2 Who Ends Up Selling to Whom?

This grid shows how 100 percent of all selling situations are distributed across our four combinations. For example, if early-market buyers are 20 percent of selling situations and customercentric salespeople are 13 percent, then that combination results in 2.6 percent of the overall total.

In other words, 2.6 percent of selling situations consist of customer-centric sellers calling on early-market buyers. This situation yields the highest ratio of success. In fact, it may be overkill, because the early market typically buys; it doesn't have to be sold.

Similarly, 17.4 percent of selling situations consist of traditional sellers calling on early-market buyers. Let's assume the traditional salesperson is capable of delivering the standard PowerPoint presentation that describes the new offering as if it were a noun. Early-market buyers are willing to endure a "spray and pray," and are also capable of determining if this offering can be used to their benefit. Despite the fact that the salesperson cannot describe how the offering could be used, the vendor still has a high probability of a sale. The biggest challenge, in this case, is finding those early-market buyers.

In 10.4 percent of selling situations, customercentric sellers are calling on mainstream-market buyers. This is the best use of a customercentric seller's talents. The mainstream-market buyers need help in understanding what the offering will enable them to do, and how they will benefit as a result. The customercentric seller has the ability and patience to navigate through the buying cycle and maximize the chances of getting the business.

The most disturbing fact that emerges from this chart is that 69.6 percent of the time, salespeople who are selling risk (that is, focusing on technology and features) are calling on people (mainstream-market buyers) who are highly risk-averse.

Buying cycles with this combination are arduous at best. In our 69 percent zone, a far higher percentage of sell cycles ends with no decision. For example, in our experience, information technology vendors selling to the mainstream market win about 15 percent of opportunities that go to the end of a decision cycle, and another 15 percent of the time, a competitive vendor wins. But in a discouraging 70 percent of these situations, buyers make no decision at all.

In the late 1990s, vendors of technology had the huge advantage of the looming Y2K threat, which forced mainstream-market buyers to make decisions in a hurry. Absent that kind of external pressure, these buyers would have been far less likely to move—and the salespeople of the day would have had far less reason to be smug.

We worked with a CEO who concluded that there *was* no early market for his company's offerings—that is, no easy sell. He then took it a step further. He also concluded he had no customercentric sellers within his sales organization. His calculation of who was calling on whom was simple: 100 percent of his sales situations were the least desirable—traditional salespeople calling on mainstream-market buyers, which can be considered as having the inept call on the unable.

Figure 5.3 is simply another way of illustrating that the majority of a potential market is post-chasm and that therefore potential buyers are unable to understand on their own why they need a new capability or technology, or how they might use it. For companies selling technology, delays in crossing the chasm can be devastating. While most everyone would agree that delays provide competitors time to catch up and adversely affect overall market share, many have not considered the impact of price erosion as a technology goes through its life cycle. Companies with unique offerings can command a premium, but as other companies enter the market, there is a tendency to migrate toward commodity pricing. In the late stages of a product's life cycle, reduced pricing is often the tactic to stay competitive with newer technologies. Companies failing to cross the chasm are adversely affected by both lower market share and margins.

We tell our clients that if they start preparing to sell to the early majority (the pragmatist) from day one, they can virtually eliminate the chasm and change the shape of the bell curve in Figure 5.3 by bringing in mainstream-market sales sooner. Note that in Figure 5.4 the duration of the product life cycle does not change but that now the categories of buyers can be sold to concurrently rather than serially. By empowering traditional salespeople to have conversations about usage with key players, market-

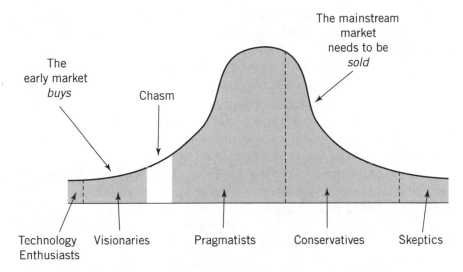

Figure 5.3 Waiting for the Mainstream Market to "Get It"

ing can accelerate acceptance and market share at higher margins. If time and revenue is the question, then Sales-Ready Messaging from day one is the answer.

What happens when a company fails to drive top-line revenues? The most common result is mutual finger-pointing by sales and marketing. We believe that both sales and marketing have failed to do their jobs. Traditionally, there is a great deal of tension, even conflict, between these two

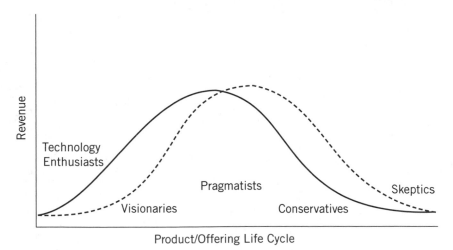

Figure 5.4 Eliminating the Chasm: Helping the Mainstream Market "Get It" by incorporating Sales-Ready Messaging into product launches (solid line curve = without chasm; broken line curve = with chasm)

functional areas. Later in this book, we'll explore this relationship more closely, and offer suggestions for effective interfacing between sales and marketing.

To summarize, there are circumstances in which new offerings can enjoy success even without Sales-Ready Messaging for the sales organization. As markets and sales organizations mature, however, penetration of the mainstream market proves to be more challenging (aka "hard rock mining"). To sustain success, companies have to realize how different mainstream-market buyers really are and act on that insight.

Mainstream-market buyers don't buy; they need help in understanding how offerings can enable them to achieve goals, solve problems, or satisfy needs. So, companies can maximize their chances of prospering if they enable their growing number of salespeople to have conversations with buyers in a way that positions offerings more consistently and leverages best practices.

Chapter 6

Core Concepts of CustomerCentric Selling

Customercentric selling empowers sellers to execute Sales-Ready Messaging to help their buyers visualize how to use offerings to achieve goals, solve problems, and satisfy needs. In our conversations with selling organizations, we believe that most of them would benefit from *reframing the concept of selling*. Why? Because by changing the way people think about the sales function, the idea of selling becomes palatable to people who otherwise would never view themselves as salespeople. Over the years, we have helped large numbers of engineers, scientists, accountants, and consultants become successful salespeople by allowing them to do what they like to do naturally—that is, help their clients achieve goals, solve problems, and satisfy needs. Is this sales? Sure. But it's not traditional selling, which is viewed as distasteful to many people who would otherwise make excellent salespeople. Despite this healthy attitude of wanting to help, engineers or experts often try to tell people what they need, rather than listen to what buyers need. The irony is that even if they are right, buyers don't like to be told what they need to buy. The change to empower buying comes by learning to develop the patience needed to ask questions that allow buyers to draw their own conclusions.

A client who sells enterprise information technology recently asked us to help them fine-tune their hiring model. We studied the backgrounds of their top salespeople going back 10 years and discovered that 7 of the top 10 salespeople came out of some form of customer support. This was a validation of something we had long believed. People who enjoy helping their customers, using their offering to achieve goals, and solving problems make excellent salespeople.

Many clients ask us, "Which is better: hiring an experienced salesperson and teaching him or her our product or teaching an employee who already knows our product how to sell?" Good question. We believe the answer lies in the individual. If the experienced salesperson believes that selling means persuading, convincing, closing, and so on, then he or she is very likely to create more of the bad experiences that buyers disdain—this time in your company's name. If the existing employee likes to help people, has the confidence to approach strangers, and knows how to use the product offering, then we vote for teaching that person how to sell. People without previous sales experience more readily accept new approaches versus salespeople who are skeptical of changing their behavior.

Think of the frame of mind of the traditional persuading/convincing salesperson in the minutes just before an initial meeting with a prospect. What is he or she thinking? Most likely, "What can I sell this person?" Or maybe, even worse, "What do I need this person to buy?" And how long do you think it takes the prospect to sense this and to start to feel uncomfortable?

But what if the seller's primary agenda is finding out whether the prospect has a goal, problem, or need that the seller might be able to help with? And what if the seller is actually willing to leave if he or she doesn't have anything to offer in this particular context? Again, we believe that reframing the concept of selling will cause the sales call—and the entire relationship—to be far more productive and rewarding for all parties.

In this chapter, we present 13 core concepts that collectively begin to reframe the concept of selling and constitute the philosophical foundation of CustomerCentric Selling:

1. No goal means no prospect.
2. It's not about where to show up; it's about what to say when you get there.
3. You get delegated to the people you sound like.
4. People buy from people who are sincere and competent and who empower them.
5. Take the time to diagnose before you offer a prescription.

6. People are best convinced by reasons they themselves discover.
7. The only person who can call it a solution is the buyer.
8. Don't give without getting (quid pro quo).
9. You can't sell to someone who can't buy.
10. Emotional decisions are justified by value and logic.
11. Make yourself equal, then make yourself different; otherwise, all you'll be is different.
12. Don't close before the decision maker is ready to buy.
13. Bad news early is good news.

Let's explore each of these in detail.

No Goal Means No Prospect

When meeting buyers for the first time, the salesperson's primary focus should be to build rapport and trust. Without rapport and trust, it is unlikely that buyers will share their goals and virtually certain that they will not admit problems to a salesperson.

When we help our clients define their sales process, we suggest that an opportunity should go from inactive to active status when the buyer shares a goal. In Mike Bosworth's book *Solution Selling, Creating Buyers in Difficult Selling Markets* (McGraw-Hill, 1994), a prospect was defined as a buyer who has admitted a problem. This may sound easy, but it's not. Over the years, we've discovered that there are very few sellers (particularly young sellers) who are able to get senior-level executives to admit critical business problems. Additionally, when observing how salespeople execute this in real-life situations, the focus on the business pain would often lead to a fairly tactical discussion. For instance, "I don't have the reports I need when I need them" or "Our CRM system is client-server-based and is a bear to try and synchronize."

In reality, a goal and a problem are really just two sides of the same sheet of paper. While buyers are typically reluctant to admit to salespeople what they aren't doing well, they usually are willing to share what they'd like to accomplish. Experience has taught us that it is far easier for salespeople to get a buyer to share a goal than to admit a problem. In fact, if you think about the terminology associated with goals versus problems, the former you usually share with someone, and the latter you are forced to admit.

Let's look at it from the other end of the telescope. We—the authors—are in our forties and fifties. You will have a much easier time getting one of us to share that he would like to lose a few pounds (goal) than to admit that he is getting fat (problem). In fact, there are cases where the salesperson should help the buyer turn the admitted problem into a goal, since it's more fun to talk about goals than about problems.

A sales cycle begins once a buyer shares a goal with a seller. The seller now has the opportunity to use our solution development process (or their own) to ask a series of questions to understand the current situation and to empower the buyer with usage scenarios that will help the buyer understand how he or she can achieve the goal by use of the seller's offering. But without a goal, there can be no solution development and therefore no prospect.

Goals may have longer-term value as well. In longer sales cycles, sellers often get to a point where they are working with delegatees—lower-level implementers—who may get lost in the details of evaluating particular features. In such cases, the seller may find it helpful to refocus the implementer on the previously stated goals of the business buyer.

It's Not about Where to Show Up; It's about What to Say When You Get There

As discussed earlier, effective Sales-Ready Messaging can be the difference between success and failure when you are navigating through a complex conversation with a savvy buyer.

Many salespeople are prodded and cajoled by their manager to "call high in the organization" and "get to the C level," yet they are never given the tools, whether it is training or messaging, that will allow them to succeed once they do enter that rarified air.

Think back to our prior discussion on product training versus product usage. In many companies salespeople are trained by product marketing on the features and functionality of their offering, not necessarily why different buyers of different job titles might need it and, as importantly, how they would use it.

Several years ago, we had a client that sold temporary housing (i.e., furnished apartments available for short-term lease). It was the only "product" they sold, and they would often find themselves pitching the human resources department as to why it made more sense than simply renting hotel rooms for the consultants they were putting on-site for months at a time. When we worked with them to identify who all the different potential buyers were, they realized that how the offering was positioned should vary based on the value each different stakeholder would realize. In other words, for the consultant using the housing, it was about choice, convenience, and not having to live out of a suitcase; for the consultant's manager, it was all about budgets, job satisfaction, and higher productivity levels; for the HR manager, it was about job satisfaction, reduced turnover, and lower recruiting costs; and finally, for the CFO, it was all about the bottom line.

You Get Delegated to the People You Sound Like

Sales executives have complained to us forever that their salespeople don't (or can't) call high enough. Many of them lament the fact that their sellers prefer to call on the potential users of their offering, rather than on the decision makers who can actually buy the product or service. As you can imagine, bottom-up selling has many pitfalls and results in longer sales cycles and lower win rates. The seller talks to many people who can't say yes but can say no when trying to reach a decision maker.

What happens when sellers do get an opportunity to talk directly to the decision maker either early in the sales cycle or after making many calls? In many cases, they present product features and functions to someone who has no interest or time for such a presentation, and so they get delegated. They get delegated to someone else in the organization that shares their interest in product features and functions, but—almost by definition—lacks the power to buy.

When you step back and look at B2B situations, senior executives don't have a need for many offerings. They are motivated to improve business results. To create a need, the seller's challenge is to help executives realize that through the usage of an offering (often by lower levels in the organization), business results can be improved. These buyers only need and want a conceptual understanding of how offerings will work in their environment, but B Players who get the opportunity to talk to decision makers open with product pitches that don't align with high-level buyers.

Why does this happen? As we have already seen, part of the problem probably lies in the product training the salespeople received. If they are trained in the hundreds of features and marketing hype of their offering, then isn't it reasonable to expect them to regurgitate features and hype, regardless of the buyer's title?

Most senior executives will allocate about 30 minutes to a sales call with a salesperson that has proved competent enough to get an appointment with them. But few executive calls last a full 30 minutes. If the seller begins expounding on technology, features, platforms, network architecture, and so on, senior executives are quick to delegate them to the people in their organization who *care* about technology, features, platforms, network architecture, and so on. In many such cases, it would have been far better not to have met with the executive at all. Your company's position may have been compromised in the eyes of the buyer. Access to decision makers is a high-risk, high-reward proposition.

When we work with marketing departments to create Sales-Ready Messaging—that is, messaging that allows sellers to converse with decision makers—one of the major difficulties we face is the shortage of people in our client organizations who know how decision makers (by job title) view the use of their offerings.

This is true whether you're talking with product development, or marketing, or sales. There is a notable exception, however. The people who understand how their customers think about using the product tend to be the professional-services people. Why? The answer is clear: because it is their job to help customers achieve goals, solve problems, and satisfy needs through the use of their offering.

It's not that complicated. Our goal in CustomerCentric Selling is simply to help our clients develop Sales-Ready Messaging to enable their salespeople to have peer-to-peer conversations regardless of buyer title, in turn creating visions in the buyer's mind of using the seller's offering to achieve goals, solve problems, or satisfy needs.

People Buy from People Who Are Sincere and Competent and Who Empower Them

When we do role-playing exercises in our workshops, we stress that it is as important for our attendees to play the role of buyers as it is for them to play the role of sellers. This is the best way for them to learn to think like a buyer. What they tend to discover through that process is that buyers want to deal with sellers who (1) are sincere, (2) are competent, and (3) allow the buyer to participate in the conversation. This is a welcome change from the "Here's what you need" approach taken by traditional salespeople.

In today's competitive market, a salesperson must be sincere and competent merely to get the opportunity to compete. But that's just the price of admission. Lots of companies know how to recruit sincere and competent salespeople (at least of a traditional sort). We submit, therefore, that conversing with buyers as a peer is the most sure-fire way for sellers to differentiate themselves from the pack.

The key to further differentiation lies in making sure that buyers retain ownership of their goals, problems, and needs. One of the quickest ways for a seller to lose credibility with a buyer is to look the buyer in the eye and say that a particular offering is going to "solve your company's problems." Solving the company's problems is what the buyer and his or her colleagues are paid to do, day in and day out. They don't want to hear that someone who drops in once a month, or once a year, is going to meet all their needs. Experience has taught them that no company, salesperson, or product can take responsibility for achieving the desired business result.

Many companies believe they can win simply by putting a superior product on the table and talking up its features. But think about it. Doesn't this force the buyer to lose control of the conversation and talk about what *you* want to talk about? Yes, if you are selling to expert buyers, you can win with a superior product. But did you really sell anything? Or did you simply take an order from a buyer who was smart enough to figure out how to use your product? And if the latter, why wouldn't this savvy buyer simply purchase online next time and cut you (and your associated costs) out of the loop?

It's a simple concept, but a critically important one. The buyer must own achievement of the goal. If your buyer concludes that you understand the current situation, goals, or problems, then—and only then—you have earned yourself the opportunity to help your buyer understand how he or she can achieve the goal, or solve the problem, with the specific capabilities of your offering.

Take the Time to Diagnose before You Offer a Prescription

If you were to see a physician with a goal (losing weight) or a problem (lower back spasms), you would expect the physician to ask you a series of specific diagnostic questions. Your trust and confidence in the physician would increase with each intelligent, probing, on-target question that he or she asked you. When you have confidence in the diagnostic process, you are far more likely to have confidence in the prescription.

Why should selling be any different?

What we are talking about here is *process*. The ability to ask diagnostic questions is a key differentiator between great salespeople and traditional salespeople. Customercentric sellers do this intuitively. Traditional sellers need help not only with content but with process as well. They need help with the process of asking the right questions to learn how the customer operates today, and the associated costs of the current method.

In many of our consulting engagements, we help marketing develop the diagnostic questions about (1) the buyer's current situation and (2) the potential usage of the offering to help the buyer achieve a goal, solve a problem, or satisfy a need. Most human beings (particularly, it must be said, male human beings) do not appreciate unsolicited advice. But if the potential buyer is being asked intelligent questions that he or she is capable of answering, the advice that emerges from that process is, in a very real sense, solicited advice. The buyer has participated in, and partly directed, the conversation that developed both the diagnosis and the prescription.

Have you ever noticed how once you know something, it is difficult to have patience with or empathy for people who don't know what you know?

This can be a curse for salespeople, and experienced salespeople can be most cursed. They've seen it all before. When they see a solution to the buyer's need, they get enthusiastic and impatient, and start projecting their solution onto the buyer. They forget their own learning curve, stop asking questions, and start saying, "What you need is. . . ."

In the late 1970s, the Xerox Corporation hired a consultant to study the behavioral habits of their best salespeople. He discovered that newly hired Xerox salespeople went through a quite predictable performance curve over time. Their sales performance steadily improved from their date of hire through about their 18th month—and then, inexplicably, suddenly declined.

Why? Eventually, he concluded that it took these sellers 18 months to become "experts." After a year and a half, they understood every goal, problem, or need that their product set would address, in every combination and permutation. Given that expertise—plus, of course, the sincere desire to help their buyers and make a sale—they began going too fast for their buyers. A buyer would begin explaining his or her situation, and the overeager seller would see a perfect fit for the Xerox solution and start telling the prospect why he or she needed this product.

It's a paradox. Of course your clients want expert salespeople. (That's what this book is all about.) At the same time, if your salesperson is tempted to use his or her expertise on the buyer, a lack of expertise can make for a better sales call. Without expertise, your seller's only course of action is to ask questions. As a buyer, do you prefer salespeople who ask or who tell?

People Are Best Convinced by Reasons They Themselves Discover

We believe that with the benefit of a strong selling process and the belief that prospects have IQs above room temperature, sellers can allow buyers to reach their own conclusions.

Customercentric salespeople leverage their expertise by asking questions, rather than by making statements. We provide our clients with a dialogue model for asking questions and Sales-Ready Messaging in the form of a Solution Development Prompter. This enables the seller to facilitate an intelligent conversation with the buyer about a specific goal. The process of asking questions helps buyers discover their own reasons that prevent them from achieving a specific business result.

Expert buyers are able to convince themselves that they should buy something, because they figure out on their own how to use the proposed offering. But most buyers *aren't* experts and therefore need help buying. By using a process that allows the buyer to feel that he or she is in control, by helping rather than pressuring, and by using content that is aimed at the buyer's specific situation, sellers can shape their customers' experiences. They can lead the buyer to discover the solution and therefore own it.

The Only Person Who Can Call It a Solution Is the Buyer

We've already talked about solutions. We believe that *solution* is one of the most misused words in the English language, certainly within the sales profession.

The *American Heritage Dictionary* defines a solution as "the answer to or disposition of a problem." But isn't it enormously presumptuous for someone with the title "salesperson" on a business card to announce to a buyer that he or she has the solution, even before the buyer has shared a single goal? Is it surprising that buyers find this offensive?

In our CustomerCentric Selling workshops, we take a different approach to solutions. We believe that a salesperson can't and shouldn't define a solution. Only the buyer can call something a solution. The seller can help the buyer get there but can't get there first. When the seller—using the right process and content—leads the buyer to conclude that he or she needs the specific capabilities the seller has posed, only then do we have a solution. Because the buyer said so.

Don't Give without Getting

Almost all sales involve some kind of negotiation. And like sales, negotiation is not an event; it is a process. In this process, we believe, the seller should strive to create a reciprocal relationship. He or she should get something in return for giving something. We call this our "quid pro quo philosophy."

This begins as a psychological adjustment: how the seller looks at himself or herself. The seller should remember that he or she is not a supplicant, looking for a handout or a favor; instead, he or she is providing a valuable service to the buyer (assuming, of course, that the offering actually can help the buyer solve a problem or meet a goal).

We've already talked about how the buyer's time is valuable. Well, so is the seller's time. Research has shown that salespeople typically spend only 29 percent of their time actually selling. The balance is spent on administration, travel, and so on. Therefore, we believe that if a salesperson gives a buyer an hour of time, he or she has the right—and even the obligation—to get something in return, before giving up another hour. What's the practical benefit? If quid pro quo becomes a habit early in the relationship, sellers can become more effective negotiators and deliver more profitable business.

When our potential clients try to assess whether to engage us and implement CustomerCentric Selling, many wind up focusing their cost-benefit analysis on discounting. Once our client decision makers understand our quid pro quo philosophy, many realize that the entire Sales-Ready Messaging and sales process implementation will more than pay for itself if sellers can reduce discounting by 1 percent.

The math isn't complicated. Let's say that the total cost of one of our standard sales-training programs is between $3,000 and $4,000 per salesperson. If each of those salespeople has an annual quota of $2 million and can reduce discounting by 1 percent, that's $20,000 a head. And, of course, this is the proverbial gift that keeps on giving, in that once salespeople understand quid pro quo, they keep on thinking and acting that way.

You Can't Sell to Someone Who Can't Buy

Stated more positively, this core concept means, "You can sell only to someone who can buy."

Many salespeople end up in the free education business. Think about knowledge workers in corporate America—engineers, software developers, scientists, and so on. How do they become educated in new technologies and new ways of doing business? The answer is through salespeople who spend their time and effort presenting their offerings. The problem is that the vast majority of knowledge workers embrace learning yet can't buy. The length of the sales cycle is often inversely proportional to the level at which it is initiated.

This is most severe with breakthrough products and services. If you are first to market with a new concept or technology, then by definition, no budgets exist to buy what you are selling. This means you have to gain access to the very small minority of people who can spend unbudgeted funds. We were working with a large software company in the mid-1990s. Of the 14,000 people on their payroll, only four could spend unbudgeted funds.

For salespeople selling continuous-improvement products and services, they still need access to the person who can spend budgeted funds. This is where homework pays off. Ideally, your prospect is both the user of your product or service and the head of a department that already has the money budgeted.

Emotional Decisions Are Justified by Value and Logic

Buying is almost always an emotional act. Depending on the specifics of the situation, those emotions may or may not have to be justified—but they're still there.

When a buyer decides to buy from a particular seller, it is an emotional decision. Equally, when a buying committee decides to buy from a particular vendor, it is an emotional decision. When a buyer decides to pay an asking price rather than holding out for a lower price, it is an emotional decision. When a buyer decides to buy from a person or company he or she is comfortable with, rather than shopping for the lowest possible price, it is an emotional decision.

If the buyer answers to no one and does not care what other people think, then he or she can buy strictly on emotion. The rest of us, though, need some kind of logic to explain to peers, superiors, subordinates, friends, or family why we chose to buy what we bought.

An acquaintance of ours bought a very expensive, stunningly beautiful, fun-to-drive German car. We asked him why. His rationale included things like "it will be a classic," "it will go up in value," "it has an aluminum body and will never rust," and so on. All very logical reasons, right? The truth is, he bought that car because he loved it at first sight, wanted to drive it, and felt he looked more handsome driving it. If a close friend asked him why he bought that car, the emotional reason would flow along with the question: "Don't I look good in it?" If a stranger asked, most likely the logical reasons would be offered.

In our CustomerCentric Selling workshops, we teach salespeople to be prepared to sell to both logic and emotion. A non-decision maker will make an emotional decision to buy from a salesperson first, but then should be armed with the logical reasons so that the buying decision can be defended.

Make Yourself Equal, Then Make Yourself Different— or You'll Just Be Different

When salespeople are in competitive situations, they frequently fall into a trap that is set—usually unintentionally—by their buyer.

It goes like this. The buyer, usually not a decision maker, is required to interview multiple vendors, but is predisposed to go with Salesperson A's product. More or less innocently, he asks Salesperson B how his offering compares to that of Salesperson A.

At this point, Salesperson B—along with something like 90 percent of all salespeople in the universe—responds with something like the following:

"Mr. Prospect, I'm so glad you asked that question. Here's how our product is different from Salesperson A's offering!" And from there, on to the specifics.

Uh-oh! Salesperson B is describing how her product is different from the one the prospect likes the best—before trust has been established, before goals have been articulated, before diagnosis has occurred, and before the buyer has become convinced of the seller's expertise. Think about it: The *worst* thing Salesperson B can do at this point in the relationship is to contrast her offering to Salesperson A's. After losing, should the buyer be asked to help fill out the loss report?

Instead, Salesperson B could have asked: "What are you hoping to accomplish?" If the buyer responds with a goal, the seller now has a prospect (see preceding discussion). Now the seller can use patience, process, and content to establish credibility, diagnose the current situation, and pose some usage scenarios that will differentiate the product from Salesperson A's. We have found, with client after client, that you have to get on an equal footing from a personal, competence, and capability standpoint first, before you differentiate your offering. Otherwise, you'll just be different—and you'll lose.

As mentioned in an earlier chapter, the Internet has allowed buyers to become knowledgeable about offerings. After a buyer has used search engines, visited multiple Web sites, and leveraged social networking, it is important for the seller to learn what requirements the buyer has established. In such cases, as we'll discuss later, the requirements may not represent a single vendor; rather, it can be a conglomerate spread across multiple vendors of what the buyer believes he or she needs.

We make the distinction that there are two types of interactions with buyers:

1. Interest development when a buyer is unaware of their requirements.
2. Interest processing describes an initial encounter a seller has with a buyer who has a good idea of what the requirements are. Those requirements can either be as a result of talking with a competitive salesperson or can reflect the research that has been done via the Internet.

As you would expect, there are different alignment issues when encountering knowledgeable or even expert buyers. Later on, we'll discuss our recommended approach to each of these types of buyers. Traditional selling approaches are especially ineffective with expert buyers.

Don't Close before the Buyer (Decision Maker) Is Ready to Buy

We like to ask our audiences if any of them have ever gone out with the intention of getting a particular order on a particular day and failed to get it. Almost everyone who has been selling for more than a couple of months (and responds honestly) raises his or her hand. We then ask them to quote their buyer's reasons for not signing on the dotted line that day. The reasons do not vary much from workshop to workshop:

- He needs to get someone else's approval.
- The contract is still in legal.
- The CFO has not approved it yet.
- They are working on their implementation plan.
- They are still waiting for another proposal.
- We are not on their approved vendor list.
- They're still on the fence.
- And the dreaded Something's come up.

But what was *really* going on here? In most cases, the seller was asking for the business before the buyer was ready to buy. This is a big mistake. We tell sellers that once they close the first time, their relationship with their buyer will never be the same. It will be either better or worse, but it won't be the same. And almost without exception, it will be better if they were ready to buy, and worse if they weren't.

Sellers are often justified in blaming their own management for closing prematurely. It was the final 10 days of the quarter, and management is pressuring the sales force to see what opportunities they can pull in from the next quarter to this one. Again, big mistake: The saddest situations we see are salespeople who sincerely want to help their buyer achieve a goal, solve a problem, or satisfy a need but are pressured by their management to close early. In many cases, this trades a long-term relationship for potential short-term gain and increases the likelihood of a significant discount.

We live in the real world, and we understand that there are exceptional circumstances under which it's necessary to attempt to close early. When this is the case, the sales manager needs to acknowledge that this is the situation and explain why he or she is asking the salesperson to accelerate the buying process. But this should be the exception rather than the rule. When management pressures salespeople to close early at the end of each quarter, there's a structural problem, and it's likely that larger future gains are being traded away for smaller short-term gains.

Before asking a buyer to buy, sellers should ask themselves:

- Have I documented the buyer's goal(s)?
- Have I diagnosed the buyer's current situation?
- Have I documented how the buyer's goal(s) can be achieved by using my offering?
- Have I helped the buyer cost-justify the decision?
- Have I documented what will happen between signing my order and having our offering fully available for the buyer's use?
- Have I provided the buyer proof that our offering and organization are for real?
- Have I asked the buyer about and mapped out organizational decision requirements—legal review, approved vendor list, and so on?

The salesperson should have some version of this list in mind very early on. He or she should be prepared to share it with the sales manager, if and when pressure comes down the pipeline, and explain which preconditions to a sale haven't been met yet, and why. Sometimes, being able to respond to these questions—or most of them—with a "yes" helps the salesperson get comfortable with the idea of moving up his or her timetable for closing.

Bad News Early Is Good News

This particular core concept of CustomerCentric Selling is for salespeople who have long sell cycles. Prior to hiring us, it is not uncommon for our clients, when initiating opportunities, to have nine-month sell cycles, in part because in the enterprise sales environment, the selection process usually requires the evaluation of multiple vendors. When a corporation is considering a large purchase, it typically wants three or more quotes. For vendors reacting, it will be a short sales cycle with little or no chance of winning. In many such cases, the buyers knew from the start which vendor they wanted to buy from, but they still had to get others to bid. In other words, these buyers are simply going through the motions to demonstrate to senior management that they did sufficient due diligence.

If you are not the predetermined vendor, bad news early is good news. The worst thing a salesperson can do to him- or herself and the company is to go the distance and lose. This feels a little counterintuitive, but it's true. Two vendors win in every predetermined sales cycle: the company that is awarded the business and the company that has pulled out early, giving itself the chance to pursue other winnable opportunities. All the other vendors invited in go the distance, only to be awarded a silver medal.

Again, the key is to do your homework, keep your ear to the ground, and be realistic about your chances of success. A salesperson has to qualify opportunities, which in many cases means disqualifying opportunities—including those buyers who are simply putting them through the motions. Sales managers, too, have a role to play. They can help their salespeople recognize bad news early and disqualify nonopportunities.

Chapter 7

Defining the Sales Process

People view sales as being an art rather than a science.

This belief is sustained, in part, by the existence of customercentric salespeople with innate skills who make selling look so easy. But there are two problems with this assumption. The first is that, as we've already seen, there aren't enough customercentric salespeople out there to go around— perhaps 13 percent of sales professionals.

The other problem is that it presents a self-fulfilling excuse for not getting better. If selling is an art, and I'm not an artist, then I'm off the hook, right? All I can do is plod along in my traditional selling mode and hope for the best.

We disagree. What if the "artful" behaviors of the customercentric sellers could be codified? What if those behaviors could be built into both sales processes and messaging? The truth is that all salespeople, and in particular traditional salespeople, can become more customercentric and can produce at higher, more predictable levels. In fact, we have found over the years that a traditional seller following a good process has at least a fighting chance to win when competing with a naturally talented seller who is winging it. Without process, the natural seller, or A Player, will prevail.

Sometimes we cite the example of two different types of musicians— those in a jazz trio versus those in a symphony orchestra. Jazz musicians improvise, in real time. They rarely play the same piece the same way twice.

But if you dig a little deeper, you find that there is a great deal of structure and discipline behind most of their improvisation. Meanwhile, musicians in the orchestra try their hardest to play a Mozart piece, for example, perfectly. For the most part, the members of the orchestra couldn't write music like Mozart's (how many of us can?). But because Mozart's music has been codified, they can replicate it brilliantly.

Naturally talented sellers are akin to jazz musicians. A new company can be launched with a few naturally talented salespeople (jazz musicians), but to build it big enough to go public and capture its share of market, traditional salespeople (the orchestra) will have to learn to execute a customer-centric sales process. The orchestra must be taught how to play a little jazz. At the risk of overworking the metaphor, we have to look for the structure that underlies the jazz.

In the enterprise selling world, there are many complicating factors—multiple decision makers, platform sales, commodity sales, relationship sales, application sales, new-name sales, add-on sales, sales through channels, and so on. When we work with client organizations, one of our first tasks is to help them document, define, and understand all their sales processes. In other words, we help them identify their selling behaviors for the different selling situations they encounter.

Is this necessary? We think so. Many companies define the *what,* in other words, the things that *should* be done at each step in their sales process. Most are not so good at identifying a message that guides the behavior of their sellers and provides the *how* for these same steps. Unless you establish a set of standards or rules—the how—at each step of the selling process, you have to depend on unreliable data (i.e., the opinions of those around you) or data that come far too late (i.e., your closed orders). If management can proactively assess the quality of what is in the pipeline and help salespeople disqualify low-probability opportunities earlier, pipelines won't be filled with hopes and dreams. Without a process, conversely, management tends to be a series of autopsies performed on dead proposals or lost orders. With process, corrective surgery might have been possible, and the outcome could have been a win. As Larry Tuck, the editor of *CRM* magazine, once said:

> Have you thought about your sales process? CRM works best
> for companies with well-defined processes already in place.
> Automate chaos and it's still chaos.

Defining the Sales Process

Companies that establish milestones believe they have process. For traditional sellers, however, this is analogous to giving a destination without a map or directions and occasionally asking if they are going the right way.

If you are going to treat sales as a process, then you have to align it with all other processes at a foundational level. In other words, any process you look at has three fundamental components: a series of defined steps, inputs, and outputs. Think about manufacturing as a process. There is a clearly defined sequence that is followed. The inputs into the process are raw materials or component parts. The output is finished goods.

In order to define sales as a process, we need to chart a different course. In doing so, it will be necessary to establish some definitions that we can build on:

- *Process:* A defined set of repeatable, interrelated activities with outcomes that feed another activity in the process. Each outcome can be measured, so that adjustments can be made to the activities, the outcomes, or the process itself.
- *Sales process:* A defined set of repeatable, interrelated activities from market awareness through servicing customers that allows communication of progress to date to others within the company. Each activity has an owner and a standard, measurable outcome that provides inputs to another activity. Each result can be assessed, so that improvements can be made to (1) the skills of people performing the activities and/or (2) the sales process itself.
- *Sales pipeline milestones:* Measurable events that take place during sales cycles that enable sales management to assess the status of opportunities for the purpose of forecasting. Ideally, most of these milestones are (1) objective and (2) auditable.
- *Sales funnel milestones:* Measurable events that take place on specific opportunities that enable sales management to assess the quality of selling skills and the quantity of activity needed at the salesperson level. Again, these milestones are (1) objective and (2) auditable.

Because of the predominant perception that selling is more of an art than a science, few companies have sales processes that traditional sellers can execute. We believe that this deficiency is the single most significant factor contributing to the disappointing results achieved with SFA and CRM systems. As suggested in the preceding definitions, the chances of building and sustaining an executable and therefore successful sales process are slim in the absence of the following prerequisites:

1. Pipeline milestones
2. Repeatable process
3. Sales-Ready Messaging
4. CustomerCentric Selling skills
5. Consistent, auditable input

Today companies of all sizes have SFA and CRM applications. The allure of these systems is to gain better control and visibility over sales efforts, culminating in more accurate forecasting. But companies that attempt to implement SFA or CRM and only have one of these five components in place—the pipeline milestones—must depend primarily on the opinions of salespeople as their input.

Repeatable Process

We've already introduced this idea. What is the "code" that allows the traditional salesperson to become more customercentric? What constitutes success, and how can more people achieve it?

We should point out at this juncture that companies have more than one sales process. For example, the selling activities will vary when selling major accounts, national accounts, mid-size accounts, add-on business, professional services, contract renewals, and so forth. Most people quickly realize that one size does not fit all; in fact, it can be a recipe for disaster to impose a single sales process on all sales. (Salespeople are fully within their rights to complain about being asked to kill mosquitoes with a cannon.) Later in this chapter, we address how to handle these different types of sales.

Consistent Input

The majority of the input to SFA/CRM systems consists of salespeople's opinions of the outcome of sales calls they make. By definition, this input is subjective and variable. Compounding the problem is the fact that the positioning of offerings falls almost exclusively on the shoulders of individual salespeople.

Consider how odd this situation is in the larger context of a business enterprise. How many other functional groups get to make this kind of report on their work, without fear of contradiction? How many other numbers that are critically important to the corporation have so much subjectivity built into them?

Auditable Input

As noted, many companies have defined milestones—that is, clearly identified steps in a sell cycle that are used to determine where the company stands vis-à-vis a given opportunity. But asking traditional salespeople to tell what milestones they have achieved invites them to provide the answer they think their manager wants to hear, and in some cases do so in order to secure their position for another quarter. Unless or until milestones have components specific to job title and business goal that can be audited by someone other than the salesperson, input will continue to be variable. We'll discuss this topic later in the chapter.

The Trouble with the Data

We don't mean to imply that companies implementing SFA/CRM systems have failed to realize any benefit, especially in the realm of improvements in forecasting accuracy. Indeed, many have experienced some success in that area. But in many cases, part of the difficulty with these implementations has to do with poorly managed expectations about how much forecasting accuracy will increase, and when.

A few years ago, while working with a CRM vendor, we asked the VP of sales if the company "ate its own dog food" (i.e., used its own software to forecast). This question elicited an enthusiastic "yes!" from this executive. He then went on to say that he usually came within 5 percent of his quarterly forecast—a level of accuracy most sales executives can only dream about. We asked for details, and within seconds, he had his laptop fired up so that he could share his forecasting secrets with us.

He showed us that the company had defined seven milestones in its sales pipeline. Beginning with the first month that a salesperson joined the company and started reporting on his or her pipeline, the software heuristically captured close rates at each of the seven milestones. When it came time to forecast, the software took each salesperson's gross pipeline and applied that salesperson's unique factors to the dollar volume represented by each of the seven milestones. In this way, he achieved his enviable forecasting accuracy.

We then asked: "Are your salespeople telling their prospects that if they use your software package, they will achieve a similar degree of forecasting accuracy?" He acknowledged that, as we expected, they were.

Next, we began to dissect how these miraculous results were being achieved, and the degree to which other companies would be able to replicate them. The hard fact was that it would take months or years for other companies to gain the historical close rates by salesperson that were the key component in our client's ability to predict revenue. Ironically, the only reason he could be so accurate with his forecast is that the software tracked historically how inaccurate (i.e., overoptimistic) his salespeople tended to be, in that they overstated their pipelines at each of their seven pipeline milestones. Any new users of this CRM system—in other words, all the new purchasers of the software—could only assign estimates of close rates at various milestones. Most likely, these would be across the board for all salespeople and would hone in at the individual salesperson level only over time.

Even with the software in place and defined milestones, moreover, forecasting accuracy could continue to be adversely affected by a range of internal and external factors:

- When salespeople leave, their historical data are no longer relevant.
- When new hires join, they have no historical data.
- New offerings don't have the benefit of historical data.
- New vertical industries present new challenges.
- A changing economic climate can undercut the relevance of historical data.
- The changing fortunes of clients within the product segment can similarly undercut historical data.
- Offerings by competitors may raise the bar.

Fire Drills and Hail Marys

Under the best of circumstances, the analysis of the pipeline is based on input from the sales organization. Notable by its absence is any input from the buyer (which, as you'll see in later chapters, could give sales management a way to audit where the buyer stands in the buying cycle and therefore provide a sanity check). With or without a CRM system, leaving the buyer out of the picture means that the timing of asking for the business is more a function of when the company wants (or needs) the order rather than when the prospect or customer is ready to buy. In other words, it is rarely customercentric.

Companies spend the last few days of nearly every quarter attempting to squeeze out business in order to make their numbers. Many senior executives leave their calendars open during the last weeks of a quarter, allowing them to embark on "closing junkets." The tool commonly used to get buyers to commit earlier than planned is substantial discounting. Some buyers are so offended by this approach ("I was naïve to assume that the initial price they quoted was real!" or worse, "They must think I'm an idiot!") that they ultimately decide not to do business with companies that employ these kinds of traditional closing techniques.

One difficulty with selling in this fashion is that it can become standard operating procedure. Emptying the pipeline at the end of March transforms April and May into the months for rebuilding the pipeline, but not closing much business. This culminates in another high-pressure closing toward the end of June. Another difficulty is that savvy buyers learn to delay buying decisions, in the knowledge that they will get the absolute best price at quarter's end.

If you doubt that such "fire drills" are commonplace among established and reputable companies, consider the following quote by Computer Associates' former chief financial officer, Ira Zar, from an article in *Forbes*:

> Negotiations [at Computer Associates] came down to the last day of the quarter, with Hail Mary discounts of up to 55 percent fairly common in the business. In the quarter ended September 30, 2000, CA did $1 billion of its $1.6 billion in revenues in the last week. We ended up trading phone calls at 11 at night.

Prior to our working with them, one company entered the last quarter of a year with a chance to achieve $300 million in revenue—a threshold they had never before attained. Senior management decided that this target was within their reach, and instructed managers and salespeople to close everything they could (i.e., go as low as necessary) so that the goal could be achieved. The good news is they succeeded, booking a few million dollars beyond the magic number. At the subsequent January kick-off meeting, jackets were distributed to everyone with that record year's revenue figure embroidered on the sleeves. The meeting proceeded with a general sense of satisfaction, accomplishment, and even euphoria. Success was in the air!

Then came the bad news. As a division of a larger organization, the company received its quota for the following year. The objective assigned by the parent company was $360 million— a 20 percent increase over the record revenue that had just been delivered. As you might expect, virtually nothing closed in January and February, as a result of emptying the pipeline in December. The company finished the first quarter with bookings below 50 percent year-to-date. Ultimately, it stumbled its way toward matching the revenue delivered the previous year—but not before both the CEO and the VP of marketing were relieved of their duties midway through the second quarter. With 20-20 hindsight, the results were predictable, as the company effectively had a 10-month year to produce the revenue. You can imagine the resulting impact on profitability.

Even without being instructed to do so by their management team, traditional salespeople are frequently guilty of closing prematurely, often attempting to close the wrong person. Attempting to close non-decision makers (and close them prematurely) can cause several bad things to happen:

- Closing the buyer may make the buyer feel inadequate or insignificant.
- Sellers may convey the stress they are experiencing to buyers, even to the point of appearing desperate.
- The buyer may become a messenger to the decision maker about your discounted pricing.
- If the decision maker is serious about doing business, the discount offered to the person who cannot buy may become the starting point for negotiating further concessions.
- If the order is not closed during the quarter, sellers may have set expectations of pricing that their companies are unwilling to honor early in the following quarter when the buyer is ready to buy.
- Transactions may be lost because of this stereotypical seller behavior.

A sales process should contain a specified time to close that was agreed to by the buyer. Senior management can attempt to accelerate orders at their own risk.

Shaping Your Perception in the Marketplace

In most cases, companies think of their sales process as a way to control cost of sales, facilitate management of the sales force, and forecast top-line revenue more accurately.

These are all valid objectives, of course. But we take things a step further. We believe that a sales process should create a framework for relating to customers and prospects. Think about it: Many organizations develop reputations and are assigned a personality by their behavior in the marketplace. Companies become known as aggressive (Oracle), predatory (Microsoft), arrogant (Accenture), and so on. How does this happen? In part, it happens through corporate policies, public utterances of the CEO, and similar high-level actions. But we believe that the behavior of the company's representatives in the field deserves at least as much credit (or blame).

By extension, we believe that it is possible to shape the marketplace's opinion of you by designing a customercentric sales process that reflects the way you want your customers and prospects to be treated. In other words, the CEO can create a blueprint for customers' experience that will influence the words that salespeople use when developing buyer needs and setting expectations.

The reality of today's information-rich marketplace is that it is becoming increasingly difficult to rely on new or unique product features as a key to competitive differentiation. Once a particular vendor releases a new version of its offering, in most cases it's only a matter of months before the other vendors have matched it or figured out how to sell around it. We believe with equal or even slightly inferior offerings, companies can make the way their salespeople sell a differentiator, and these organizations can win on sales process.

What Are the Component Parts?

A customercentric sales process needs to cover all the steps, from market awareness through measuring results achieved by customers. It should define and include the following:

- When buying cycles begin
- The steps involved in making a recommendation or generating a proposal
- The steps necessary to have the buyers fully understand their requirements
- The steps needed for buyers to understand how your offering addresses their goals and problems
- An estimated decision date documented to confirm the buyer's agreement
- Built-in feedback loops, to permit a rapid adjustment to timing issues, competitive pressures, client feedback, market issues, and external events (e.g., 9/11, Y2K)

One way of structuring a sales process is to define an appropriate set of pipeline milestones, as mentioned earlier. Consider, for example, the following set of milestones in a typical sales process:

- Access to the decision maker
- Cost versus benefit completed
- Cost versus benefit agreed to by prospect
- Billable events
- Customer resources committed
- Budget allocated (whose?)
- Meeting with IT
- Business goal(s) shared or problems admitted
- IT technical approval
- Corporate visit
- Implementation plan
- Executive calls
- Professional services calls
- Specific titles called on
- Non-IT champion

- Demonstration
- Proposal submitted
- Reference site visit
- Site survey
- References provided
- References checked
- Verbal agreement
- Client financials received
- On-site survey
- Financials requested by prospect
- Pilot agreed to
- Competitors identified
- Projected decision date
- Price quotation
- Compelling reason to buy
- Contracts submitted to legal
- Call made by services staff
- Contracts approved
- Billable education
- IT approval of cutover
- First-level manager call
- Trial
- Project start date defined
- Credit approval

How do you identify milestones? In addition to drawing on your own experience and process, as well as the preceding list, we recommend analyzing transactions from the past year or so to determine if you can isolate common factors and patterns in opportunities that you've won and lost. By so doing, you can begin to identify and incorporate specific best-practice events and use them as milestones. This allows organizations to begin to institutionalize their best practices within a sales process and to improve win rates on opportunities in the pipeline.

One company we worked with sells software and would not allow opportunities to be qualified past a certain level unless the salesperson had made calls on businesspeople outside of the IT department. This milestone was created because history showed that many sales cycles that began within IT ended suddenly, and unhappily, as soon as a request for funds was made without having built a business case that end users could present to their line of business executives. On the more positive side, another client discovered that when prospects came for a corporate visit, they had an 88 percent close rate on those opportunities. Guess what recommendation we made that became a step in their sales process?

These milestones allow salespeople and management to better understand where they are in a given sell cycle. Just as important—or maybe more important—they provide insight into whether opportunities are qualified, and therefore worthy of resources. As noted in earlier chapters, traditional salespeople take comfort in having quantity, rather than quality, in their pipelines. They are competing to keep busy, rather than to win.

Key steps in every sales process must be documented in order to be auditable. In other words, there must be a letter, fax, or e-mail from the salesperson to the buyer that summarizes key conversations. Such documentation serves multiple purposes:

1. It maximizes the chances that both the salesperson and the buyer understand where they are in the deal process.
2. It allows consistent internal messaging by the buyer, within his or her organization.
3. It allows the first key player in a committee sale to communicate his or her vision clearly to peers and superiors.
4. It minimizes the chance that the salesperson is overoptimistic ("happy ears").
5. Most important, it allows the manager to audit and grade the opportunity.

Note that not all milestones need to be auditable. Your goal should be to define those critical ones that will allow you (or your sales managers) to grade opportunities. This is the only way to get away from the unbridled optimism (i.e., in salespeople's opinions) described earlier.

Senior management must take ownership of the customer experience and ownership for the corresponding sales process, in part by defining deliverables based on the size and complexity of a given transaction. If this is not done by management, salespeople will do it in a more informal manner—often at the annual kick-off meeting—in ways that undercut the sales process. Consider this imaginary (but entirely plausible) exchange:

Salesperson 1: What was your largest transaction this year without following the process?

Salesperson 2: $60,000.

Salesperson 1: Wow, mine was $30,000.

Salesperson 3: Got you both. Mine was $85,000!

The simple fact is, salespeople resist following a process. As a rule, they don't like documenting their sales efforts. Even those who can clearly articulate their buyer's goals, problems, and needs; understand the buyers buying process; and so on rarely take the time to put it down in writing and confirm it with the prospect. If they win, it appears to be based solely on the sales expertise of the salesperson. If they lose, there's no tangible evidence—no "fingerprints on the gun," if you will.

Consider for a moment how much money it costs an organization to compete on a major transaction and lose. According to Sales Benchmark Index, the cost of sale for an average company is 22 percent of the final transaction amount. On a major opportunity (let's say $250,000), if you were to add in management calls, support people, demonstrations, plane trips, and so on, the cost to compete on a major opportunity over the course of six months could easily be $60,000 or more. When you start looking at the number of opportunities that salespeople compete for where they go the distance and lose anyway, it doesn't take many of those marathon losses to wipe out the profits made on the winning transactions.

Seen in that context, is it reasonable to require that the salesperson be able to document where he or she is in the opportunity, so that the sales manager can determine if it is qualified and warrants the allocation of additional resources?

Salespeople (especially those who are not year-to-date against quota) intuitively know how much needs to be in their pipelines to keep their managers off their backs. When their pipelines are thin, salespeople become less selective about what they are working on. Along with the compromise in quality of opportunities comes an increasingly unbridled optimism. Here's another dialogue that may sound familiar:

> Salesperson: As you know, boss, things have been slow for me the last four months. I've been in a slump. But this is my month! Grab onto my coattails, because I'm going to have a huge month!

> Manager: Let's run through your forecast.

> Salesperson: OK. Unexpectedly, I received an RFP this week. It looks like it was wired for us. They're going to make a decision by the end of the month. I figure it to be about an 80 percent chance. I just spoke with the ABC Company. The proposal has been sitting there for 90 days, but my friend in the account says management is getting serious again. And there's another one sitting out there! . . .

Most likely, this salesperson will continue in this vein until the manager is persuaded that things are OK. And most likely, that won't be too difficult, because managers want to believe. Optimistic forecasts from the sales force, as noted earlier, permit the sales manager to make his or her own forecast more optimistic. And—on the downside—asking a salesperson to leave is likely to cause disruption, distract the sales manager from more important tasks at hand, and perhaps reflect poorly on the manager.

We've presented these two dialogues in part to underscore the critical importance of having a process and managing with the process in mind. Discipline and structure are as important to sales as they are to basketball, military maneuvers, and the opera. Yes, creativity and spontaneity have their place—but not in a conversation between a salesperson and a manager of a publicly traded company about what opportunities make up the revenue forecast.

By reviewing progress (or lack thereof) against defined and auditable best practices, managers can assess the probability of winning a particular opportunity and help salespeople do something that they are loathe to do themselves: withdraw from low-probability opportunities. (For a salesperson, removing a low-probability account from the forecast generally means that a replacement will have to be found by prospecting (an activity that many salespeople like less than a root canal). The role of salespeople is to *build* pipeline by executing the sales process; the role of the manager is to *grade* that pipeline, with an eye toward *disqualification*. Managers should own the quality of the opportunities they allow their salespeople to spend time and resources on.

By invoking and sticking to a strong sales process, managers should be able to increase the percentage of winnable situations in the pipeline.

More Than One Process

A common misconception is that companies have a single sales process. In fact, most organizations have multiple offerings, serve different vertical industries, and engage in several different types of sales. Following are some examples:

- Add-on business with an existing client
- Sale of professional services
- Renewal of a maintenance agreement
- Sale to a prospect
- Sale involving a partner
- Sale through a reseller
- Major account
- National account

Given this diversity of transactions, many companies find that one size (or process) does not and cannot fit all of their selling situations. We suggest defining customercentric steps and deliverables for your most complex sale, and then determining subsets of steps and deliverables for smaller transactions.

Targeted Conversations

In our view, a sales cycle can be distilled into a series of conversations between the seller and the buyer(s) for each defined step in a sales process. But the emphasis is on the *buyer*—that is, someone who is qualified and empowered to buy. This means that conversations have to be targeted. Sales-Ready Messaging involves defining the titles or functions of people within a prospect whom salespeople will have to call on in order to get their proposed offering sold and installed.

Once those titles have been identified, a menu of business objectives for each title should be developed. As explained in our previous discussions, a buying cycle does not begin unless or until the buyer shares a goal that your offering can help them achieve. Once you have a title and a business objective, you are in a position to have a targeted conversation.

See the Targeted Conversations examples in Table 7.1. This simply lists four titles at a prospect company and assigns a total of eight goals to them.

Title	Goal
VP Finance	Achieve profit projections with accurate sales forecasting
VP Finance	Reduce the cost of sales
VP Sales	Improved forecasting accuracy
VP Sales	Shorten start-up time for new sales reps
VP Sales	Increase the number of B and C reps who make quota
VP Mktg	Provide Sales-Ready Messaging to sales force
CIO	Support implementation with limited resources
CIO	Secure customer/pipeline data from competition

Table 7.1 Integrating Marketing and Sales Targeted Conversations for Selling: Sales Force Automation

Obvious? Perhaps. But we've seen most salespeople start making sales calls without this kind of structured and focused approach.

Another advantage of developing this kind of list is that it can include inputs from more than just the salespeople. In fact, people at many levels in the selling organization can contribute. In addition, targeting conversations permits a more consistent positioning of offerings, because the responsibility for positioning no longer falls solely on the shoulders of the salespeople. And finally, we find that targeting conversations tends to push conversations up higher in the hierarchy—and the higher in the organization a salesperson calls, the shorter the potential menu of business issues, the more predictable the ensuing conversation, and the more likely the sale.

The Wired versus the Unwired

Here's a piece of traditional sales wisdom: "Winners never quit, and quitters never win."

Nonsense. We believe that most organizations don't quit often enough, or early enough, when the odds are against them. Without a defined sales process, they don't know that the odds are against them.

Consider the case where a firm receives a "wired" RFP that requests responses from 10 vendors, and a sales manager authorizes the 60 hours needed (by multiple people) to prepare a response. (By *wired*, we mean that the fix is on, and the process is not truly open because Column A helped write it.) Would you agree that the salesperson who generated the initial interest, and shaped the RFP's requirements with a bias toward his or her own organization's strengths, has a 90-plus percent probability of getting the work? We would.

Now let's say that six other organizations choose to respond. What probability will the salespeople from those six firms enter on their respective forecasts? In most cases, the win rate on unsolicited RFPs is less than 5 percent. But if a salesperson was honest and assigned a 5 percent probability to this effort, his manager would almost certainly ask why 60 hours should be spent in crafting such a careful response to such a low-percentage opportunity.

Experienced salespeople skirt this issue by assigning even the wildest long shots at least a 50 percent probability. If you think about it, being a salesperson is one of the most measurable jobs in the world (percentage of quota obtained), but one of the least accountable. The 60 hours are spent, and when the order goes somewhere else, that opportunity quietly falls off the radar screen. In this example, even though only one favorable decision could possibly be made, six organizations within the vendor community have acted as if they all had at least a 50-50 chance at getting the contract.

The fact is that in defining your sales process, it makes sense for your organization to define two RFP processes. One should be for RFPs that your company has proactively uncovered and driven. A second one could be defined for RFPs in which you have been mainly reactive—that is, not well positioned to influence any of the requirements in the RFP prior to your receiving it.

To give you an idea of win percentages: We worked with a company selling enterprise software that had an entire department that did nothing but respond to RFPs. The previous year, they had reviewed their records and divided RFPs into proactive and reactive initiation. They discovered that in one year, they had responded to 143 unsolicited RFPs that required an average of 75 hours—and got the business a grand total of three times! Long story short: Responding to RFPs that you did not initiate can be a huge drain on your resources. Consider segmenting your sales process and investing your limited resources where they'll give you the most return.

At the end of the day, when a deal finally does close, there are two winners: the vendor who gets the business and the vendor who was the first to walk away because they determined early on that they never had a real chance to win.

Further Segmentation Opportunities

For companies that have multiple divisions with independent sales forces, and/or those using value-added resellers (VARs), it may be helpful to take a step back and decide who you want calling, and where. While this seems fundamental, sales organizations evolve over time, and they can get out of touch with a changing reality. A fresh look—a "clean sheet of paper" approach— can be helpful in stepping away from the forest and looking at the trees.

One account we worked with sold engineering software and over time had developed an extensive reseller channel. They shared with us their desire to migrate their direct sales force from departmental technical sales to Fortune 1000 enterprise sales. After better understanding their direction, we attempted to segment their territories and markets and how they were being covered. We ultimately came up with a grid (see Chapter 19 and Figure 19.1) with the key demarcations they wanted:

1. Sales below $10,000 should be handled by their Telesales group.
2. Transactions with F1000 companies should be sold by their direct sales force.
3. Transactions with non-F1000 companies below $50,000 should be done by resellers.
4. Non-F1000 transactions over $50,000 should be handled jointly.

After defining these thresholds and where they wanted people to be calling, we asked the firm's sales executives what their coverage looked like. They sheepishly admitted that they had the small company/small transaction quadrant covered jointly, transactions over $50,000 with small companies were rare, and virtually none of their direct salespeople were capable of executing an enterprise sale to the F1000. Further investigation uncovered the roots of the problem:

1. Their traditional salespeople were comfortable leading with product and talking to engineers, but they were unable to relate to business-people.
2. Their compensation plan provided an override on business sold by resellers in the direct salesperson territories. Some direct salespeople were making a great living by doing nothing more than overseeing the efforts of their assigned partners and hadn't closed any business of their own in over a year.

The executives realized that in order to achieve the desired coverage, it would be necessary to train their salespeople to make higher-level calls, and that the compensation plan had to change. Because of their concern about the potential turnover of many of their direct salespeople, we suggested a 12-month weaning period, during which the override would be phased out. This approach allowed the pipeline on larger accounts to be built. Turnover was minimal, and a high percentage of direct salespeople who were either unable or unwilling to make the adjustment to large account enterprise sales voluntarily joined reseller organizations—a favorable outcome for everyone concerned.

This situation was discussed, and an approach to resolving it was completed, in about an hour. We don't claim to be geniuses, and in fact, none of the concepts came close to being rocket science. But we think the example underscores the fact that sales processes evolve over time and that a fresh look periodically is a good idea. In many cases, inviting in an outsider for a new perspective turns out to be productive.

The Clean Sheet of Paper

When it comes to sales process, an occasional clean-sheet-of-paper look is a good idea.

Take, for example, a company that starts with a few salespeople and co-founders selling the first few accounts, then evolves into a $250 million organization using both direct and indirect sales. The VP of sales was the first salesperson hired all those years ago. A wonderful success story, all around—and yet, in our experience, the company could derive a great deal of benefit from a third party facilitating a session to evaluate (1) where the business is heading, (2) what markets they are attempting to penetrate, and (3) who is calling where.

Just as offerings, markets, and sales situations are dynamic, sales processes, too, must be reviewed and adjusted on an ongoing basis, if they are to reflect how your buyers buying patterns change over time. Reviewing your sales process is recommended, and milestones should be either verified or modified by analyzing the results. This may be done as often as quarterly, for a relatively new market or offering, or on an annual basis for mature organizations.

As suggested previously, consider reviewing your top five wins to highlight best practices in selling. And as unpleasant a task as it may be, it's important to review your toughest five losses as well, in an attempt to see if your process needs to be changed.

Process Is Structure

Our view is that a sales process represents the management team's best understanding of how buying cycles take place and how to fit into those cycles.

As with most processes involving human behavior, there can and will be exceptions that must be made under certain circumstances. While some sales methodologies treat selling situations as being black or white, experience has taught us there are many, many shades of gray.

If the potential usages of your offerings are highly variable (i.e., consulting, professional services), process becomes more important. The worst-case scenario is a salesperson calling on a buyer who has a wide spectrum of responses and reactions without a plan of how to handle the call. In one sense, sales process tries to put structure around the number of sales calls made during a sales cycle.

Without sales process, every situation is an exception based on the seller's opinions. Despite the potential benefit of repetition, everything gets done "once in a row." This can be costly at several levels:

1. Salespeople are determining when and how to compete. These are people whose compensation is based on gross revenue, without regard for the amount of resources required either to win or to lose. Their qualification skills in filtering out low-probability opportunities may be proportional to their year-to-date quota positions. For someone behind quota who is working marginal opportunities, things are likely to get worse, not better.

2. Without putting structure around sales situations, selling organizations lack the ability to drill down and better understand the kinds of circumstances that are likely to result in unsuccessful sales cycles—or, conversely, are likely to lead to sales.

CEOs frequently proclaim to the investment community that their firms embody "best practices." Unfortunately, we rarely hear this claim made in regard to sales—probably because most companies don't do so, and wouldn't dare to claim to. In fact, when it comes to sales, they're not even sure that best practices exist. (It's an art, right?)

We believe that a milestone-based road map that can be audited is absolutely essential. Sales is less an art, and more of a craft. While the design and implementation of an effective sales process are formidable tasks, the upside—having better control over top-line revenue generation—can be absolutely invaluable.

Chapter 8

INTEGRATING THE SALES AND MARKETING PROCESSES

In many cases, the difference between a company that is enjoying success and one that is struggling is the degree of integration and cooperation among the functional departments. If the relationships among engineering, manufacturing, purchasing, finished goods, accounting, and so on are poorly defined, you can have anything ranging from disorganization to chaos. CEOs are hired, in part, to create and maintain effective relationships among functional organizational "silos," and—in the best of cases—to break down the walls between those silos. And most CEOs will tell you that they're pretty good at that role.

Our professional experience has focused us on the interface between two of these functional areas: sales and marketing. (We'll use the generic term *marketing,* but in this and subsequent chapters, our focus is on product and tactical marketing rather than, say, institutional marketing, strategic marketing, or consumer packaged goods marketing.) We believe strategic marketing means looking at the convergence of market factors, technology trends, productivity improvements, and the like and asking questions like "Who and where do we want to be three years out? Five years out? What decisions must we make today to position ourselves for where we want to be in the future?" Tactical marketing's mission is to figure out how to achieve today's revenue targets with today's offerings.

In the B2B world, our experience tells us that the interface between sales and tactical marketing is often neglected, and frequently tenuous—limited, in some cases, to a lead being passed from one to the other. On the face of it, this most common touch point is a weak reed to lean on. Imagine if the VPs of sales and marketing were each asked to define a lead. How closely do you think those two definitions would resemble each other?

If we dig deeper, the root cause of problems between sales and marketing is a lack of formal awareness and process to gather knowledge about how customers use offerings to achieve goals, solve problems, and satisfy needs. In most organizations we work with, product development is also at fault. How many technology companies have been founded by a technologist who created a solution in search of a problem?

Later in this book we show you how to create an organization's "core content"—content that will enable business conversations with decision makers and influencers. Content that will enable Web visitors to understand how they might use your offerings. Content that will permeate the rest of your tactical marketing vehicles—white papers, brochures, advertising, trade shows, and so forth—and make its way into your customer and sales training.

We believe that a key component of creating B2B core content is tapping the experience of a client's customer service people and professional services people. These are the people that are responsible every day for helping customers use their offerings to do their jobs and satisfy their needs. They have the customer usage knowledge we need to help them create Sales-Ready Messaging.

In most organizations, sales and marketing are expected somehow to collaborate or "align." Of course, sales thinks that marketing should align with them while marketing thinks it should be just the opposite. These two functions ultimately drive top-line revenue, and yet few companies have a working definition of how they are supposed to interact. Further complicating matters is the fact that in many organizations, marketing activity is neither clearly defined nor readily measurable. This overall lack of clearly defined roles and responsibilities contributes to what is frequently a strained relationship. In extreme cases, when revenue targets and market share numbers are not achieved, the result is a rash of finger-pointing.

An all-too-typical example of how each side views the other, when things get testy:

Sales on Marketing: Ivory-tower big-picture people with no clue as to what customers need!

Marketing on Sales: Overpaid order-takers who will promise anything to get the business!

The executive to whom both sales and marketing report—the CEO or another senior-level person—is sometimes called on to "referee" their relationship, especially after the finger-pointing sets in. This is a difficult and unpleasant role. Who's to blame for the fact that revenue objectives are not being met? We've already seen how selling (in most organizations) is a haphazard activity. And inside the walls of the organization, the assessment of marketing's performance is almost entirely subjective.

Often, in the early stages of our interactions with a client CEO, we find an opportunity to ask him or her to describe marketing's role as it relates to sales. Usually, there's a long pause, meaning that the executive doesn't have a ready answer to this question. (There would not be a similar pause if the question focused, for example, on the relationship between engineering and manufacturing.) After some hemming and hawing, we get responses like the following:

- They support sales.
- They position our offerings.
- They generate leads for sales.
- They create collateral for our offerings.
- They run our seminars and trade shows.

From the CEO's perspective, the good news is that over the past several decades, many companies have made huge progress in establishing clear and effective processes to govern the relationships among accounting, engineering, manufacturing, and so on. The bad news is that sales and marketing have resisted this kind of progress. By any measure, this is an enormous lost opportunity. These two functions define, almost exclusively, the company's relationship with its customers, and ultimately are responsible for driving and achieving top-line revenue. Think how much a business could benefit from putting processes in place that would get these two functional silos—traditionally uncooperative—to (1) work together, and (2) work for the good of the customer.

A Natural Integration

For at least the last 20 years there have been articles and seminars geared toward the concept of integrating sales and marketing. So few companies have been successful in this endeavor it is a topic that won't generate much interest. Executives have concluded it is "mission impossible" despite the fact that it is a vitally important issue. As with many things, a name change can resurrect an issue. The whole concept of Customer Experience Management (CEM) cannot be addressed unless sales and marketing get on the same page.

We'd like to propose a necessary first step: marketing must view itself as the front end of the sales process, rather than the back end of product development. Especially in this new world of the well-educated, informed buyer, marketing plays a critical role. If you agree with the concept that sellers are typically engaged much later in the buying process (i.e., after the buyer has already identified an active need, researched potential solutions, and formulated at least a preliminary vision), then marketing—the people creating the publicly available, customer-facing content—can often determine if the salesperson even gets a chance to compete.

Sounds simple, right, like some sort of psychological sleight of hand? Not really. Before two groups can coordinate their efforts, they need to settle on one or more common objectives. We've already described CustomerCentric Selling as a way of helping buyers achieve a goal, solve a problem, or satisfy a need. Well, shouldn't that also be marketing's objective as well—to help potential customers understand how they can achieve a goal, solve a problem, or satisfy a need with the company's offering? If, in addition to creating the "view from 30,000 feet," marketing could contribute effectively to the conversations that salespeople have with their prospects and customers—the "view from 3½ feet"—all would benefit.

But this can't happen unless marketing joins forces with sales. To restate the imperative: marketing has to believe that they are the first car on the train of sales, rather than the last car on the train of product development. Marketing has to learn to face the customer, learn from the customer, and enable the customer, rather than look toward the lab.

Marketing executives, of course, claim that they are already supporting sales. They are handling messaging; generating leads for sales (but what really *is* a lead?—see Chapter 11); creating collateral for product and service offerings, seminars, and trade shows; and, of course, cranking out PowerPoint presentations for senior executives. But the evidence suggests that whatever they're doing, it's not working. Research done by the American Marketing Association's Customer Message Management Forums indicated that between 50 and 90 percent of the collateral prepared by marketing is not used by salespeople in the field.

Clearly, a new approach is needed. We suggest that the first change needs to be a shift of affiliation within the organization. This is primarily a psychological shift, but it can also take many procedural and even physical forms. (How is the organizational chart drawn? Whose office is next to whose? Which departments are physically adjacent?)

A second step is to formally charge marketing with the responsibility for developing and maintaining the company's core content—in other words, its sales messaging. Sales-Ready Messaging can be created to support targeted conversations with decision makers and decision influencers. As stated in earlier chapters, this cannot be accomplished with product information; it requires product *usage* information positioned specifically for decision-maker job titles within targeted industries. We strongly recommend to many of our clients that they consider creating the post of chief content officer. This is an individual who takes responsibility for all product usage messaging—the positioning of an organization's offerings at all levels and through all channels.

In today's business environment, companies are trying to eliminate positions, and we don't make this recommendation lightly. But think about the potential benefit that grows out of this kind of change. We now have a way to begin a natural, organic integration of the marketing and sales functions: Both marketing and sales share the common mission of helping customers achieve goals, solve problems, and satisfy needs through the use of the company's offerings.

The sales and support teams in the field are closest to the customers and prospects. If a tool doesn't work in making a call, they're the first to know. They therefore have to serve as constructive malcontents—meaning that they have to suggest how messaging tools can be improved and kept up to date. They have to bring back from the field new insights into how offerings are actually used, and not used, by customers.

Marketing, meanwhile, must own the content. They have the responsibility of achieving consistency of message and dissemination across multiple sales channels, multiple product lines, and so on. In the past 10 years we have seen technology increase the touch points that are now available to marketing. Consider e-mail, Web sites, blogs, social networking, Webinars, banner ads, CDs, and so forth. Adding the responsibility of Sales-Ready Messaging dramatically increases the scope of marketing's job, which is the reason we believe the title chief content officer is more appropriate.

Learning from the Web

For a number of reasons, we love the Web.

One reason, relevant to this chapter, is that it puts marketing directly in touch with buyers. Think about it. In most organizations, marketing owns the Web site. Every day, dozens—or hundreds, or thousands—of visitors show up on the organization's electronic doorstep. Some are only window-shopping, of course. But in many cases, they are trying to buy. Companies are slowly coming to the realization that more and more buying experiences begin electronically. Along with this trend, salespeople are getting involved much later in buying cycles because buyers can leverage search engines, blogs, Webinars, and social networking to learn about offerings and develop their requirements prior to talking with a salesperson.

Some buyers have gotten there as a result of a salesperson making an in-person sales call or through a demand creation campaign. But now they're at the doorstep, and ready to be influenced, if the Web site is up to the challenge. As a result, the Web is giving organizations—and specifically marketing groups within those organizations—the opportunity to develop a rich and nuanced understanding of what customers want to accomplish. In addition to disseminating information or even order fulfillment, Web sites can be designed to help marketing learn the following: "How do you use our products?" "What were you able to accomplish?" "How would you like to use our products in the future?" One client, a software company in the Washington, D.C., area, reported a 400 percent increase in inquiries once they shifted the focus of their site to customer goals versus company product. Additionally, according to the VP of marketing, the tone of the inquiries changed from "send me some literature about your product" to "our goals for the coming year are . . . how could you help?"

This understanding can profoundly influence subsequent messaging (and ultimately, perhaps, research and development, product development, and engineering). When marketing relates directly to buyers by means of a Web site, they begin to understand the necessity for facilitating the buying process with meaningful electronic dialogues. You don't handle an objection on a Web site; instead, you make it easy for buyers to get good answers to and work through their questions. You don't close a sale on the Web site; instead, you make it easy for buyers to take action to satisfy their own needs. When the Web visitor hits Enter and buys, it may be because marketing was able to facilitate the buying process. In other words, in the electronic manifestation, marketing has acted exactly like an effective, customercentric salesperson.

However, the Web is not the answer to everything. In enterprise selling situations, for example, salespeople are necessary. But think how much more effective marketing can be, in providing tools and collateral to support enterprise selling, when they have had sustained, iterative contact with the customer base through the Web. They are far better prepared to develop Sales-Ready Messaging to support all the many conversations that add up to an effective customercentric sales process.

Toward a Selling Architecture

Sales-Ready Messaging, as we've already noted, means empowering salespeople to have meaningful conversations with decision makers and decision influencers about how they can achieve a goal, solve a problem, or satisfy a need through the use of the offering. Sales-Ready Messaging also empowers Web visitors to understand how they can achieve a goal, solve a problem, or satisfy a need through the use of the offering. When you combine this effective core content with sales process, you gain the capability of codifying, or architecting, sales conversations, and sales cycles.

As we've already seen, many organizations are currently struggling to implement CRM systems. With sales and marketing integrated at the salesperson level, the desired return on a company's CRM investment now becomes achievable. CRM systems are failing because the SFA component is failing. We believe that by integrating product usage messaging with defined sales processes, the manual sales productivity system can now be automated. We have developed "best practice" sales processes for multiple industries. With the SFA component enhanced with sales process and just-in-time Sales-Ready Messaging, CRM systems can begin to produce tangible, measurable results.

If sales processes can be integrated with marketing processes, which include Sales-Ready Messaging, CEOs can gain control over generating top-line revenue, and organizations can improve their relationships with their customers.

In later chapters, we'll describe the components of a sales process that allows sharing of best sales practices, defines the relationship between sales and marketing, facilitates creation of Sales-Ready Messaging, allows managers to ensure pipeline quality while assessing and developing their direct reports, and ultimately results in an improved ability to forecast revenue at the opportunity level.

Chapter 9

FEATURES VERSUS CUSTOMER USAGE

In this chapter, we pick up on a theme introduced earlier: the need to focus on how a customer might use a particular offering—growing out of conversations about that customer's needs—rather than on a presentation focused on features.

Here's a question you might want to ask us at this point: Is Customer-Centric Selling applicable in a range of situations? For example, is it applicable when a product is viewed as a commodity with no distinguishing features? Is it applicable when you sell professional services rather than a tangible product?

Our methodology is based in large part on our experiences, many of which initially involved selling information technology at the enterprise level and later evolved into selling our own professional services and sales methodology. The principle of positioning offerings applies whether you are trying to make an enterprise sale for an intangible offering such as business intelligence software, selling the phone company's services, or helping a bank that is trying to cross-sell additional features or services directly to consumers.

Over the years, we have worked with a wide range of companies in a variety of industries. These have included professional services providers, retail banks, companies offering credit card sales to merchants, overnight delivery services, and temporary housing providers, to name a few. All have benefited from our approach, even in cases where the offering was only one of many in a crowded field of entries. In fact, our experience suggests that in situations where the offering is perceived as a commodity—that is, interchangeable with the competition—the most powerful differentiator is the buyer's experience with the salesperson or sales process.

The Pinocchio Effect

As noted in earlier chapters, traditional sellers tend to lead with product—that is, to push hard on what they perceive to be the distinguishing characteristics of their offering. In the case of business software, they are quick to jump to the demo. For professional services, it is often a detailed (and lengthy) PowerPoint presentation that serves up the opinion of the service provider as to how they impact the prospective buyers' business results. But this approach is fraught with peril. It often fails, for example, to establish a salesperson's competence. It short-circuits meaningful discussion of the buyer's needs. It may lead to premature price discussions, causing sticker shock, and ultimately result in no sale. Many traditional salespeople fail to realize that only those differentiators that the buyers agree they want or need are applicable.

Part of the problem is the seller's familiarity with the offering—most often thought of as a great asset. Think about how traditional salespeople learn about their offerings. In many cases, newly hired salespeople are sent off to what their employers call *product training* during their very first week on the job. In many organizations, this instruction is referred to as *sales training*, but it should not be, in our estimation. This training is frequently conducted by the product marketing department.[1]

More and more companies are building infrastructures in product marketing. In many cases, these efforts lead to what might be called a Pinocchio effect: The product begins to take on a life of its own, aside from any customer-related considerations. The apparent mission of product marketing is to talk about what "it" will do—"it" being the product. It will lower your inventory costs, it will build your market share, it will improve your profitability, it will reduce your employee turnover . . . (feel free to fill in any unsubstantiated claims your Pinocchio can accomplish).

This is a backward approach. At the end of a call made by a customer-centric seller, the buyers shouldn't be focusing on what *it* can do for them; they should be focusing on what *they* can do with it. The conclusion is inescapable: The focus of both salespeople and buyers should be on usage, not the features of an offering.

---

1. In this case, we'll use the specific term *product marketing*, rather than the broader *marketing*.

Features and Benefits

What's a feature? For our purposes, a feature is an attribute of a product or service. Features include things like size, weight, color, material used, modules, and specifications. Product marketing people take artistic license with these facts, adding adjectives to heighten the feature's presumed sex appeal and thereby make the product even more irresistible. This is where words like *robust*, *seamless*, and *integrated* begin to creep in.

The primary problem we have with sellers being taught to lead with features is that this approach counts on the buyer knowing whether or not the feature is useful and therefore relevant. Yes, there are hundreds of thousands of salespeople who lead with product or service features in their sales pitches every day, and yes, in a lot of cases, it actually works. But it works best when buyers already understand how to use the proposed product or service, understand the value or benefit of using it, trust the seller, and trust the seller's company.

Information or Irritation?

Let's say that you are a satisfied BMW customer and you go into a BMW dealership shopping for your next Beamer. You already know the product line, already trust the company, and already have a pretty good idea of which model you are interested in. Up comes the salesperson, who begins lecturing you on the cool new features of something called "I-Drive." As a buyer, can you get past this feature presentation? Probably. You'll listen for a while, take a test drive, and—all else being equal—you'll buy your BMW. Were you impressed by the salesperson or by I-Drive? Not really. How much selling was done here? Not much. You came in the door as an expert buyer, and you bought. If you didn't buy, has the salesperson earned your loyalty? Wouldn't you buy the same car for $500 less from another dealer? The seller has missed an opportunity to become part of your buying decision.

So is it a good idea for salespeople to spew features? Almost never. The expert buyer already knows about, or knows enough not to care much about, I-Drive. As for the rest of the buying population—most people, in other words—those who do not understand I-Drive might not ask for an explanation that could expose their ignorance to someone they don't trust. They could be intimidated and start to distance themselves from the salesperson. Most people have their own version of I-Drive in their buying past. For example, have you ever been told that the car you are thinking about buying has an overhead camshaft? Well, do you know or care what an overhead cam is, or how that feature might be useful to you? How about a McPherson strut?

Does that sound like something you might put to good use? Could you explain the benefits or value of these features at a cocktail party?

The CustomerCentric definition of selling is "helping a buyer achieve goals, solve problems, or satisfy needs." So what do we do if we're not BMW—if our buyer has no clue as to why he or she might need our product, or how to use it? Presumably, our product has some features that are of interest. So how do we position our features to nonexpert buyers?

The first step in a buying process, of course, is having someone decide to look. Assuming that our business-development efforts succeed in stimulating some measure of curiosity or interest on the part of prospective buyers who we believe should be looking at our offering, what then? They will stay interested only as long as they are curious about what we are selling, understand the importance of our offering to them, or have hope for a solution from us. If we launch into a feature presentation, we will lose most nonexpert buyers very quickly. They will stay interested only as long as they perceive the conversation, and therefore the seller, to be relevant.

Many salespeople experience a 6- to 12-month learning curve when they join companies selling enterprise solutions. In those weeks and months, they frequently get their heads stuffed with the features of their company's offerings—which in the case of a complex offering may number in the hundreds or even the thousands. Then they go out into their territories and attempt to convey their own interpretations of countless features in a 30-minute presentation—and are surprised, and frustrated, when their prospects don't get it. How well can CEOs sleep when they come to the realization that each of their 200 salespeople has developed his or her own boiled-down version (opinions) of what the company sells?

In most cases, the buyer who doesn't get it isn't stupid. So what's going on in a buyer's head when he or she encounters a seller describing an offering as a noun (as opposed to a verb)? Here are some of the questions a buyer may be asking:

- "Is the salesperson trying to sell me?"
- "Am I supposed to understand what the salesperson is talking about?"
- "Why is the salesperson telling me this?"
- "Why does the salesperson think I would be interested in *that*?"
- "Am I supposed to take the salesperson's word for it?"
- "Are these facts or opinions?"

In situations like this, buyers defend themselves with objections. Dozens of sales courses over the years have had modules on handling objections, as if an objection were an ailment or character flaw in the buyer. Many companies have taught the "feel, felt, found" approach. When encountering objections, the seller takes three steps:

- "I understand how you feel."
- "Others have felt that way."
- "But they found that (insert phrase here indicating that the buyer is mistaken in his or her concerns)."

The fact is, most objections that salespeople encounter are induced by the seller. Sellers invite objections by the way they present their offerings.

Even some sales approaches that seem customer-friendly are really "spray-and-pray" presentations in disguise. In early Xerox sales training, for example, salespeople were taught to talk about benefits: "Because of Feature X, dear buyer, you can expect to get Benefit Y!" But strangely enough, Xerox's sellers were not encouraged to find out what the buyer wanted to accomplish before they made their initial benefit statement. In that sales culture, therefore, the alleged benefit of a feature resided mainly in the mind of the seller.

And Xerox was not unique in this regard. We sometimes ask our audiences the question, "What sales culture did you grow up in?" Most large selling organizations have their subtle sales-culture idiosyncrasies, but virtually all of them encourage presumptuous benefit statements by sellers to buyers.

The Power of Usage Scenarios

Our experience has taught us that great salespeople rarely have to close, and that great sales calls are conversations, rather than presentations. Customercentric salespeople are able—usually with very little help from their marketing department—to translate the feature knowledge they are given by product marketing into usage scenarios. These are simply hypothetical examples that are highly relevant to the buyer and that the seller can use to conduct intelligent conversations. They somehow just roll off the tongue of a customercentric salesperson.

As noted, those are the lucky 13 percent. But what about the other 87 percent? What about salespeople who are unable to do the feature-to-usage-scenario translation on their own?

Let's say we have a seller in his late twenties who is going to make a sales call on a senior executive in her mid-fifties—let's have her be the vice president of sales of a Fortune 1000 company. The seller's mission is to have the buyer spend hundreds of thousands of dollars on a CRM system, which is an application she does not fully understand. How can we help this young seller relate to this buyer? How can we help him have a conversation, rather than make a presentation?

One of the features of the CRM application is control over access to specific data—that is, who can see what—in a company's database. Most likely, an expert buyer can understand this feature and relate it easily to his or her own use. Most senior executives, however, are not adept at understanding how software can help them achieve their business goals. What can the seller do?

Well, most senior sales executives understand high employee turnover. Suppose the seller asked a question like, "What if you heard through a reliable source that one of your top salespeople was going to leave to go to work for your competition?" If the executive expressed interest, the salesperson could then pose another question: "Would it be useful to you to be able to go into your CRM system and suspend that person's access to your prospect and buyer data—from any location, even if you were traveling?"

This is an example of converting a feature into a usage scenario. It works because it is so specific. It shows the prospective buyer how the data security feature could be used by the executive to protect company assets in the event of employee turnover. Usage scenarios help buyers visualize how they could use the seller's offering to solve a problem, achieve a goal, make money, or save money. The preceding example involves a complex enterprise software sale, but what about simple retail sales? Would converting from product presentations to usage scenarios also be preferable?

We gave a presentation at a Silicon Valley marketing executive symposium at the Stanford Business School. At the end of our talk, a senior vice president of a retail bank approached us with the idea of trying out our ideas in a banking context. Specifically, their issue was cross-selling. At that time, the average number of bank products (savings account, checking account, ATM card, CD, and so on) for a retail bank buyer was 2.2. His bank was below average—at 1.9—and he was under heavy pressure to increase cross-selling.

First, we needed to learn how they were currently selling before we could suggest any changes. We were observing one morning when a couple from out of state came into a branch near one of the campuses of the state university system. They had their daughter in tow. After a brief wait, they were steered toward the desk of a 23-year-old retail banker, whom we'll call "Sarah."

"Our daughter will be going to school here," the father told Sarah. "We want to open up a checking account for her."

Sarah immediately brought out her sales kit, which included details about the four checking account plans. She detailed each and asked the buyers if they were prepared to select one. Then she remembered the new corporate priority—cross-selling—and asked politely, "Would you also like a savings account?"

"No, thanks," said the father; they did their banking back home in Iowa. They simply needed a local checking account for their daughter while she was in college.

We told the bank that this was one approach to cross-selling, but that we thought there was room for improvement. The bank's marketing head decided to let us try out our ideas on a pilot basis. After we studied how consumers actually used each of the bank's products, we developed usage scenarios and (in a predetermined pilot region) trained their retail people in the use of these scenarios.

Here is an example of adopting a customercentric approach to cross-selling: A couple from Nebraska visited a branch office to open a checking account for their daughter, who would be attending school near the bank. This time, before working through the specifics of the checking account, the retail banker asked a number of usage-scenario questions:

- When you are back in Nebraska, would there be times when you would like to be able to check your daughter's balance by using the Internet?
- When you are back home, would you like to be able to transfer money from your bank account there to your daughter's account here simply by using the Internet?
- If your daughter has a roadside emergency, would you like her to be able to get emergency funds anytime she wants—but still not have her hand in your wallet?

Good questions, right? Questions that you would like to be asked by a representative of a bank that you're doing business with, and that demonstrate customercentric expertise in dealing with circumstances like your own. Well, guess what happened. By using these kinds of usage-scenario questions, cross-selling in the pilot region went up 400 percent. In truth, the bank had no product differentiation whatsoever from its competition. The difference is in patience, process, and content—in architecting the buyer's experience with the seller. It was in shifting from feature selling to customer-usage selling.

Another, slightly more complicated, example of converting from feature to customer-usage selling involved the call center of a telecommunications company in a large metropolitan area. When new residents moved into the area, they typically called to set up their phone service—service initiation. We're willing to bet that almost everyone reading this book understands what call waiting is, and what it allows you to do. But imagine it's the early 1980s, you *don't* understand call waiting, and someone is trying to sell it to you. Chances are that you'll have to ask some follow-up questions before you get it—and maybe even buy it. Even then, the phone company greatly hopes that you would keep that service for at least six months, so that it could break even.

Let's assume that a call center representative of a phone company today were speaking with a retired couple in their late seventies or early eighties. During the service-initiation process, the call center representative asks a series of "do you want . . ." questions regarding the company's various products, like call forwarding, voice mail, call waiting, paging, caller ID, and so on. If a free trial were offered, would people say yes to these features?

The problem for the phone company arose when many of these services were discontinued three to six months after initiation. The phone company needed these additional services to stay installed for at least six months to break even on them; after that, the arithmetic was good. So how do you keep new services installed? Customers must realize the value of the services and understand how to use them.

In the case of our client, our analysis revealed that many buyers didn't know *why* they needed the additional services they were saying yes to, or *how* they would use them. Some elderly purchasers of call waiting called customer service to complain that their phones "keep on beeping." Others firmly objected when their phone bills went up in the fourth month—perhaps forgetting that the premium services that they had subscribed to (and that they had never used) were offered free of charge for the first three months.

When designing an approach to address this customer issue, we first developed a simple spreadsheet of available features (the y-axis) and their related buyer issues (the x-axis). We then worked through a series of diagnostic questions and usage scenarios for their customer service representatives to use while taking orders during service initiation.

Example

Call center representative:

  "Have friends or family tried to reach you while you have been on the phone?"
  "Have they been frustrated by busy signals?"
  "Have you missed, or been delayed in receiving, important calls?"

If (and *only* if) the buyer says yes to these questions, the call center representative then asks:

> *"If someone attempts to call you while you are already on a call, would you want to hear a tone, and—at your option— click the receiver to put the first call on hold, take the incoming call, and when finished, click the receiver to resume your original call?"*
>
> If the buyer answers with a yes, the call center representative can then close the sale:
>
> *"Our Call Waiting feature provides this capability at a cost of only $4.95 per month. Would you like to try it for 30 days, at no charge?"*

It's not rocket science, right? But it works. By taking the time to ask a few simple questions about need and customer usage—and, importantly, to educate the consumer about the usage and value of particular services— the company was able to cut discontinuances dramatically. And, we should stress, the company was able to deliver services to people who understood and appreciated them, and were willing to pay for them. A win-win outcome for everyone.

The Shared Mission

A shared mission is critical. We often tell our clients to reinvent their marketing efforts away from product marketing and toward customer-usage marketing.

The best way to facilitate this reinvention process is through the CustomerCentric Selling Solution Development Prompter, which we'll explain in the chapters that follow. Once the theme of customer usage replaces the traditional emphasis on product features, all kinds of good things begin to happen across multiple marketing vehicles. For example:

- Prospect and customer correspondence
- Product development
- Advertising
- Success stories
- White papers
- Web site
- Trade-show strategies
- Demand-creation strategies

- Buyer training
- Sales training
- Professional-services training

When marketing becomes focused on customer usage, only then will marketing share a mission with sales: helping buyers discover how they can achieve their goals, solve their problems, and satisfy their needs through their company's offerings. For companies without this shared mission, CEOs will continue to lose sleep, knowing that the forecast consists of the opinions of sellers who each developed their own interpretation of what they're selling, rather than selling with a shared mission.

Chapter 10

CREATING SALES-READY MESSAGING

Selling at its best consists of a series of conversations with buyers. During these conversations, the salesperson's objective is to identify and understand the buyer's needs, problems, desires, and goals. As the salesperson learns about the buyer's circumstances, he or she also begins to position the company's offerings. Another benefit of competently diagnosing a buyer's need is discovering why the buyer cannot achieve a goal, solve a problem, or satisfy a need.

Selling organizations would love to influence and direct these conversations. But this seems like an impossibly ambitious and far-reaching goal. It's not. In this chapter, we lay out a strategy to accomplish that goal.

No, you can't anticipate all potential interactions with buyers at all levels. So our approach is to help the salesperson orchestrate conversations with targeted decision makers and influencers about specific business issues that are addressable through the use of their offering. After a buyer shares a goal, we help the salesperson follow one of a number of flexible scenarios.

Looking at this issue from another perspective, companies that fail to step up to the challenge of influencing sales conversations, give an enormous amount of responsibility to their salespeople. They are asking their salespeople to interpret and communicate the capabilities of their products single-handedly and on-the-fly.

So let's begin with the three conditions that must exist in order to orchestrate an effective, more consistent sales conversation about an offering:

- The buyer's title (or function) and vertical industry must be known.
- The buyer must share a business goal or admit a business problem.
- The seller's offerings must have capabilities that a targeted buyer can use to achieve a goal, solve a problem, or satisfy a need—and, of course, the seller must understand and articulate those capabilities.

Given these three conditions, we believe, organizations can help their traditional salespeople have far more effective sales conversations. They can create Sales-Ready Messaging—a way of approaching a conversation that greatly increases the chances of success.

A Caveat

We will return to the premise of Sales-Ready Messaging throughout the rest of the chapters, but we want to offer a caveat at this point: The higher up in an organization a salesperson calls, the more predictable the conversation. Traditional sales managers will respond well to this observation, of course, since they always want their salespeople to call higher. But we're making the same point for a different reason: The higher in the organization you call, the smaller the number of business objectives you are likely to encounter. This sounds counterintuitive, but it's not: In general, more senior people worry about a finite number of important issues. Conversations with senior management are shorter, more conceptual, and less technical—which in many cases means they're more interesting and more productive.

Analyzing this from a different perspective, there is a level within every target organization below which people tend to have personal goals or agendas, but these are not usually issues their organizations are willing to fund. Designing dialogues at these lower levels is nearly impossible. These people may want to learn all about your offerings, but they don't usually have either (1) the title or (2) overall business goals in mind. Without these prerequisites, Sales-Ready Messaging is impractical.

In the enterprise-solution world, conversations eventually take place with technical people and end users. Our concern is when in the sales cycle these meetings take place. If they constitute the initial meeting, brace yourself for a long sales cycle, and one that can fall apart at any one of several places, as you'll be talking to people who can't say yes but can say no, ending the sales cycle. In contrast, if your initial conversations are with targeted businesspeople who share their business goals, your meetings with the people who report to them will be more productive. After having high-level conversations, calls on lower-level buyers can be more focused by having the buyer understand senior management's goals as they relate to the offerings that are being discussed.

In other words, we advocate, and are attempting to illustrate, a top-down approach to sales. The structured approach described in this chapter lets salespeople spend far less time with people who cannot, or are not going to buy. Whenever possible, we advocate calls being made on people who can't buy, only after qualifying one or more people within the organization who can.

Titles + Goals = Targeted Conversations

We typically initiate our Sales-Ready Messaging projects by asking our clients a fairly basic question: "What are the typical job titles or job functions of the decision makers and influencers with whom your salespeople will have to have meaningful conversations?" Or, phrased differently, "Who is in a position to cost-justify, fund, buy, and implement your products and services?"

The first step in answering this question is to list your vertical industries. Even if you have horizontal offerings, keep in mind that mainstream-market buyers (as described in earlier chapters) like to feel that the selling organization understands and has done business with their industry.

For each industry, make a list of the titles (or job functions) a salesperson is likely to call in order to get your offering sold, funded, and implemented. This exercise is often dependent on the size of the potential transaction and the size of the prospect organization. For now, let's concentrate on large transactions to large organizations, since you can scale down this process at any time.

The problem with this task is directly related to the complexity of the offering. In some instances, salespeople enjoy the luxury of calling just one person who can make the decision. For enterprise sales, the challenge is heightened as the number of people and the accompanying number of business issues increase. Having said that, most of our clients find this to be a fairly easy exercise. They can do it from past experiences, because they encounter the same job titles in sale after sale.

Answering the next questions, though, requires more thought: "For each of these job titles, what goals or business objectives do they have in that function? Which of those goals are addressable through the use of your offering?"

Every goal on your list should be a business variable that your company's offering can help a particular job title achieve. Ideally, the goal should be monetarily based, as the financial benefit of achieving the goal will be used to determine if the cost of the offering can be justified. In other words, a business should be willing to spend money to achieve a goal.

Let's imagine that you are selling an enterprisewide CRM system to a large company. Your amended list might look as follows:

CEO	Achieve revenue growth targets.
	Improve company image.
	Improve share price via improved forecasting.
	Shape the customer experience.

CFO	Improve profitability by lowering cost of sales.
	Lower IT cost for providing a single view of the customers.
	Improve forecasting accuracy.

VP Sales	Increase revenue through improved win rates.
	Shorten sales cycles.
	Improve cross-selling.
	Increase close rates by tracking leads.
	Improve forecasting accuracy.
	Reduce start-up times for new salespeople.

VP Marketing	Increase market share.
	Track results by campaign to justify programs.
	Reduce expense of collateral.
	Deliver just-in-time (JIT) Sales-Ready Messaging to the field.

CIO	Support end users.
	Protect valuable company data.
	Reduce IT expenses.
	Achieve service-level commitments.

In this example, the objectives of the CIO are especially telling (and this turns out to be true in many cases). Buyers generally need the opportunity to quantify solutions. But how would someone determine, for example, if it would be worth $1 million to better support end users? The only way to make that business judgment would be to go out and get the perspectives of the end users—certainly possible, but not an easy task. So the goal that the CIO's office is best able to quantify is that of staying within budget, and that may turn out to be your most fertile ground. Focusing on staying within budget, however, does not bode well for funding new initiatives.

Creating this merged list—job titles with associated goals—sets the stage for what we call Targeted Conversations. But before those conversations can begin, more homework needs to be done.

Solution Development Prompters

As a next step with our clients, we begin to develop questioning templates, which we call Solution Development Prompters, or SDPs.

We recommend that marketing take responsibility for developing these materials and maintaining them. They represent the core content of a company's Sales-Ready Messaging, and they give selling organizations the ability to influence the conversations that their salespeople have with buyers. Simply put, they constitute a sort of road map for a salesperson—a tool that he or she can use to lead a specific job title to a specific vision of using the company's offering to achieve a specific goal.

Unlike a movie, where the writer and director exert full control over the interactions among the actors, no dialogue between a buyer and seller will go exactly according to a script or a plan. Instead, our approach is about increasing the odds in the salesperson's favor by setting the stage for a Targeted Conversation. If a seller can approach a call with a clear idea of (1) whom he or she is talking to and (2) where he or she hopes the conversation will wind up, the chances of success improve. On average, the seller will make better calls.[1]

Solution Development Prompters, as noted, are the core content of a company's Sales-Ready Messaging. So it may surprise you to learn that the messaging in SDPs takes the form of questions. Why? Because questions keep salespeople from "telling." As long as they are asking intelligent questions that their buyer is capable of answering, they are not selling (at least in the buyer's mind). They are consulting. This is a welcome change for the buyer and allows the seller to provide a better customer buying experience.

We believe the role of the salesperson is to become a buying facilitator by leading the buyer with questions that are biased toward the seller's particular offering. SDPs help develop "buyer visions" that have a bias toward your offering.

Some people have difficulty with the term *bias*, feeling that it implies a manipulation of the buyer. We disagree. When we talk about creating a bias, we mean that the salesperson should be making an attempt to help the buyer put his or her stated goal in a context in which the seller's offering will help the buyer achieve that goal. It's analogous to trying on a new pair of running shoes to solve the problem of recurring blisters. If the shoe fits, great. If the seller's offering doesn't fit the problem as defined by the user, then the "opportunity" should be disqualified.

Here's another analogy: Let's say you injured your back, and you consulted with three doctors—one trained in the United States, another in China,

---

1. The phrase "better calls" involves a subjective judgment, but in Chapter 14, we'll show you a more objective way to debrief and assess calls.

and a third in Sweden. Most likely, their methods of treating you would vary drastically, based on their training and experience. And most likely, each would attempt to create in you a bias in favor of his or her specific therapies. Are they manipulating you? No. They are offering solutions based on how they have been successful in treating similar conditions in the past. They are attempting to help you solve your problem (very patient-centric). And ultimately, you will choose your doctor based on the trust and confidence the doctor created during the diagnosis.

Once you have created your Targeted Conversations List for a given offering, you are ready to create Sales-Ready Messaging, in the form of SDPs. You do this by assembling four components: offering, industry, title, and goal. Using an example from the list developed previously, the result would look like the following:

Offering:	CRM software
Industry:	Fortune 1000 company
Title:	CFO
Goal:	Improve forecasting accuracy

The next step is to position your offerings. With the CFO's goal of improving forecasting accuracy in mind, you now identify all the features of your CRM software that could be used to achieve this goal. As you do so, keep in mind that up at the CFO's 30,000-foot level, multiple features are likely to merge into one overarching feature and that there may be features that are vital to users but will be of no interest to a senior executive. We recommend distilling your features down to your top four.

That said, here is an example, with the features that could be helpful to a CFO who wants to improve forecasting accuracy in italics:

Password administration
Single view across platforms
24/7 access
Contact information
Account history
Cross-selling
Standard milestones
Political mapping
Electronic coaching
Historical close rates
Lead tracking
Passing of leads
Analysis of past campaigns

This may seem like a small step, but we believe it is a significant one. It is the start of positioning the CRM offering in a way that is targeted on a specific conversation—and is being done on behalf of the salesperson. In the same way that a tailor takes a client's measurements prior to an initial fitting, this is an attempt to put some structure around the prospective conversation by identifying the parts of the CRM offering most likely to be relevant to a CFO who wants to improve forecasting accuracy.

Nearly as important are the features *not* chosen for each key player conversation. They have been eliminated because they have little potential relevance to the topic of forecasting accuracy. Note, too, that they probably are not of interest to a CFO under most conceivable circumstances. Discussing them is likely to confuse the CFO, waste time, and/or cause a seller to be delegated to a lower level. Even though this exercise so far has done executive buyers of the world a tremendous service, there is still work to be done.

Revisiting the Usage Scenario

A problem remains. If a salesperson simply blurted out "24/7 access!" to a CFO, that probably wouldn't be meaningful and the buyer wouldn't understand why 24/7 access is relevant. Most likely, the phrase would mean more to the seller than to the buyer. Feature names (nouns) don't help buyers understand how the features can or could be used (verbs). Therefore, an additional step is needed to convert features into usage scenarios, as introduced in the previous chapter. Here again there are four components:

Event: The circumstance causing a need for the specific feature.
Question: Asking versus telling doesn't feel like selling to the buyer.
Player: Who (or what system) will take action to respond to the event.
Action: How the feature can be used, stated in terms buyers can
   understand and relate to their job title. The description of the action
   should be specific enough so buyers can visualize how the result will
   be achieved. Terms used in a call with a CIO, for example, would be
   different from those used when calling on a CFO.

Let's take a closer look at the feature 24/7 access to create a usage scenario for a conversation with a CFO about the goal of improving forecasting accuracy:

Event: When trying to determine the status of large opportunities,
Question: Could visibility be improved if
Player: You

Action: Could access your pipeline via the Internet, anytime, anywhere, and review progress against standard milestones, without needing to talk with anyone in your sales organization?

Please note that the action refers to the ability to "access pipeline information via the Internet." This degree of specificity and concreteness is deliberate. If it simply read, "could review progress against milestones without needing to talk with anyone in your sales organization," the CFO probably would have no way of understanding how this would be accomplished.

In other words, the salesperson would be asking the CFO to either (1) imagine how it might work or (2) trust that it would work. But buyers—especially those who have authorized previous expenditures that haven't performed as advertised—are likely to be skeptical. (They will be short on imagination and trust.) And keep in mind that we want all buyers to be able to articulate what they are buying and why. If asked by another person within the buyer's organization to explain the offering, the empowered buyer can answer with confidence (e.g., "I can use my laptop to access specific opportunities in the pipeline even when I am on the road").

Here are the other three features selected for a discussion with a CFO about forecasting accuracy that have been converted to usage-scenario format:

Event: After making calls,
Question: Could input be more consistent if
Player: Your salespeople
Action: Were prompted on their laptops to report progress against a standard set of milestones for each opportunity in their pipeline?

Event: When reviewing a salesperson's pipeline
Question: Could stalled opportunities be reduced if
Player: Your sales managers
Action: Could access the pipeline database for their salespeople, evaluate the status of specific opportunities, and e-mail suggestions to reps to improve their chances of winning the business?

Event: On an ongoing basis,
Question: Could accuracy be improved if
Player: The system
Action: Tracked historical close rates for each salesperson by pipeline milestone and applied them to each of the salesperson's opportunities to predict revenue?

The next step would be to sequence these usage scenarios. This is usually driven by the order in which the buyer would be likely to encounter them. In this example, you want to lead the CFO to a vision of creating an accurate monthly forecast. The right sequence, therefore, would be as follows: pipeline milestones, electronic coaching, historical close rates, and 24/7 access.

Note that the feature we considered first—24/7 access—winds up being the last in the sequence. This kind of reshuffling is quite common and illustrates the importance of approaching this task systematically.

The Templates

Let's formalize this template—in part to emphasize that salespeople need structure for using Sales-Ready Messaging to make calls, and in part to underscore the systematic nature of our approach.

The header information in the blank SDP template (Figure 10.1) contains the prerequisites for the targeted sales conversation (offering, vertical industry, title, goal). Figure 10.2 shows the partially developed SDP that we are building for the CFO of a software company whose goal is improving forecasting accuracy. The right column has been populated with the usage scenarios we developed earlier that were relevant to the buyer's goal.

But what's that column labeled "Diagnostic Questions" on the left of Figure 10.1? We have just created four usage scenarios that *might* be used to enable a CFO to visualize how he or she could improve forecasting accuracy. But the real test for this system comes when a salesperson tries to determine which of these usage scenarios a CFO would agree he or she needed, during a structured conversation. Consider how important the diagnostic process would have been in the selection of a doctor earlier in this chapter. In sales, since the diagnosis is so critical, does it make sense to abdicate this step to traditional salespeople?

For each usage scenario, therefore, we now create corresponding best-practice diagnostic questions for the salesperson to ask in order to determine if the buyer has a need for the usage scenario described in the "event, question, player, action" (EQPA) question. In addition, it is helpful to seed questions that can be used to determine the potential value of a usage scenario to the buyer.

Diagnostic questions are used to better understand how the buyer is performing a function today—for example, forecasting—and, ideally, the cost of doing it the way he or she is currently doing it. At the same time, good diagnostic questions help the seller build credibility, in the same way that a physician you meet for the first time builds credibility with you by asking insightful, intelligent questions that you are capable of answering.

Title: **Goal:**

Product/Service:

How do you _____ today?

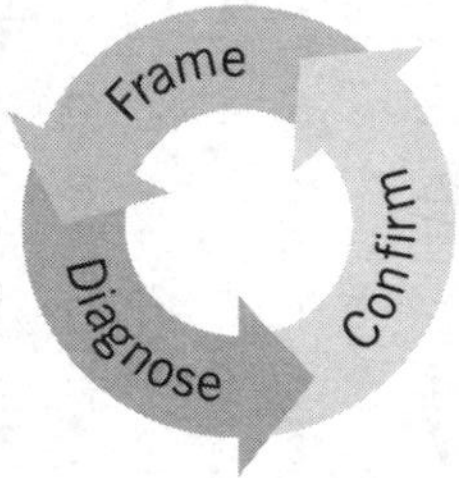

What solutions have you considered?

Frame
Confirm
Diagnose

Diagnostic Questions

Usage Scenarios

Event:
Question:
Player:
Action:

Event:
Question:
Player:
Action:

Event:
Question:
Player:
Action:

Event:
Question:
Player:
Action:

Figure 10.1 Solution Development Prompter Template

Developing Solution Development Prompters

Targeted Conversation:

Title: VP Finance

Goal: Achieve profit projections with more accurate revenue forecasting

Offering: Enterprise SFA Software

Potential Usage Scenarios

Pipeline milestones →

Event: After making calls
Question: Could opportunity status be more current if
Player: Salespeople
Action: Were prompted to report progress against a standard set of milestones for each opportunity in their pipeline?

Electronic coaching →

Event: When reviewing a salesperson's pipeline
Question: Could qualifications be improved if
Player: Sales managers
Action: Accessed a central database, evaluated the status of opportunities, and e-mailed suggestions to reps to improve the chances of winning the business?

Historical close rates →

Event: On an ongoing basis
Question: Could revenue projections be more accurate if
Player: The system
Action: Tracked historical close rates for each salesperson and applied them to the pipeline to predict revenue?

24/7 access →

Event: When evaluating the status of large opportunities
Question: Could you be more confident if
Player: You
Action: Had the ability to access a centralized database via your laptop anytime/anywhere and review progress against milestones?

Figure 10.2 Solution Development Prompter-in-Progress

Now refer to Figure 10.3. This fills in the Diagnostic Questions column with the questions that a competent diagnostician would ask a buyer. (Remember: These are good questions only if the person with whom you're having the conversation can answer them—the point is *not* to embarrass someone with unanswerable questions.) Every conversation is different, and *no* conversation would follow the script outlined in Sections 1, 2, 3, and 4. Conversations have to follow their own flow; otherwise, they're not conversations. But if you look at these questions, you'll get the idea.

How many usage scenarios will a given CFO agree would be helpful to achieve his or her goal? The answer lies between zero and four. (Zero means you're not calling on a qualified buyer as relates to forecasting accuracy; four approaches the upper limit that can be dealt with in a conversation that's scheduled for a half hour.) Later, we'll describe a structured way for salespeople to navigate through SDPs so they can lead the buyer to understand why he or she is having difficulty achieving a goal (diagnostic questions) and what is needed to achieve the goal (usage-scenario questions).

So we've now completed the first SDP. Additional SDPs would be created for each remaining goal on the menu for CFOs. After that, this same process would be repeated for each title/menu that is specific to an offering and vertical title. The final result is Sales-Ready Messaging to enable sellers to have targeted conversations with the titles needed to sell, fund, and implement an enterprise CRM system.

Closing Observations

Is this a significant effort? Absolutely. But we believe the result is well worth that effort. If properly prepared, SDPs provide a more consistent positioning of offerings by all salespeople, and should help your sales effort overall.

A few other observations about creating SDPs:

- They get easier to prepare after you have created the initial ones, because usage scenarios tend to be reusable for multiple targeted conversations. However, be sure that the way the usage scenarios are positioned are relevant to the job title of the person you are positioning it with. In other words, the Event portion of the EQPA is probably going to be different for the CFO than it is for the VP of sales.
- While marketing should take responsibility for the creation and maintenance of SDPs, it also requires significant involvement from the sales organization. There has to be a continuous feedback loop of what is working and what isn't. The reality is that the messaging is never really "done"; it's a living set of documents.

Title: VP Finance   **Goal:**   Achieve profit projections with more accurate sales forecasting

Product/Service: SPA

How do you forecast today?

What solutions have you considered?

Diagnostic Questions

Usage Scenarios

1. How do forecasting metrics vary by district? How are they enforced? No. of reps? Do reps rush and feel pressured to forecast numbers? Are some overoptimistic? How do they report progress on sales to their managers?

2. How are unqualified opportunities in the pipeline identified? How do managers assess the current status of opportunities? How do they coach reps to qualify/disqualify prospects? How are "stalled" opportunities identified, and what action is taken?

3. How do forecast probabilities vary by salesperson? How do sales managers adjust their forecasts for this? Do you adjust the numbers you get? How? Why?

4. Can one or two large opportunities "make or break" a forecast? How do you track those prospects? Would better visibility into these accounts be helpful?

Event: After making calls
Question: Could opportunity status be more current if
Player: Salespeople
Action: Were prompted to report progress against a standard set of milestones for each opportunity in their pipeline?

Event: When reviewing a salesperson's pipeline
Question: Could qualifications be improved if
Player: Sales managers
Action: Accessed a central database, evaluated the status of opportunities, and e-mailed suggestions to reps to improve the chances of winning the business?

Event: On an ongoing basis
Question: Could revenue projections be more accurate if
Player: The system
Action: Tracked historical close rates for each salesperson and applied them to the pipeline to predict revenue?

Event: When evaluating the status of large opportunities
Question: Could you be more confident if
Player: You
Action: Had the ability to access a centralized database via your laptop anytime/anywhere and review progress against milestones?

Figure 10.3 Solution Development Prompter Example

- The true test of an SDP is whether it can be used in making a call. If it cannot, salespeople must offer constructive feedback on how it needs to be modified.
- At executive levels, anticipate that a salesperson has only 15 to 20 minutes to have a discussion. This means limiting the number of usage scenarios to a maximum of four (perhaps with a fifth in reserve).
- While you may view SDPs merely as questioning templates, they go much further in that they define the outcome of a successful call. A buyer's solution will be composed of the usage scenarios they agreed were needed to achieve their goal.
- A single usage scenario may require integration of multiple product features.
- SDPs are indexed by vertical market, title, and business goals and objectives. Therefore, they are geared more toward management discussions than toward product presentations. If you are selling a complex offering with 847 features, eventually someone in the organization will want to know about all of them—and maybe more—in discussing potential future enhancements. SDPs won't be useful in these calls, which are often associated with due diligence.

But we'd turn this on its head by asking a key question: "Where in the buying cycle are these detailed feature discussions taking place?" If they are during the first meetings in an enterprise sale, it may take months of effort to get in front of the right person. It is far better to have these "due diligence" meetings take place after you have generated interest at business/executive levels.

- Whenever possible, SDPs should bias buyers toward usage scenarios that represent a company's strengths against competitors that either (1) are in the account today or (2) are likely to be invited to compete at a later time.
- SDPs should be developed for offerings besides product. As an example, software companies should create templates for selling professional services and ongoing consulting. We work with a company selling copiers and printers that has an SDP for positioning equipment leasing (which is more lucrative for them than a straight purchase).
- New product or service announcements should be accompanied by (even preceded by) the preparation of SDPs.
- Outside help may be necessary in preparing SDPs. Many people working for a company get so steeped in their offerings that they find

it hard to create SDPs; conversely, a consultant that is unfamiliar with a company's offerings often has an easier time of it. If the ultimate objective is to facilitate a dialogue with an executive who is unfamiliar with your offerings, you may find that hiring an outside person to pick the brains of your smartest people is a good investment.

- With salespeople directed to higher levels, qualification becomes easier. Most senior executives will not waste their time or their staffs' time. If they point or delegate you to others after being empowered to achieve a goal, they are serious about evaluating your offering.
- Some of our clients find that in calling high, SDPs can span multiple offerings. This is a shift from selling product-by-product at lower levels. In some cases a single usage scenario at a decision-maker level can cover an entire offering. The call on the next level down may consist of an entirely separate SDP to have a more detailed discussion.
- In creating SDPs, it is sometimes impossible to establish competitive differentiators. Consider for a moment multiple vendors selling CRM systems. To make it easier, let's assume all offer client/server applications. If salespeople are making calls at the highest levels (CEO, CFO) and having conceptual discussions, the conversations (and therefore the SDPs for any such CRM company) would be similar. Differentiators may have to be introduced at slightly lower levels.

Chapter 11

MARKETING'S ROLE IN DEMAND CREATION

In previous chapters, we've been advocates for a new psychological stance for marketing. Marketing should think of itself as being the front end of the sales process, instead of the back end of the product-development process. Why? Because we believe that this is a prerequisite for improved coordinating efforts with sales.

Marketing is a huge function, and it comprises many activities that are beyond the scope of this book, so as we look at marketing's role in demand creation, let's explicitly limit our scope. We intend to focus on marketing's direct support of salespeople by attempting to create demand for qualified buyers, to generate leads and move new opportunities into salespeople's funnels. We will *not* look at marketing from the stance of building brand recognition and awareness or strategic planning for future offerings.

Marketing and selling exist along a single continuum designed to connect a company (vendor) with buyers and customers. The most fundamental goal of marketing is to reduce the cost of selling; otherwise, why not just have every company abandon marketing and put a million sales reps on the street? Marketing can employ tactics that increase reach at a much more favorable cost than the notion of relying entirely upon salespeople to find new opportunities.

The skill set and mindset of marketing and sales "types" are quite different. This has caused disconnect and friction over time between these two related, but separate functions. Marketing is viewed as more creative, abstract, and strategic, while sales is viewed as more aggressive, single-minded, and tactical. Naturally, these differences attract people with different personality traits to marketing and sales.. Looking at these roles from an evolutionary standpoint, some view marketers as farmers and sellers as hunters. Metaphorically, they share the common objective of providing food to eat (generating revenue), but their roles require very different skill sets.

Leads and Prospects

Most marketing departments allocate a large part of their budget to creating demand for their offerings, in one way or another. In some of those organizations, salespeople are not expected to do much heavy lifting as relates to prospecting or business development. The Sales Benchmark Index, in a 2008 report sponsored by CustomerCentric Selling, surveyed World Class Sales Organizations (WCSOs) in an effort to find best practices that yielded superior results. Part of that report found that companies that performed at World Class levels relied more heavily on centralized lead generation than other organizations. The survey concluded that formal lead generation programs that had to be cost justified were more effective than ad hoc attempts at business development by individual salespeople.

Within WCSOs, the number of leads generated by territory salespeople was 47 percent lower than the norm. The report indicated that reduced business development efforts allowed salespeople more time to focus on moving opportunities in the pipeline along and this ultimately resulted in higher close rates.[1]

Despite the common objective that sales and marketing have—generating top-line revenue—often the coordination between the two groups leaves much to be desired. The touch point between the two groups is often a "lead," but often there is no standard definition. Rather, it is a nebulous term that reflects (1) the poorly defined relationship between sales and marketing and (2) a lack of understanding about what a good prospect looks like.

Let's start with this second issue. Does your company approach demand creation systematically? If so, are you learning enough from your customer base to leverage how they've used your offerings to achieve goals, solve problems, or satisfy needs?

Here's an exercise you might want to try. Figure out, in rough terms, the entire potential of your territory, district, region, or total target mar-

---

1. *Source: Sales Benchmark Index 2008 Survey* of the World Class Sales Organization.

ket. By potential, we mean the total number of people or entities that could benefit from using your offerings. Once you've established that figure, estimate what percentage of the people or organizations in that universe are currently conducting evaluations for offerings comparable to yours.

What do we mean by an evaluation? Here are five important criteria that suggest that a legitimate evaluation is under way:

1. The buyers have identified a business goal they want to achieve or a problem they want to solve that you believe can be addressed by your offering.
2. One or more decision makers are involved.
3. Requirements are documented.
4. A buying decision will be made within your average sell cycle.
5. Budget for the project has been earmarked.

As they conduct this exercise, most vendors conclude that only a small percentage of their potential prospects meets these criteria. (Most people find that between 0 and 10 percent of their potential market are currently evaluating.) In other words, there aren't many legitimate evaluations going on out there.

There is another "slice of the pie," perhaps another 10 percent, that is curious but not yet ready to buy. This segment of the market has at least a high-level interest (perhaps due to a marketing campaign, a conversation with a peer executive, a magazine article, etc.), but the need has not developed to the point where they've documented requirements or established a budget. They are curious but not yet truly evaluating.

Though at the same time, they discover something very interesting. The majority of prospects that are not actively evaluating have goals that are similar to those of the prospects who are evaluating. This brings up the question: Why would a buyer not attempt to improve an important business variable? Our experience suggests that there are three common answers:

- The company or buyer is aware that the variable could be improved, but doesn't consider it to be a priority (including a budgetary priority).
- The company or buyer failed in previous attempts to achieve the goal and is reluctant to try again.
- The company or buyer is unaware that it is possible to improve the business variable.

So if the vast majority of your targeted marketplace is not looking to change, that's bad news, right? Yes and no. It's bad news if your organization knows only how to be reactive. But it may be good news if your organization knows how to be proactive—that is, how to cause buyers to begin considering change. Two advantages come to mind immediately:

- There is a huge, untapped pool of prospects out there.
- If you help initiate an evaluation, there's every chance that if the buyer ultimately considers other alternatives, you will be "Column A"—the vendor whose offering is perceived from the outset as the best match with the requirements of the buyer, and therefore is the standard against which other competitors are measured.

Many salespeople believe the best way to build a pipeline is to find and pursue active evaluations. Why? They are qualified in that budget, perceived need, and time frame have already been established. We suggest that the real marketing challenge is to target potential decision makers (people who can spend or allocate unbudgeted funds) who are not looking to change with your Sales-Ready Messaging. If you disagree, please keep an open mind while reading the next section.

The Bottom Line on Budgets

Having already singled out salespeople, many companies steer their salespeople toward finding opportunities where buyers already have active evaluations under way. They do that by making budget an early qualification question that sales managers ask. Is that smart? Let's examine why companies have budgets and what salespeople can learn from the budgeting process.

Let's first take a look at why budgets are a way of life for buyers and sellers. Senior executives must predict and deliver a bottom line to investors. The two major variables are top-line revenue, which is speculative, and spending, which is more controllable.

Going into a fiscal year, would it be prudent for a CFO to give, let's say, the top 20 executives in the company permission to spend whatever they felt was necessary to run their functions within the business? If he or she did so, it is possible that toward the end of the first quarter, it would turn out that each manager had spent $1 million more than what was expected. The CFO would then have the unpleasant task of informing the CEO that the company was $20 million over on the spending side—which would in turn mean that the CEO would have to alert investors that earnings projections were not likely to be achieved. So budgets are established to control the expenditures of people within the organization, and to allow the CEO and CFO to sleep at night.

If given the choice between reporting missed earnings due to a revenue shortfall or due to a budget overage, most CEOs would opt for the former in a heartbeat. Even the most hard-nosed analysts and investors recognize that the CEO exerts a tenuous control over revenue generation. These same people, however, would view the failure to control spending as a sign of gross executive incompetence.

Here's the theory: Budgets are set at the beginning of the year and are cast in stone, and everybody sleeps well. The reality, though, is very different. In real life, companies retain a great deal of control over how they will spend their money, month-to-month or week-to-week. If a compelling case can be made that expending unbudgeted funds will (1) increase top-line revenues by (significantly) more than the cost of the outlay or (2) cut costs to a similar degree, most companies can find the necessary funds.

So—to bring this back to the perspective of the salesperson—if a buyer claims their budget won't allow them to buy the offering, so long as the target organization doesn't have financial or other insurmountable constraints, the salesperson and manager should conclude that he or she is not calling high enough within the prospect organization.

Here's a real-life example from our own experience of how funds can be freed up for unbudgeted expenditures. A VP of sales who had attended one of our workshops told us after the session that he wanted to conduct an internal workshop for his staff, but he couldn't authorize the funds. He asked us to do an executive overview of our methodology for his VP of marketing, his CFO, and his CEO. This required a flight to Utah, so we agreed to do the overview if he would cover our travel expenses, which he agreed to do (quid pro quo in action).

Near the end of our discussion, the CEO asked how much it would cost to implement a sales process in his company. Because he already had a vision of how the process could be used and the accompanying value, we reviewed pricing with him.

After discussing costs, the CEO turned to his CFO, Ed, and asked how the company's cash flow looked. Ed gave the answer that all good CFOs give when asked that question in front of a salesperson: "Things are a bit tight." The CEO turned to the VP of marketing. "Caroline," he asked, "of the three trade shows we plan to participate in this year, which one provides us the least value?" She quickly identified the laggard. On the spot, with the consensus of his colleagues, the CEO decided to skip that trade show, thereby freeing up funds for the sales-training program. The CEO told us to work out the details and contact him with any questions, and then he left the meeting.

In other words, when you call on decision makers, budget alone does not prevent buyers from going forward. Having said that, even the most senior decision makers can't print money, so if they set a new priority, it is likely that some other project may have to be deferred or canceled. This is part of the reason so many buying cycles wind up with no decision.

So salespeople not only compete with other vendors; they also compete for "mindshare" of business executives who have to decide how best to invest their company's limited capital, and how to adjust allocations that have—in most cases—already been fought for through the previous budgeting cycle.

Starting Out as Column B

We've already alluded to the advantages of starting out as Column A—that is, of being the vendor whose offering is perceived from the outset as the best match with the requirements of the buyer.

We believe salespeople who are called into or stumble on opportunities where buyers already have the budget for the project should assume that they are not Column A. (The vendor who has initiated the evaluation that led to this opportunity is Column A and will continue to enjoy this position unless another vendor is able to change the buyer's requirements.) Therefore, in creating demand, we believe it is important for organizations that are not currently looking to change to start looking to change.

Let's examine how much better your chances are as Column A versus Columns B, C, D, and so on, which we sometimes refer to as "silver medal" vendors. The vendor that closes the order gets the gold medal. The other four are told: "We liked your proposal, but I'm sorry to tell you we awarded the business to another vendor. You came in second." Here is a scenario that may be familiar.

A salesperson sits at her desk, debating whether to work on overdue expense reports or make some cold calls, when the phone rings. A prospect in her territory begins the call with:

> I'm Ray Jones, project manager for XYZ Company. The reason for my call is that we are going to make a buying decision within the next month. I already have budget approval for the project. We've heard good reports about your company and products and would like to give you a shot at earning our business. We'll need a demonstration, price quotation, references, and a proposal as soon as possible. You should be aware that this ultimately is my decision, so there's no point in looking for ways to go around me. How soon can we meet to discuss these items?

In the wake of this kind of call, most traditional salespeople would feel fortunate to have been invited to compete for the business. The appointment would be scheduled for the earliest possible time, the salesperson's manager would be informed that there was a "hot one" in the funnel, and this opportunity would appear on the salesperson's next forecast. The pricing, references, demonstration, and proposal would be expedited to meet the prospect's tight time frame. Everyone in the selling organization would be feeling a little giddy.

Before we allow ourselves to get *too* excited, however, let's examine the sequence of events that most likely preceded the call to the salesperson. (This is a composite, based on lots of stories like this that we've heard.) Is this a hot prospect?

Requirements[1]	Column A [2]	Column B [3]	Column C [3]
___	___		___
___	___		___
___	___	___	
___	___	___	
___	___		___
___	___	___	___
___	___		
___		___	
___	___	___	
___	___		
___	___	___	___
___	___	___	
___	___		
___	___		

[1] Often vary by buyer.

[2] Vendor whose offering best matches the requirements. Can change during a sales cycle.

[3] Winning vendor often is known before others are invited to bid.

Table 11.1 Vendor Evaluation

Six months ago, Salesperson A uncovered a requirement for a product that XYZ Company had never considered, which meant that no budget had been established for this purpose. The sales cycle started at a lower level within the organization. After months of effort and research, an overwhelming business case was built for Salesperson A's product, which cost $100,000. The buyer could see the value of buying the product but needed to obtain approval for an unbudgeted expenditure.

After the business case and an attractive payback were presented, the CFO said: "You've put a lot of effort into this evaluation, and it sure looks as though the benefits far outweigh the costs. What other vendors have you looked at?" The internal champion answered, truthfully, that no other alternatives had been considered. "Well," the CFO continued, "Our corporate policy is never to consider just one vendor for a purchase of this magnitude. Get other quotes so we can make product and pricing comparisons. And by the way, please don't bring any salespeople in to meet with me. How soon can you perform this analysis and get back to me?"

After this meeting, the buyer at XYZ Company has a sense of urgency about completing the requested analysis. To get funds allocated, he must perform due diligence by considering other options. But how objective will his evaluation really be? Naturally, he wants his initial vendor recommendation to be the chosen alternative. After all, Salesperson A initiated the sales cycle, showed strong potential payback, and spent months developing a relationship. The buyer may confess to Salesperson A that he is required to look at other vendors, and solicit her advice on which ones to consider. What he may not fully understand is that Salesperson A also anticipated that her prospect would be instructed to look at competitors, and provides a biased requirements list to play to her product's strengths.

What does this list (see Table 11.1) look like? The requirements column on the left is filled out first: a detailed description of the only product that has been evaluated to date. Column A is just to the right of this column. It is filled in completely, and—not surprisingly—it is more or less an exact restatement of the requirements column. To the right of Column A are blank columns for Competitors B, C, and D to fill out. The internal champion is now ready to call and invite the silver-medalist candidates to bid on the business, provided they can pull all the numbers together by the deadline.

How well will the competitors compare? If Salesperson A's product is price-competitive, Competitors B, C, and D have little chance of getting the business. If Salespeople B, C, and D ask for the opportunity to meet the CFO—who could potentially change the requirements—they will be denied that opportunity. Even if one of them were successful in adding new features to the requirements list, weighting factors could still be used to ensure that Column A would win. If a lower bid comes in, Salesperson A may be given a clandestine opportunity to sharpen her pencil after all quotes are received. In other words, Competitors B, C, and D have been invited to compete, lose, and ultimately help the internal champion do business with the vendor he wanted from the start. In most cases, the reward for Columns B, C, and D is the silver medal.

Column A's internal champion next schedules a follow-up meeting with the CFO. Although multiple alternatives are shown, there is a clear choice. Reallocated money for Column A is approved. Vendors B, C, and D are thanked for their responsiveness, complimented on doing an excellent job, and told that it was a difficult decision, but that they were not chosen this time. All three are told that they came in second, and that if future requirements arise, they'll be invited to bid. The losing vendors remove XYZ Company from their forecasts as a competitive loss, feeling—correctly, in many cases—that they could have turned the situation around, if only they had gotten into the account sooner.

In short, when you are told early in a sales cycle that the budget has been approved, you should *always* assume that your competition has set the criteria. The prospect has already started to evaluate the merits of comparable products or services being offered, and has obtained cost estimates. If this were not the case, how could they possibly know already how much money to budget?

Being called by prospects with preapproved budgets and tight deadlines for providing demonstrations, pricing, references, and proposals should warn you that you are being asked to provide a column. If the answer to the question, "Is there a budget?" is yes, sales managers may want to ask an additional question: "Whose numbers did the prospect use for obtaining budget approval?"

In our client engagements, we try to get our audiences focused on the advantages of being Column A, as opposed to being silver medalists. One way we do so is to ask them to look back on the competitions they've won over time and to estimate the percentage of those wins that represented situations in which they started as Column A.

Most people wind up giving a number in the 80 percent range. Flipped the other way around, this means that they have a 400 percent better chance of success if they can proactively cause people to look to change. Yes, individual salespeople should prospect to fill their funnels, but marketing also has a critical role to play as the front end of the sales process.

It should be noted here that the perceived average sales cycle for a company could be misleading. Even if you are calling someone at a higher level, if you are Column A, a fair amount of time is needed to get to the point of having a closable order. When you are coming in as a potential silver medalist, the good news is that it will be a short sell cycle (Column A has already done most of the selling). The bad news is that the sales cycle is likely to have an unhappy ending.

Marketing and Leads

If you want to start a buying cycle where none exists already, it is necessary to get mindshare. As suggested in previous chapters, you can't win over a decision maker's mind if you lead with a pitch of your offerings. What we suggest, instead, is leading with business issues to generate curiosity and interest. Leading with business issues offers organizations the benefit of higher entry points into prospect organizations, leading to shorter sales cycles and quicker access to mainstream-market buyers because the buyers are now being shown product usage or potential results rather than starting with your offerings.

Which issues should you consider first? Well, let's revisit the Targeted Conversations List—containing a menu of goals by offering, vertical industry, and job title—that we created in the previous chapter. Using the list, we would now like to give you a definition of a lead that sales and marketing can agree on, because the three components of a lead are the same as the Targeted Conversations List:

- Vertical industry
- Title (or job function)
- Business goal identified

In our model, an organization (or salesperson) cannot begin selling until a Targeted Conversations list is evaluated and the buyer expresses a goal that can be achieved or a problem that can be addressed with an offering. When that happens, you have a legitimate and qualified lead that sales and marketing can agree on. For companies with no standard definition for a lead, how meaningful is the process of tracking close rates?

Now let's discuss the various avenues that most marketing groups currently use in an attempt to generate interest—brochures and collateral, trade shows, seminars, Web sites, and so on—and how these approaches can be improved (by leading with either business goals or business problems) or replaced.

Brochures and Collateral

Just as traditional salespeople feel compelled to "spray and pray" when contacting prospects, so do most brochures and collateral literature. These materials more or less offer product specifications, often with some graphics and a sampling of nebulous terms (seamless, robust, synergistic, leading edge, and the like) thrown in to make them slightly more readable.

But this is silly. When you go fishing, you choose a specific location, type of bait, type of hook, and method (trolling, casting, and so on), all based on the particular type of fish you are attempting to catch, right? Why would you not do as much, or more, when trolling for prospects?

Here's a useful exercise. Pick up a brochure that is likely to be sent to a prospect, and turn the pages. As you do, ask yourself:

- What level within the organization would want to read this?
- Can this level allocate unbudgeted funds?
- What business issues does the brochure attempt to raise?
- What action is it intended to prompt?

Yes, there is always a role for strong technical information—but is it something you want to lead with, in attempting to get an entry point into a prospect organization? In most cases, the answer is no. Brochures with extensive technical detail are best at (1) answering a deep question from an expert, (2) informing those who are not decision makers about your offerings, and (3) reinforcing credibility that you've built up in other ways.

Another generally dangerous approach is to provide traditional salespeople with glossy "pocket folders," large folders into which smaller brochures, letters, and business cards are inserted. In many cases, when a prospect asks, "Can you send me some information?" traditional salespeople start emptying out their drawers of printed material. The result? Twenty-five dollars in printing out the door and a three-dollar charge for the mailing, at the end of which buyers feel that they have received too much information and therefore don't read much (or any) of the material. (We hear this story all the time as we follow up on clients' salespeople.) This, in turn, prompts the classic response from the prospect's assistant: "I'm sure she's seen it, and if there is any interest, she'll get back to you." We don't recommend putting this prospect on your forecast. Does it belong there?

Of course, marketing can reduce this exposure to some extent by being selective about the types of marketing material it produces. But in addition, we suggest that when they receive RFIs, salespeople respond by asking for a brief discussion to better understand the buyer's area of interest, so that they can send only material that is relevant. It doesn't hurt to be explicit about this: "We have lots of offerings with different capabilities, and we'd prefer not to subject you to saturation bombing. What, exactly, do you want to know about?" Another alternative is to ask the buyer: "What are you hoping to accomplish?"

Here are some possible alternatives to spec sheets and too many brochures falling out of pocket folders:

- Lists of business goals or problems
- Success Stories
- Sample cost-benefit results achieved by customers

Note that the list of business goals or problems can be taken directly from a Targeted Conversations List, as described in the last chapter. The point of this approach, of course, is to allow sellers to use examples of common business problems to lead the buyer into a discussion. It's often easier for the buyer to say, "Hey—we have this same problem!" than to say, "Let me describe this odd problem we, and only we, seem to be having."

Success Stories are one of the oldest techniques in the sales profession. For understandable reasons, buyers are much more comfortable if they are not among the first to buy the seller's offering. Keeping in mind the concept of product usage and Targeted Conversations, consider the CustomerCentric Selling Success Story format in Table 11.2.

1. Key Player (industry/title)	From Targeted Conversations List
2. Goal	From the list of goals
3. Contributing reason	Prior to implementing your offering, cite a reason they could not accomplish their goal. This reason should come from the left side of the key player's SDP.
4. Corresponding capability	Choose the capability from the left side of the SDP that addresses the corresponding reason cited.
5. Capability statement	State that you or your company provided the capability.
6. Quantified results	Share quantified results that were achieved, and be sure they link to the goal being discussed.

Table 11.2 Success Story Components

Note that the first two components (Key Player and Goal) are from a Targeted Conversations List. Once a seller gets a buyer to share a goal, the next element is a "contributing reason" for the customer's not being able to achieve the goal. This reason is naturally aligned with a capability. The benefit statement now allows the seller to finally say, "We gave him that capability," and then finishes with the actual benefit derived from the customer's use of the offering.

In Figure 11.1, we have reproduced an actual CustomerCentric Selling client Success Story. This particular client sells a host of manufacturing productivity-enhancing products and services, and the key player and goal are from their Targeted Conversations List. The contributing reason is aligned with one of their key capabilities: early warning notifications. After their salesperson delivers a benefit statement, she can then finish by quantifying the actual financial benefit.

"We worked with a *(VP Sales of a software company)*[1] who wanted to *(improve his forecasting accuracy)*.[2] Forecasting was difficult because *(qualifications varied by salesperson and there was no standard way of assessing progress in an opportunity)*.[3] His salespeople updated forecasts when pressed for time at the end of the month. He said he needed a way to *(define milestones for the whole company so after making calls, the salespeople could sign onto a Web site and be prompted to update the status of opportunities against a standard grading system)*.[4] *(We provided him with this capability)*.[5] Over the last six months *(his forecasting accuracy improved by 35 percent)*.[6]"

1. Key Player (industry/title). 2. Goal. 3. Contributing reason. 4. Corresponding capability. 5. Capability statement. 6. Quantified results.

Figure 11.1 Establishing Credibility: The Success Story

Note that this Success Story was crafted by marketing, published by marketing, used by the training department in training salespeople, and finally used by the salespeople when engaging potential new prospects. This is the kind of collaboration that leads to sales success.

The third alternative to the standard marketing materials listed previously is sample cost-benefit results achieved by customers. These can be extremely powerful tools, because they let customers speak to customers, without any intermediation by the salesperson.

Trade Shows

By now, it should be clear that we don't approve of vendors leading with offerings. So you can guess how we feel about the ways in which many vendors—especially technology vendors—display their wares at trade shows. Product, feature; product, feature; product, feature; and so on. Suffice it to say that there's almost always room for improvement. The exception, of course, may arise in the case of an early-market offering, where just putting your product in front of early-market buyers—and letting *them* figure out how to use it—may be a valid short-term approach to getting help in understanding how your offering can help a buyer achieve a goal, solve a problem, or satisfy a need.

But let's assume that you're not pursuing Innovators and Early Adopters. So first things first: Exactly what are you trying to accomplish by participating in a trade show? Are you trying to generate leads? Many marketing departments pound their chests in triumph after a trade show generates 500 "bingo cards" requesting information. But the hapless salespeople who follow up on these so-called leads soon discover that 95-plus percent of them are dead ends. They turn out to be consultants just trying to pick their brains, college students interested in the technology or looking for employment opportunities, window shoppers, trinket gatherers, and so on—in other words, people who may be intrigued by your offering but can't buy.

If you were to take the total cost of participating in the trade show (including all personnel) and divide by the number of bingo cards generated, you might be shocked at how expensive these leads are—especially in light of the fact that many or most are not leads at all. And it gets worse: According to Gartner Group, a face-to-face call by a high-tech salesperson costs over $400, when all costs are taken into account. So if you called on just one in five of those 500 bingo-card contacts, you'd be out another $40,000!

Remember, too, that your initial contact becomes your point of entry into an organization. In the case of an enterprise sale, entering at the user level almost guarantees a long sell cycle. You'll probably spend a lot of time, along the way, with people who can't say yes but can say no.

We suggest taking a different approach to trade shows. Just as companies can differentiate themselves with a sales process, we believe they can do the same with trade shows. When seeking mainstream-market buyers, consider scaling back your participation in traditional trade shows. Choose shows that businesspeople are more likely to attend.

Get a small booth, and resist the temptation to load it up with equipment. Use prominently displayed quotes, or likely lists of goals or problems, to get Targeted Conversation attendees (who are not necessarily thinking about change) to slow down, enter your booth, and share a business goal. This puts your staff in a position to begin asking intelligent questions that the prospect is able and willing to answer.

If demos are appropriate, we suggest asking interested prospects if they'd like to see the offering. If they agree, fill out a card with (1) their goal and (2) the capabilities they'd like to see. Direct them to a suite away from the floor, where they can have refreshments and make phone calls. When they're ready, they visit the suite and give the card to one of your staff, who can then tailor the demo to the specific capabilities the buyer is interested in seeing.

Seminars and Webinars

In a newly assigned territory, or in the case of a new announcement, seminars or Webinars can be an effective way to jump-start pipelines. Despite the differences in how they are delivered, the content and objectives of both are similar. Seminars take time and effort to coordinate, but they provide an opportunity to sell one-to-many, and therefore should not be overlooked. The goal should be to structure them in a way that provides maximum benefit. Again, the ultimate goal here—as with the tools and techniques suggested previously—is to get buyers who were not looking to change to realize the potential benefits of change, and initiate an evaluation. Your prospect pool gets bigger, and you're in Column A.

An important first step is to bring together a group of attendees who have something significant in common; for example, they work in the same industry, or do more or less the same job. A good way to do this is to feature one of your customers—preferably from a familiar company—who holds the same position and is willing to share a problem that your offering has helped them solve. When it works, this is a win-win-win: Your customer is flattered, the attendees can readily relate to material presented by someone with credibility who speaks their language, and you get access to a pool of prospects.

Little things count for a lot. Schedule your seminar for first thing in the morning—before people go into the office—and limit it to between one and two hours. Prepare your invitation carefully: It is very important in laying out the agenda and setting expectations. If you hope to attract an executive audience, spend enough money on invitations so that it looks like an executive event.

Consider preparing a list of goals or problems that are likely to be relevant to this target audience, and include that list—and a preaddressed envelope—along with the invitation. Encourage them to highlight topics that they would like to have covered during the session. (You may want to post this menu on your Web site as well, so that invitees can do their highlighting electronically.) You can tabulate the results in advance of the seminar, thereby maximizing alignment with your audience.

Follow-up is just as important as the invitation—and maybe even more so. Call the people you've invited, and ask if they plan to attend, if they have looked at the agenda, and if they have any questions that you can address. Above all, see if you can get them to commit. Then be sure to call the day before—under the pretense of needing a head count for refreshments—and confirm that they still plan to attend. You don't want a half-empty room, and sometimes it's worth making a full room (of high-potential people) the responsibility of one of your more reliable and creative people.

Start the session with a brief overview of your company—no more than five minutes, tops. If you were able to collect and write up the list of business issues before the meeting, then go over them now. Otherwise, build a list on a flip chart by asking for suggestions, and then use that list to settle on two or three goals that are of general interest. (Assure your guests that concerns that are not dealt with at this session can be revisited one-on-one at a later date.) In some cases, you may want to use a Success Story to prime the pump. Or, you may want to survey the entire room to pin down common reasons why attendees can't achieve the kinds of results they are looking for. After the session, if appropriate, you may have demos set up, which are focused on the specific capabilities that were discussed and presented.

Your objective, again, is to get them to think about change. We don't believe that one-on-one selling is appropriate at seminars. On the other hand, if you can get a business card and an associated goal or objective, this sets the stage for a follow-up phone call or meeting that can quickly determine if there is an opportunity to pursue.

This approach can also be effective when holding Webinars. The low cost for the vendor as well as the ease for targeted prospects to participate make it an ideal way to generate interest. As with sales introductions over the phone, with face-to-face introductions, brevity is important. A company overview in a seminar may take five minutes or so, but it should be less than half that time when conducting a Webinar. During the presentation, the speaker does not have the luxury of an interactive session, so our recommendation is to be sure to allow enough time for questions and answers toward the end of the session.

Advertising

In too many cases, advertising ignores the most basic rule of Customer-Centric Selling. It treats offerings as nouns instead of verbs. It ignores or undervalues business issues as a way of generating interest.

While the subject of advertising is large enough to justify volumes all on its own, let us suggest two CustomerCentric approaches for advertising:

1. Attempt to create "results envy" by having buyers realize that people in their own industry, and with the same job function, are achieving improved results through the use of your offerings.
2. Use a "hurt and rescue" approach, getting people to realize that there is a business problem that they are now experiencing, and that they have a means to control it.

In all cases, try to focus on the action you want buyers to take as a result of seeing your ad. Options include, for example, visiting your Web site, calling a toll-free number, contacting a local office, and sending in a response card.

Web Sites

We don't have to belabor the obvious: when it comes to the Web, the bloom is off the rose. The widely shared expectation that Web sites would be able to sell anything to anyone, 24/7, has been brought crashing to earth by mediocre results. True, an ever-increasing amount of *buying* takes place on the Web, but very little selling (or need development) actually goes on. Early Web sites were little more than electronic brochures. They lead with product, and they treated it as if it were a noun.

As mentioned previously the advent of the Internet and progression of functionality mean that buyers no longer have to contact vendors or salespeople during the initial stages of buying cycles. The reality today is that the buying experience begins for a particular vendor when a potential buyer accesses that company's Web site or signs onto a Webinar that they are hosting. The "requirements" list created before talking with a salesperson represents the aggregate of visiting multiple vendor Web sites, looking at blogs, and social networking. The buyer can readily learn a ballpark figure of what an offering will cost. This means that the buyer has entered Phase 2 of the buying cycle through self-service and is now starting to evaluate vendors to determine which one represents the best buying decision.

This presents challenges to salespeople today because when buyers finally talk with them, they are more expert than novice buyers. Many salespeople treat buyers as "blank canvases" in terms of their requirements during the initial conversation. This approach will be out of alignment with what the buyer wants. Later in the book, we'll describe how to learn what requirements the buyer has established and earn enough credibility to be able to take the buyer back to Phase 1 and potentially add or delete requirements.

Although technology has broken down barriers, the majority of Web sites are plodding and mechanical. We have yet to see a Web site that begins to simulate the work of a CustomerCentric salesperson. Perhaps it's unfair to expect a machine to interact with a person as well as another person would, especially since computers are still largely limited to seeing the world in a binary, on/off way. But Web sites do have the potential to engage a dialogue with buyers, and we think they should begin to live up to that potential. In fact, a client of ours in the Washington, D.C., area, sells membership management software to large associations used to redesign Web sites to focus on goals and objectives that interested buyers might have. When they launched the new site, according to their VP of marketing, the volume of prospects increased by 400 percent. More importantly, the "tone" of the inquiries changed from "send me some information on your product" to "I'm interested in improving my cross-selling abilities."

The Solution Development Prompter described in previous chapters is all about dialogues, based on "conversation architecture." There's no inherent reason why this kind of architecture can't be re-created in the context of the Web. Given adequate investments in programming, a Web site should be able to discover the interests of the Web visitor and, based on those interests, present content in a sequence that simulates a sales call.

We remain optimistic. Think how far these technologies have come. With today's technologies, we believe, it will be possible to build a Web site capable of developing a visitor's vision, either to qualify a buyer or—depending on the type of offering and expense—to take a sale all the way to closure. With tomorrow's technologies, it should be far easier, provided the Sales-Ready Messaging has been created.

Letters, Faxes, and E-mails

Letters, faxes, and e-mails can be effective ways to create demand, either on a companywide basis or within a salesperson's territory. If best practices are going to be shared companywide, marketing should provide a readily accessible inventory of sales-ready messages that are industry- and title-specific, so that individuals are not reinventing the wheel. Let's defer this discussion until the next chapter, where we'll focus on prospecting efforts using these methods of communication.

Nurturing Curious Buyers

One of our clients indicated that they typically have a four-month sales cycle once a buyer is ready to evaluate an offering, but it often takes months or even years for the organization to get ready. For that reason, we have added a third category for buyers. In addition to looking to change and not looking to change, we believe there is a need to add a category for curious buyers. These people are interested in offerings, but not ready to begin buying cycles.

Given they are interested but not ready to buy, they do not want to talk with salespeople, and so most likely they will do searches and visit selected Web sites of potential vendors. The key is that the relationship ideally becomes "sticky" so that if and when the visitor is ready to consider buying, vendors that have provided a positive electronic experience will be the ones that will be contacted. Consider for a moment that a salesperson you didn't know left you a voice mail, causing you to consider looking to change for an offering you hadn't been considering. Would you call that seller back, or would you go to the Internet and do some research yourself? More and more people would opt for the second choice.

Salespeople and marketing people are stereotyped as having different personalities. Sellers are perceived to be tactical, hunters, and so forth, while people in marketing are thought to be more strategic, farmers, and so on. Sellers are driven by quota pressure and therefore are not good candidates to nurture prospects that may not be ready to consider buying until some future time. That task should be done by marketing, and a Web site is the most cost-effective way to accomplish this task.

In our opinion, many Web sites are too aggressive in trying to qualify curious buyers prematurely. We suspect the reason is the desire to generate leads that will be passed onto salespeople. For example, in order to access a PDF (Portable Document Format) article, the visitor must provide his or her e-mail address. According to Brainshark, a rich media distribution company that is one of our customers, the viewing of an online presentation goes down by 30 percent if the viewer is required to provide contact info. Consider that when a curious buyer visits your site, it would be helpful to provide general information about offerings, but without much attempt to qualify or try to "sell" that person on your offerings. Over time, you can make attempts to introduce issues and see if a buying cycle can begin. Based upon frequency and duration of visits, many vendors can grade curious buyers as to their level of interest.

The key point is that buying experiences usually start electronically. Your objective is to establish credibility through electronic media so that the buyer will return. If and when the buyer is ready to consider buying, your hope is that you will be one of the vendors that will be contacted.

Redefining Marketing's Role in Demand Creation

Marketing can play a critical role in creating demand for a company's offerings. If marketing is going to serve as the front end of sales cycles, then its messages across all media should be consistent with the salesperson behavior, namely, leading with business issues with people who can make decisions and allocated unbudgeted funds.

Marketing should be the keeper of Sales-Ready Messaging, but should not be expected to accomplish this in a vacuum. Sales should provide constructive input, continuing to fine-tune material so that it reflects best practices in the field.

Marketing and sales have to agree on the definition of a lead. To reiterate, legitimate leads are made up of three components:

- Vertical industry
- Title (or job function)
- Goal

There are only a certain number of people out there who are already looking to change. Chances are, they already have a preferred vendor in mind. Demand generation entails causing people who weren't looking to change to begin a buying cycle and nurturing curious buyers in the hope that over time they will start the buying cycle. This segment, oftentimes, represents the potential number of people who are already looking, and offers the advantage of allowing salespeople to be proactive and become Column A, instead of being reactive and competing for a silver medal.

People who are not already looking to change have no budget allocated, so the focus in those organizations should be on people who have the authority to free up unbudgeted funds. And, as always, we strongly recommended leading with business issues and usage, rather than the traditional "spray and pray" approach.

As we have discussed, CustomerCentric Selling cannot begin until buyers share either a business goal or a problem that a vendor's offering can help them address. Whether you are designing advertising campaigns, participating in trade shows, or putting on seminars, you should begin with the end in mind: creating qualified leads for the sales organization.

In summary, few companies have a working definition of the interrelationship between sales and marketing. Companies implementing Customer-Centric Selling embrace the following description of each function's role:

- Marketing, through its programs, is responsible for getting buyers who are not currently looking to change to consider change. Marketing is also the keeper of the tools needed to lead buyers from a perceived goal to the vision of a solution.
- Salespeople execute the sales process by using Sales-Ready Messaging. In doing so, they are responsible for documenting calls so that sales managers can audit and grade the opportunities that are in the pipeline.

Chapter 12

Business Development: The Hardest Part of a Salesperson's Job

One of the biggest challenges that salespeople face is generating and maintaining sufficient opportunities in their pipeline so they can meet their quotas. When pipelines are inadequate, many salespeople are subjected to intense pressure—whether imposed internally (by their own desire to excel) or externally (by their manager). In many cases, salespeople fail because they are unable to generate interest, and thereby do not initiate buying cycles with buyers. Once they are in front of a prospective buyer, they can do a creditable job, but they just have a hard time getting their foot in the door.

While we believe marketing should be responsible for nurturing curious buyers and generating leads (as defined in the previous chapter) that are passed to salespeople, the ultimate responsibility for achieving quotas lies with each salesperson. Many leads that will be passed from marketing to salespeople will be mid-level or lower people that may not be able to obtain budget, are already down the road with a Column A vendor, or have done a great deal of research via the Internet and think they know their requirements.

For that reason our thought is that prospecting efforts of territory salespeople should aim at high-level titles in organizations assigned to them.

Executives aren't apt to visit Web sites multiple times, nor do they have the patience to be nurtured. Getting access to these executives requires a focused effort that territory salespeople are best suited to execute. While leads generated from marketing are welcome, in most cases these will be fairly knowledgeable buyers. Initiating buying cycles at key player levels provides the best chance to establish yourself as Column A. As a result, close rates should be higher than when sellers attempt to start buying cycles with mid-level staff.

In this chapter, we look at the different ways that salespeople generate interest from prospects—including telephone prospecting, referrals, and written communications—and suggest techniques for making the prospecting process more customercentric, and therefore more successful.

The Psychology of Prospecting

The difficulties salespeople struggle with when it comes to prospecting can generally be put into one of two categories—"cannot" and "will not." Each category requires a very different response.

On an ongoing basis, most sales managers assess whether a pipeline contains sufficient opportunities to allow a salesperson to achieve his or her assigned quota. This analysis is usually done without regard for the mix of new accounts versus add-on business. If a pipeline is thin, sales managers tend to focus on the quantity of prospecting activity, often without helping salespeople improve the quality of their efforts. After a period of time, if a manager determines that one of the salespeople is not generating enough prospects, the knee-jerk reaction is to mandate that a higher percentage of his or her time be spent uncovering new opportunities. And in some cases—namely, cases of "will not"—this is the best way to go. Order for more activity, and monitor subsequent prospecting behavior closely.

But ordering someone to spend more time on a given task does little good if the individual lacks the skills required to accomplish what is expected, which brings us to the more common problem: "cannot." By and large, salespeople are proud and highly motivated individuals; in fact, in many cases, the desire to excel takes precedence over financial motivation. So lackluster prospecting is most often due to skill deficiencies. And poor results due to poor skills quickly plant and reinforce the notion that prospecting is a chore. In other words, "cannot" turns into "will not."

On a recent client engagement, we were hired to assist a VP of sales in reviewing the pipeline of all 18 of the company's sales force. We scheduled 45-minute conference calls with each of the salespeople, with the VP sitting in as well. Each salesperson was asked in advance to be prepared to discuss his or her top three opportunities.

During each discussion, we asked—at different times, and in different ways—how the salesperson first learned about each opportunity. Out of 54 opportunities in their collective pipelines, a total of four had been proactively prospected. It turned out that in many cases, the salesperson's entire prospecting activities were limited to calling marketing and asking a direct question: "Where are the leads from the last trade show?" This opened the eyes of the VP of sales, who had no idea how little proactive prospecting was being done by his salespeople.

Sales performance is largely driven by human nature. It's very common for salespeople to follow an outstanding quarter with a lackluster one. Why? Because they stopped prospecting as soon as the pipeline looked reasonably healthy. Dreaded activities get put on tomorrow's list. How many times have you made a to-do list and discovered at the end of the day that you had done only the tasks you detested the least? So it is with prospecting. Salespeople are extremely creative at finding reasons why they are too busy to prospect.

Everyone who has tried it will agree on one thing. Prospecting can be a humbling experience. Nevertheless, it needs to be done. Closing business is good news. You get the transaction. But there's accompanying bad news. One opportunity has been removed from your funnel and now needs to be replaced.

In many cases, the first place prospectors turn to is the telephone.

Telephone Prospecting and Stereotypes

We've already touched on the negative stereotype of sales as a profession. Pretty consistently, public opinion polls place salespeople and lawyers on the bottom two rungs of the ladder of honorable careers. At the very bottom of the bottom, we would guess, are telemarketers. While the "Do Not Call List" has been effective, most people on occasions do get interrupted during dinner by people trying to sell products and calling them at home. Most of us try to introduce salespeople that call us to Mr. Dial Tone as quickly as possible.

Understanding that they have to sink the hook as quickly as possible, telemarketers resort to one or more techniques that they've been taught to get your attention and keep you on the line. For example, they:

- Overuse (and frequently mispronounce) your name.
- Ask, "How are you today?"
- Begin with, "I'm not trying to sell you anything."
- Ask inane questions, such as, "How would you like to get a higher return on your money?"
- Talk nonstop for the first 90 seconds (if you give them that long).

Since nothing we write will make telemarketers go away—and since you may be on the hook to be an effective telemarketer—let's look at some sample dialogues and think about what works and what doesn't through the lens of CustomerCentric salespersonship. Imagine you are sitting in your den and the phone rings. You pick up the receiver, and you hear the following:

> This is Mike Kenney with Acme Heating. How are you this evening? (brief pause) Acme takes pride in our outstanding reputation for customer service. We offer a complete line of furnaces and would welcome an opportunity to spend about 30 minutes discussing your heating requirements. We'll be in your area Wednesday evening. Would 7:00 or 8:00 work better for you?

Not bad enough to set your teeth on edge—probably—but there are several things that prospects might find objectionable in this approach, all of which reduce the likelihood of the seller's getting that appointment. For example:

- The script contains an insincere, personal question in the second sentence. They are calling to sell you something—do they really care how you are?
- Next, a biased opinion regarding customer service is offered. Doesn't every company say its service is outstanding?
- The script mentions a specific product (a furnace). What are the chances that you were thinking about a new furnace—in other words, that you were already looking to change? Leading with the product makes it likely that the buyer will ask about cost early in the conversation (assuming that there *is* a conversation). It would be virtually impossible for the seller to provide a meaningful response, given the variables of house size, insulation, oil versus gas, and so on. And as we've already seen in other contexts, without the potential value of an offering being established in advance, virtually any figure will seem high. Of course, the salesperson can simply be evasive about price, but this can be a dire mistake, especially early in the call. The script as written gives pressure, by asking, presumptuously, for an appointment at two specific times that are convenient to the seller— and does so without having generated potential interest.

The objective of this script is to get an appointment. We suggest, however, that the script could be far more effective if there were an initial attempt to gain mindshare. Yes, there's a chance that someone is sitting out there shivering and thinking about how his or her current heating unit needs to be replaced. But in almost every case, there is little upside in leading with the product (the furnace). Let's assume we make an attempt to improve our odds by doing some planning and research before the call. By reviewing recent real estate transactions and stopping by the town hall, we learn that a particular house has been purchased within the past two months and was built in 1937. Here is a different script, which attempts to generate interest in 30 seconds or less:

> This is Mike Kenney with Acme Heating. We've been working with homeowners in Park View Estates since 1979. A common concern of people buying older homes is the high cost of heating them. I've helped my customers reduce energy costs and would welcome an opportunity to discuss some approaches with you.

Note that we've eliminated the personal question. The opinion about customer service has been replaced with a fact that helps the homeowner reach the conclusion that Acme is an established and reputable business. Rather than mentioning a furnace, we attempt to gain mindshare by referring to the "high cost of heating older homes." This keeps the potential field of discussion broad in the prospect's mind; it might have to do with insulation, water heater or burner maintenance, or other topics, all of which fall into the category of "energy costs." The script heads off a premature discussion of price and ends in a way that makes a yes/no response difficult. Unlike the first script, the second does not end with a yes/no question that would give the buyer an easy way to terminate the call.

Some Basic Techniques

The script is extremely important, and so is the way you deliver it. Following are some basic delivery techniques for successful telephone prospecting. These apply to all kinds of phone sales efforts, so keep them in mind as you read later sections of this chapter.

As you have probably already discovered, when you are prospecting, it is important that it not sound as though a script is being read. Therefore, you need to internalize the script. This is not the same as memorizing; by "internalize," we mean make it your own. Practice by delivering it to your own voice mail, then playing it back to evaluate your delivery. When actually making the calls, use a long phone cord, or a cell phone, or a headset, or any other device that will allow you to pace and gesture. Your voice and delivery tend to be more natural and animated when you are in motion than when you're sitting at your desk.

Another suggestion is to smile. While we have no research to support the notion that smiling will improve your results, it can't hurt. People can "hear" your smile. You'll feel better. So why not try it?

Generating Incremental Interest

Studies show that on average, when on the telephone, you have less than 20 seconds to generate initial interest. This window can be shorter or longer, depending on how "salesy" the person sounds and how tolerant the person receiving the call is.

In light of that sobering statistic, the initial objective of a telephone script must be to establish curiosity in the mind of the buyer about how to address a need, achieve a goal, or solve a problem. As you'll see, we recommend attempting to create incremental interest with the initial script to gain mindshare and see if you (as the seller) can earn another few minutes to uncover a goal. If you're successful in this effort, you then may want to see if the need can be further developed over the phone. Most salespeople make a mistake when they try to schedule an appointment at the earliest possible time.

We'd now like to change the scenario. Let's imagine that you are a salesperson calling a prospect at his or her office. This means that you're attempting to interrupt the prospect's business day, rather than his or her personal time, which in many cases is easier (but still not easy) to accomplish.

Our definition of prospecting is attempting to make people who weren't looking for an offering to consider one. As we've seen in earlier chapters, if the expenditure hasn't already been planned, then no budget exists for it. Therefore, your goal is to initiate contacts at levels senior enough to free up funds (create budget). Your chances of success will be improved by using a "rifle" rather than a "shotgun" approach, one that is specific to a particular job function, business issue, and industry segment.

We demonstrated this approach in Chapter 8 when we created a list of issues for a CRM offering. In looking at job functions, our approach would be to initiate contact with prospects at the CEO or CFO level, because in many cases a VP of sales or a CIO would lack the ability to get unbudgeted funds.

Let's assume that we've chosen to target CFOs of software companies. The next step would be to choose what we believe would be the highest-probability business issue a CFO is facing. This can be done across the board by making a judgment call on industry trends, but customization after visiting a company's Web site or doing some research can improve success rates.

Having said that, there is a constant risk of "paralysis by analysis" when it comes to sales. Some salespeople are so reluctant to make cold calls that they spend all their time researching. (On their to-do lists, researching is a less dreaded option than prospecting.) You simply can't afford to wait until you know the birth dates of all board members, have analyzed the past four annual reports, and have calculated the associated "acid ratios." Past a certain point, it's better to just dive in, having made some intelligent assumptions.

In looking at the list of potential business goals of a CFO, without having specific knowledge about a target company, our inclination would be to choose "forecasting accuracy" from the list. Out of 100 CFOs, how many do you feel are satisfied with the accuracy of the monthly forecast provided by their senior sales executive? The choice of this business issue provides the broadest range of potential acceptance. And while they're not happy with the current forecasting methods, most CFOs have concluded there isn't a better way to do it and haven't given thought to how to improve forecasting.

With telephone prospecting, we've found you will have a higher success rate if you lead with a business problem, find out its root cause, and finish with the corresponding goal or solution. Therefore, the goal of "improved forecasting accuracy" from the list of goals should be changed to the problem of "inaccurate forecasting." In addition, you need to get the problem to be more specific, by offering a reason (for which you have a usage scenario) that the CFO may be experiencing that problem. Because a CRM system offers the ability to capture close rates by salespeople, this represents a high-probability reason for inaccurate forecasting.

Here, then, is the suggested script:

This is Rob Sherman with the XYZ Company. I've been working with software companies since 1995. A common concern other finance executives have shared with me is missing revenue targets because close rates vary by salespeople. We've helped clients improve forecasting accuracy, and I would like to share with you how.

Experience suggests that when a person in a business setting answers the phone, you have 30 seconds or less to generate initial interest with your script. (Note that you've gained a little time over a call into the home.) For that reason, we don't suggest asking how the person is (you will be perceived as insincere), or whether this is a good time (given an out, buyers will say no).

In keeping with the "rifle" versus "shotgun" philosophy, the company or industry should be referenced. Even vendors with horizontal offerings do the majority of their business with mainstream-market buyers who don't want to be first, meaning that they want to know that your company has done business with others within their market segment. We also include the title of the person we are calling on. We suggest avoiding the use of the title "vice president," because in some industries (e.g., banking and financial services) there are multiple levels of vice presidents (such as AVP, EVP, Sr. VP, and Sr. Executive VP), and a senior vice president may be offended if you speak of "working with vice presidents." Instead, reference the job function (Sales, Marketing, Finance, IT, and so on) followed by the term *executive*. Virtually all people in organizations like to be referred to as executives.

The most important portion of the script is the wording of the business issue. In order for you to read the script in 30 seconds or less, the issue must be concise (20 words or fewer). The best hit rates we've seen have been achieved by leading with a problem, including a reason for the problem that points to one of your usage scenarios. Consider how much less compelling the script would be if it read: " . . . other finance executives have shared with me is the inaccuracy of revenue forecasts." Tweaking a few words in stating the problem and the reason behind it can dramatically affect success rates.

An important thing to notice in the above script is the transition from a business issue to a goal or objective (i.e., from "missing revenue targets" to "improve forecasting accuracy"). From the perspective of alignment between the buyer and the seller, this is a critical transition. We have found that the success rate for this script goes up dramatically if, at the conclusion of the script, the buyer is allowed to *share* that they would like to improve their forecast accuracy (a goal) rather than having to *admit* that they are missing their revenue objectives (a problem). While leading with a problem stimulates interest, transitioning to a goal facilitates a further dialogue.

A quick word here on a resource that sales organizations leave largely untapped: their customers. One of the best ways to verify that your list of goals/problems and prospecting scripts are on target is to ask a corresponding title within your existing customer base for an informal review and edit. (This is a favor that you would ask only of a satisfied customer, of course.) Two—and maybe three—good things can come out of this. First, and most important, you can gain valuable insight into how best to approach the customer's counterparts. Second, you flatter the customer by asking and valuing his or her opinion. And third, if circumstances permit, you might ask if the customer can think of any real-life prospects on which the scripts could be tested.

Some Common Scenarios

Many salespeople perceive that they fail when it comes to prospecting because they set the bar of success far too high for themselves. They typically define a successful outcome as "a meeting," "they tell me their particular goal or problem," etc. We believe that if the script simply initiates a conversation with the prospect, it was successful. In other words, the definition of a successful cold call is to get the buyer to say "I'm interested. Tell me more." Once interest is expressed, the prospecting is over. Now the salesperson must begin to leverage other skills (alignment, need, development, etc.). With that in mind, let's discuss the responses you are most likely to get and how to handle them. Keep in mind that you cannot begin to sell until a buyer shares a goal or admits a problem that you can help to address. Here are some potential buyer responses:

1. *The buyer shows no interest.* "I don't have that problem and/or I'm not interested." It could be the person is busy, is in a bad mood, doesn't have his or her attention grabbed by the business issue, doesn't like salespeople, doesn't face that problem, and so on. According to a study conducted by the Kenan-Flagler School of Business at the University of North Carolina, fully 44 percent of people surveyed said that they would *never* respond favorably to a telephone cold call. The most important thing to remember in this situation is not to take the rejection personally. This is easier if you prospect using a script and a plan, rather than winging it. (It's not *you* they don't like; it's the script.)

   When you get this response, offer the other menu items for that title. You can make the transition by saying the following:

   Other issues finance executives I've worked with are facing include:

   - Low margins due to the increasing cost of sales
   - Increasing cost of marketing efforts to generate leads
   - Lost cross-selling revenue because IT cannot provide a single view of customers

   Would you like to learn how we've helped our customers address any of these issues?

   This yes/no question ends in one of two ways. Either the buyer is curious about one or more of these items, in which case you can begin a conversation, or the buyer says he or she is not interested. In the latter case, thank the person for his or her time, get a dial tone, and make your next call. Keep in mind that prospecting can be done at several different levels in the same organization. Even if one or more people you contacted were not interested, if you have lists and scripts for other titles within that organization, you can continue your effort to begin a buying cycle at that account.

2. *The buyer shows immediate interest in discussing an issue from the list.*
3. *The buyer expresses mild interest and asks you to forward information.* Inexperienced salespeople tend to see this as a positive sign.

Experienced salespeople are more cynical. They believe (with good reason) that this is a convenient and reasonably polite way to get salespeople to leave you alone. When the time comes to follow up, the prospect (or more likely, the assistant) will say that he or she has reviewed the material and will get back to you if interested. Our suggestion is, pursue these leads systematically, but don't hold your breath in anticipation of a positive response.

When you get a request to send information, do both the prospect and yourself a favor by indicating that you have an extensive set of offerings, and you would like to get a better idea of the prospect's particular areas of interest so that the material you send will be targeted toward the prospect. Either this will allow a conversation (your desired result), or the prospect will ask that you just send the information. In this circumstance, we believe that you still have prospecting to do, as the buyer has not shared a business objective with you. Instead of sending a full set of four-color brochures, consider sending something along the lines of a prospecting letter, fax, or e-mail that is geared toward getting the buyer to consider looking to change. (We'll discuss how to use these tools later on.)

In cases where the buyers express interest but don't explicitly sign on with the goal mentioned in your script, your continuing objective is to get them engaged. This means a continuing conversation—either now or later. "Now" means extending this phone conversation, which means, in turn, that you ask if this is a convenient time. "Later" means either on the phone or in person.

To the extent that you control this choice, you should think carefully about how best to use your time. Many salespeople immediately request a face-to-face meeting, but such meetings can be time-intensive. You should consider the title of the person you are talking with, the size of the prospect company, and the amount of time needed to make a face-to-face call. Given the obligatory social niceties involved in meeting someone for the first time, you may well find that you can get more done in a 15-minute phone conversation than in a 30-minute meeting.

If a phone call sometime in the near future is the next step agreed to, make sure that the appointment is booked on both persons' calendars— yours and the prospect's—and that time is blocked out for that purpose. It's rarely good enough to agree to "talk Tuesday afternoon." Tuesday afternoon will come, and something else will replace the phone call as a priority—unless a specific time has been reserved.

Let's assume that the prospect is curious and has time now to continue. Keep in mind that a buying cycle has not yet begun because a goal has not been shared. There's more work to be done. The transitional phrase could be like the following:

It may be helpful for me to tell you about the work I did with another finance executive of a software company who wanted to improve the accuracy of her forecast. This was difficult because close rates varied widely by salesperson. Each month, this executive found that she had to discount the numbers she was getting from Sales, because they were overly optimistic. She wanted to capture close rates by salespeople at different parts of the sales cycle on an ongoing basis, so that each month, they could be applied against the gross numbers to create a forecast. We provided that capability. As a result, her forecasting accuracy has improved by 54 percent.

You'll recognize this as a Success Story, described in previous chapters. The Success Story is used to build credibility for both the salesperson and his or her company. It also attempts to cause someone who was not looking to change to share a goal. Part of that effort is to highlight an area the buyer was unaware of, had not considered, or believed was unachievable.

After sharing the Success Story, it is time to provide the prospect an opportunity to speak. The range of responses ideally has been limited to an area the salesperson would like to focus on, with the ultimate intent of having the buyer share either a business goal or a problem. About 90 seconds into the call, you've earned the right to ask, "Is forecasting accuracy an issue you'd like to discuss?" If the buyer says yes, you will see how to proceed in the next chapter. If the buyer responds with a no, thank the buyer for the time and branch to dial tone.

Thus far in our scenarios, we have given the salesperson the great luxury of being able to talk directly to the targeted title. Unfortunately, that does not happen as often as salespeople would like. Many territory salespeople rely almost exclusively on the telephone when attempting to uncover new opportunities, and while the telephone offers the advantage of minimal time and effort up front, studies suggest that it is not a very effective way of contacting executives.

Therefore, we believe, salespeople have to cover their territories with additional methods, beyond phone calling. These methods include referrals, letters, faxes, e-mails, recommendations, and seminars on an ongoing basis.

The Power of Referrals

Satisfied customers represent a huge and potentially untapped asset. People who have made a buying decision have a natural tendency to conclude that they've made a wise choice, which can be further validated if others make the same decision. Consider this: it is rare to get a negative response when you ask people how they like their expensive new car (even if they've had a less than stellar experience with it). Even unhappy customers want to validate their choices, so happy customers tend to be more than willing to help a vendor succeed by finding new accounts.

There are three common reasons why vendors fail to reap the benefit of referrals from their clients:

1. Salespeople fail to ask for referrals.
2. When getting referrals, salespeople fail to ask for a "warm" referral, meaning that their customer will make an initial call or do an introduction. Beyond that, salespeople don't make an attempt to discover from their customers what specific business goals or problems the prospect may be facing.
3. When calling prospects they are referred to, salespeople fail to go much beyond saying: "Joe Smith is one of our happy customers and suggested I contact you." With a referral, as with all other prospects, your objective is to have the prospect share a business goal or problem so you can start selling. One of the best ways to do that is to share a Success Story for the customer that referred you. One of the easiest circumstances in which to make the connection is when the titles of both your customer and the referral are the same. When they are not, be sure you are attempting to relate to business issues the prospect is facing. Go into the meeting with a plan, including a list of potential goals for the person you are calling on.

Letters, Faxes, and E-mails

Written correspondence prior to making phone contact can dramatically increase your chances of getting through on the phone and uncovering new opportunities. Here are some guidelines to follow:

1. Shorter is better. Any prospecting letter longer than one page is not going to be read by many prospects.
2. Early in the correspondence, it is critical to get the buyer's attention. This can be accomplished by offering a list of potential goals or problems.
3. Minimize hype and opinions that start the buyer in the direction of concluding that the message is too "salesy."
4. A prospecting letter is not a place to get the buyer to understand very much about your company. Instead, focus on generating curiosity. If you achieve this short-term objective and the buyer becomes interested, he or she will want to know more about your company.

5. Understand that there is a high probability that the correspondence will be screened by the executive's assistant.
6. Aim high (maybe higher than your targeted title), because if the executive is interested, you may be referred to a lower level.

Our experience has been that e-mail is the least effective way to make an initial contact in writing. Simply put, if an executive (or assistant) doesn't recognize the e-mail address of the sender, the chances that the message will be opened and read are small. The title of the e-mail becomes extremely important. It must be scripted very tightly to generate enough interest, perhaps even indicating that some research about the target company has been done, although space is limited.

Prospecting letters also have their limitations. As with direct mail, their biggest challenge is getting opened and read before getting pitched. Many salespeople handwrite addresses on envelopes and use a stamp rather than a postage meter to increase the odds that their prospecting correspondence will get read.

Many salespeople like to use letters prior to calling, because when they get the assistant on the phone and the assistant asks, "Who is this, and what is it regarding?," they have an easy response: "This is Dan Ahrens of XYZ Software, calling to follow up on my letter dated November 18. Is Joe available?" This sounds like a good tactic, but in fact, of the possible responses, most are not favorable. The possibilities, starting with the only good one, are as follows:

1. The assistant agrees to put you right through.
2. The assistant doesn't recall your letter.
3. The assistant threw your letter out.
4. The letter has been misplaced.
5. The assistant read the letter and concluded it was not of interest.
6. The assistant brushes you off: "I'm sure he's read it. We'll get back to you if we are interested."

So although letters can be effective, they face multiple barriers: getting opened, read, passed along, saved, and so on. Letter campaigns take time, can incur expense in processing and tracking, and usually involve a delay before follow-ups can be done.

For these and other reasons, faxes offer several advantages. First, consider what has happened to the volume of faxes you receive. With the advent of e-mail, scanning, and attaching documents to e-mails, the number of faxes being received has dramatically decreased. We see that as an advantage. Faxes aren't in envelopes that may be "round-filed" before being opened. Faxes sent in the morning can be followed up the very same day. Consider the fax shown in Figure 12.1, which seeks to gain mind space for our product (CustomerCentric Selling techniques) in the mind of one John Daly.

To: John Daly   From: Michele Khoury
Date: xx/xx/xx   Re: Interview on your Web Site

In the interview posted on your Web site, you stated a goal of having XYZ Company double its revenues in the next three years. To achieve this objective, do you believe sales and tactical marketing will have to work in concert? If so, here are some areas that may be important to achieving your goal:

1. Marketing campaigns should generate interest at targeted decision-maker levels.
2. When calling at executive levels, salespeople should lead with high-probability business issues, rather than your offerings.
3. When evaluating pipeline, sales managers need a consistent grading system, so they can disqualify low-probability opportunities.
4. On an ongoing basis, sales managers should be able to assess their salespeople on six individual skills to identify deficiencies, and they should be able to help their salespeople improve in these areas.
5. When making calls, salespeople should consistently position offerings specific to title/industry and business goals via Sales-Ready Messaging.

CustomerCentric Selling helps clients define and implement sales processes to address these and other issues. I would like to schedule 15 minutes to discuss your sales environment, and mutually determine if further investigation is warranted.
   I'll call this afternoon at 4:30. I look forward to talking with you.

Figure 12.1 Seeking to Gain Mind Space

   Many of our clients find that sending a letter by fax is an effective way to improve the odds of gaining a conversation with the target title. One of the advantages of this approach is that if the executive's assistant sees the fax, he or she gets a clear idea of what you would like to discuss. If the assistant feels some of the items are of interest, the fax provides Sales-Ready Messaging to help him or her explain why a phone conversation may be warranted.

Leveraging the Internet

One of the critical things in prospecting is having contact with a large network of people. Whether customers or prospects, it is important to have as many touches as possible. Many vendors offer quarterly or monthly newsletters, and territory salespeople can maintain a list and have copies sent from their e-mail addresses. This is an inexpensive way to keep your company and your name in front of prospects on a regular basis that takes very little time or effort.

Social networking is becoming an increasingly common way to leverage contacts. Salespeople should consider investing the time to establish an electronic community of people that you know can make you aware of opportunities and/or make introductions to others. One of the keys is to focus on the quality rather than the quantity of relationships. Another is to make sure that you give as well as receive introductions and referrals. LinkedIn is one of the best-known sites. For more information about how to leverage this site, there are several resources such as *LinkedIn for Dummies*, which give suggestions on how to optimize the benefits you receive.

If networking sites such as LinkedIn provide you with some "warm" introductions, it's probably not enough to fill your pipeline and allow you to meet your quota. Some work has to be done to create new relationships with prospects that you have not dealt with before. This is where the raw power of the Internet, if harnessed properly, can help you differentiate your initial message. Countless tools are available. One of our favorites is called Brainshark (www.brainshark.com), which allows anyone who has a PowerPoint deck and a telephone to create an online presentation that can be used to stimulate buyer interest, highlight a compelling event, leverage your internal experts without having prospects get on an airplane, and so on. The many advantages over a traditional e-mail include the ability to be notified when someone clicks on the link, get reports on how long they viewed it, and track who else they have forwarded it on to. Because it operates through a link to a hosted system, it avoids the trap of getting sent to the spam folder because of an unsolicited attachment.

Whether traditional, text-based e-mails or something more appealing like Brainshark, you still have to figure out whom to send it to. Here is where Web-based information services can be a huge and very cost-effective tool. We subscribe to a service called Lead411. Because one of the characteristics of many companies we do business with is a change in management (new CEO, new VP of sales, etc.), we need to know when there is a change like that in companies that fit our demographic. Lead411 scans the business wire every night and delivers to our e-mail inbox every business morning a list of all companies who have announced a new hire of interest to us, segmented by industry, geography, and so on. Additionally, more often than not, an e-mail address as well as a main contact number is available. This becomes part of our pool of new potential prospects.

Speaking Engagements

Another way to build a network and pipeline is to find speaking engagements. In most cities there are a large number of professional organizations that have meetings on a regular basis. Often they struggle to find speakers to present topics that will be of interest to the group. If you do some research on local organizations, you can target those that you feel would be a good fit. There is usually a person who is responsible for scheduling speakers (anywhere from 3 to 12 months in advance). While your talk should not be a blatant commercial for your offering, a discussion of industry trends and issues can be a good chance to bring buyers from a latent to an active need. After the talk, hopefully you can collect some business cards of people who are interested and follow up with them at a later time.

Prospecting + Qualifying = Pipeline

Salespeople generally dislike trying to contact strangers, but prospecting activity on an ongoing basis is essential to meeting or exceeding an assigned quota. For enterprise solutions, the difference between a good and a great year could boil down to causing two additional prospects per month to consider changing. The second key aspect of creating and maintaining a productive pipeline is qualifying and quantifying a buyer's need for your offering, which is the subject of our next chapter.

Chapter 13

DEVELOPING BUYER VISION THROUGH SALES-READY MESSAGING

In previous chapters, we emphasized the importance of getting to the point where a buyer has either shared a goal or admitted a problem that the CustomerCentric salesperson's offering can help them address. This is a watershed event, in that it starts a buying cycle. Buying cycles end in one of two ways:

- *A decision is made to buy*—either from you or from another sales organization.
- *Buyers decide not to buy*. The most common reasons buyers don't buy are that they conclude the proposed offering is too risky or complicated, it can't be cost-justified, or their priorities shift. The phenomenon of "no decision" is far more common with mainstream-market than with early-market buyers.

Sharing a goal makes a salesperson's job significantly easier, because the buyer now sees potential value in improving one or more business variables. This can create a sense of urgency, depending on how much potential improvement can be achieved. Sellers are usually trying to push sales cycles ahead. Now, the buyer may have a sense of a cost of delay. While the buyer is deciding what to do—change or not change—the buyer may realize the enterprise is losing money. Once a goal has been shared, the seller is positioned to start developing the buyer's vision by executing Sales-Ready Messaging.

When encountering buyers, there are three different types of interactions with which salespeople must be prepared to align:

1. Speaking with a key player (high-level) buyer most often occurs when the seller initiates the buying cycle (outbound call) by taking the buyer from latent to active need. In such cases, the buyer does not usually have requirements in mind and the conversation is more business- than offering-focused. If the call goes well, the seller most likely will become Column A and their chances of winning the business are good.
2. A non-key player contacts a salesperson (inbound call) and already has a vendor in mind as being Column A. The conversation will be more offering-focused and unless the seller can influence the requirements which start as a mirror image of Column A's offering and gain access to key players, the chances of winning such opportunities are not very high.
3. A non-key player contacts a salesperson (inbound call) after doing extensive research via the Internet and by leveraging social networking. The requirements list isn't for a particular vendor; rather, it is an aggregate of everything they felt was needed from doing their research. The seller that can best align with this buyer by respecting the research that has been done, helping define business goals, establishing value, and gaining access to key players will most likely become Column A.

Companies without a structured process leave it up to each individual salesperson to handle these calls, which we hope you appreciate present different challenges. In this chapter we describe a recommended way to execute Sales-Ready Messaging to maximize the chances a seller will become Column A.

Patience and Intelligence

While having a buyer share a goal is highly positive, it also can be the catalyst that causes traditional salespeople to blunder. Picture a traditional salesperson, for example, making a call on a finance executive. The executive says, "Our forecasting accuracy has been awful, and this is an area in which I'd like us to improve." What response will most traditional CRM salespeople make in this situation?

If a traditional salesperson's process does not have patience built into it, he or she will often attempt to project his or her vision of a solution onto the buyer, rather than developing a vision that the buyer owns. Many sellers launch right into something to the effect of, "Here's what you need to improve forecasting accuracy!" Then begins the intense "spray and pray" of features, many of which the executive doesn't understand, isn't interested in, and may not even need. Mix in some ownership for the vendor or seller achieving the buyer's goal, and you have a potential lost opportunity or sale where buyer expectations are out of alignment with what can be delivered.

Sharing a seller's opinion or trying to impose that opinion on a buyer won't work in most cases. Instead, once a goal is shared, the traditional salesperson needs two qualities in order to take a customercentric next step:

A questioning etiquette that provides artificial patience to avoid giving the seller's opinion of what the buyer needs.

Artificial intelligence in the form of questions designed to (1) understand the buyer's current environment, (2) understand what parts of the offering may be needed, and (3) propose usage scenarios to the buyer.

These two components, integrated in the Solution Development Prompter (SDP), provide a template enabling sellers to deliver Sales-Ready Messaging. These templates help traditional sellers become customercentric by leading the buyer to a vision of a solution that the buyer owns.

Let's say a salesperson proactively takes a CFO from latent to active need and a desire to improve forecasting accuracy is shared. The customercentric way for sellers to exhibit patience and frame the conversation is to ask, "How do you forecast today?" This allows the buyer to discuss his or her current approach, which in turn allows the following positive things to happen:

- The salesperson gains an understanding of how the CFO currently forecasts.
- The cost or negative impact of poor forecasting and/or the potential benefit of more accurate forecasting can be established.
- The usage scenarios the buyer is most likely to want and need can be uncovered and offered.
- Usage scenarios the buyer is unlikely to need or want can be identified and avoided.
- The buyer concludes that the salesperson is competent, by virtue of being able to ask intelligent questions related to forecasting accuracy.

- The buyer concludes that this salesperson is different from the negative stereotype.
- The seller allows the buyer to decide which usage scenarios are needed (upon buyer agreement a usage scenario becomes a capability).
- The buyer can decide if having those capabilities would empower him or her to achieve the goal of more accurate forecasting.

While few would disagree that these are all positive outcomes, it is sobering to realize that the vast majority of salespeople (87 percent) will be unable to achieve them without Sales-Ready Messaging, which ultimately positions a company's offerings. Once the components of a conversation (vertical industry/title/goal) have been established, salespeople can benefit by executing SDPs. Sales organizations can also benefit because the output of these calls becomes more objective and less dependent upon the salesperson's biased opinion.

Good Questions, in the Right Sequence

In the rest of this chapter, we'll describe, step by step, how a seller would use an SDP to develop the buyer's vision once a goal has been shared. First, though, it might be helpful to think about the different types of questions that can be asked, and when to use each:

- *Open questions* require "essay" answers, allowing the buyer to take the conversation anywhere. Buyers feel safe, but the downside is that the conversation may not go in the direction the traditional salesperson wants it to go. The only open question contained in Customer-Centric Selling is this: "What are you (or your organization) hoping to accomplish?" This allows buyers to talk—but if they don't bring up a business objective, the salesperson has the menu of goals from the Targeted Conversations List as a safety net to steer the conversation.
- *Framing questions* offer the best of both worlds, in that the buyer is free to expound, but the salesperson has placed boundaries on the direction the response can take. "How do you forecast today?" is not an open question, because the response will relate to a topic the salesperson wants to discuss: forecasting. Questions beginning with the word *how* help facilitate conversational sales calls. Buyers do not feel that they are being "sold" when salespeople ask framing questions.
- *Closed questions* require short, specific answers. Potential answers to a closed question would include yes, no, a number, and so on. Closed questions are best used after framing questions, to drill down on and

quantify specific areas. Also, note that the only way a salesperson can convert a usage scenario to a capability is by posing a yes/no question to the buyer and getting an affirmative response.

Once a buyer has shared a goal, we recommend starting with a framing question beginning with the words: "How do you _____ today?" It is a logical, safe question that is virtually guaranteed to get buyers to describe their current process, which is exactly where a customercentric salesperson wants to go. Additionally, by leading with the open-ended framing question, the salesperson is effectively giving control of the conversation over to the buyer. When the buyer responds, he or she is effectively handing that control back. In fact, it's our belief that the asking and answering of the framing question is what gives the salesperson the right to start guiding the diagnosis in a more controlled fashion. If, after sharing a goal, the salesperson launches immediately into a series of directed diagnostic questions, skipping over the framing question, it tends to feel much more like an interrogation than a conversation (more like being sold than buying).

Once a buyer has responded, it is time to follow up with diagnostic questions, ideally biased toward usage scenarios that your offering provides. In order to accomplish this, as previously noted, we adhere to Stephen Covey's concept of "starting with the end in mind." That is the reason why, in Chapter 10, we developed the potential capabilities using the EQPA (event, question, player, action) formula, in the form of usage scenarios on the right side of the SDP. We then built the diagnostic questions on the left side.

These diagnostic questions are now used to discover which usage scenarios the buyer is likely (and unlikely) to want. The salesperson follows up with the buyer by asking the questions in a sequence that flows within the call, takes detailed notes, and—when finishing the diagnosis—does a summary to make sure both the buyer and the seller are on the same page. The summary ends with a question to gain the buyer's agreement.

A Good Conversation

Let's walk through a dialogue between a customercentric salesperson and a targeted key player at the VP of finance/CFO level. (Refer back to Figure 10.3.) We'll assume the seller has proactively taken the buyer from a latent to active need and the CFO shares the goal of wanting to forecast more accurately. We'll now walk through how the salesperson would execute an SDP developed for selling CRM software:

Salesperson: How do you forecast today?

Buyer: With great difficulty. Our overly optimistic VP of sales gives me a monthly forecast that I have to reduce by about 50 percent just to be close. Even then, many of the specific opportunities he forecasts to close don't. Luckily, we get some unexpected business most months, or we would really be in trouble!

Salesperson: How do your forecasting metrics vary by district?

Buyer: We have hired sales managers from a number of different companies, and they all seem to have their own way of qualifying and grading opportunities. At this point, I don't believe we have a standard grading system that is enforceable.

Salesperson: How many salespeople do you have, and do many feel rushed or pressured to do their forecasts?

Buyer: We have 200 salespeople, and from what I hear they all despise forecasting.

Salesperson: Do you think those who are below quota are overoptimistic and attempt to show enough in their forecast so it looks as though they are going to get caught up?

Buyer: That seems logical to me. It would be best to verify that with some of our sales staff. I can say that the forecast I ultimately get is usually higher than what I'll use as a projected top line.

Salesperson: How do salespeople report progress to their managers on opportunities in the forecast?

Buyer: I'm led to believe it is done on an ad hoc basis. Sales managers are asking questions as the forecast is being created.

Salesperson: How do your managers determine which opportunities on the forecast are stalled?

Buyer: There doesn't seem to be any standard way. Even if managers know an opportunity is stalled, they seem reluctant to remove anything from the pipeline. We recently closed a deal that had been on the forecast for 13 months! When I ask if an opportunity should be removed, my VP of sales reminds me of the one that took 13 months to close.

Salesperson: How do managers assess the current status of opportunities and how do they coach reps to qualify and disqualify prospects?

Buyer: If we have a way to assess the status of an opportunity other than calling the salesperson and asking his or her opinion about an account, I am unaware of it. I believe our managers pressure more than they coach—especially at quarter's end.

Salesperson: Do forecast probabilities vary by salesperson?

Buyer: Based on the experience and year-to-date quota position of the salesperson, they vary widely. There are a limited number of reps in whom we have a high degree of confidence as relates to bringing in what they forecast in a given month.

Salesperson: How do sales managers adjust for this, and do you adjust the numbers you get?

Buyer: I would hope managers would take close rates of salespeople into account, but it must be on a seat-of-the-pants basis. Managers are under pressure as well, so their year-to-date position against the district's quota also affects forecasting at this level. As I mentioned earlier, I typically adjust the number I get from my VP of sales by about half.

Salesperson: If one or two large opportunities can make or break a forecast, how do you track them?

Buyer: We missed our year-end earnings target because two large opportunities that were supposed to close by December 31 didn't. Here it is, almost the end of March, and still neither one has closed. So yes, absolutely, large opportunities can make or break a quarter! But other than every C-level executive in the place calling the VP of sales twice a day, there is no way for us to track those large opportunities.

Salesperson: What would better visibility on these opportunities mean to you?

Buyer: As CFO, I can deal with bad news much more effectively if there is some lead time. If a large opportunity drops off the forecast early in a quarter, we can do some belt tightening and hopefully find some other sources of revenue. My job is immeasurably harder with "high-wire act" finishes to our quarters. Any bad news from sales late in the quarter becomes an unpleasant discussion in staff and board meetings.

Salesperson: Let me summarize what we have covered so far. You have difficulty forecasting revenue, and it has affected your ability to hit your earnings targets. There is no consistent, companywide standard to use when grading opportunities. Unqualified opportunities find their way into your pipeline. It is difficult for managers to track progress. Close rates vary widely between salespeople, and you have a difficult time keeping updated on make-or-break deals. Ultimately, you have to reduce the forecast you receive by as much as 50 percent. Is that a fair summary?

Buyer: Yes, that pretty much describes how things happen today.

Salesperson: What approaches have you considered to improve forecasting accuracy?

Buyer: Other than changing vice presidents of sales every couple of years, I am not sure what else we have tried or could try. I've had several sales executives in my career tell me that I just didn't understand sales.

Salesperson: Based on our discussion so far, may I offer a few suggestions?

Buyer: Please do.

Salesperson: After making sales calls, could input be more consistent if your salespeople were prompted on their laptops to report progress against a standard set of company milestones for each opportunity in their pipeline?

Buyer: I have been clamoring for a standard set of milestones we could all use and understand. Prompting the salespeople seems like a good way to collect data after each sales call. I believe it would help.

Salesperson: When reviewing a salesperson's pipeline, could stalled opportunities be reduced if your sales managers could access the pipeline database for their salespeople, evaluate the status of specific opportunities, and e-mail suggestions to reps to improve their chances of winning the business?

Buyer: I believe so. We didn't discuss it, but many salespeople work out of remote or home offices.

Salesperson: On an ongoing basis, could accuracy be improved if the system tracked historical close rates for each salesperson by milestone, and applied them to each of the salesperson's opportunities so you could predict revenue?

Buyer: I would like that! I might not have to tweak the numbers by 50 percent or more. It would be refreshing to apply a little science and logic to our forecasting process.

Salesperson: When trying to determine the status of large opportunities, could visibility be improved if you or any C-level executive could access your pipeline anytime/anywhere, and review progress against milestones without needing to talk to anyone in your sales organization?

Buyer: Yes.

Salesperson: In summary, if you had standard milestones updated after each sales call, an accessible pipeline database for coaching and reviewing progress, the ability to track historical close rates by milestone, and the ability to assess make-or-break opportunities from your laptop, could you achieve your goal of more accurately forecasting revenue?

Buyer: Yes, and I'd feel more confident going into board meetings if we had a better handle on forecasting.

This conversation, of course, is something of an ideal. It mirrors the first role-play we have attendees execute in our CustomerCentric Selling workshops. The role-play coaches, who serve as buyers, are passive and cooperative the first time through so as to allow participants to walk before they run. The subsequent role-plays become more challenging and realistic.

In the preceding example, the seller enjoyed the luxury of having a key player readily share a goal and be willing to engage in a candid and pointed conversation, with the salesperson doing a lot of directing (through questioning). In sales calls, conversations almost never follow a script. But the SDP provides a guideline for (1) diagnosing the buyer's current situation with a bias toward your offering and (2) developing a custom vision that the buyer owns. Please note that in this example, the buyer agreed to all four major diagnostic questions, and therefore the seller offered all four usage scenarios. In making calls, if a buyer does not agree to a reason the company cannot achieve a goal, the seller would not offer the corresponding usage scenario.

Competing for the Silver Medal?

Now let's look at a more difficult conversation. This is an inbound phone call, initiated by a lower-level buyer doing due diligence to justify buying from Column A. Here's how the conversation might go:

Buyer: Hello. This is Anita Quote with the ABC Company. We have decided to purchase CRM software. We have budget, and we want to make a decision soon. How quickly can you provide a demonstration, pricing, and a proposal?

Salesperson: I'd be glad to help. How did you happen to contact us?

Buyer: I visited your Web site and felt your offering could be a fit for our needs.

Salesperson: What type of organization is ABC Company?

Buyer: We provide software to shorten engineering design cycles of printed circuits.

Salesperson: What is your role at ABC Company?

Buyer: I'm a senior analyst in our IT department.

Salesperson: It sounds as though you've researched CRM offerings. What if any requirements have your organization established?

Buyer: We definitely want a hosted solution that provides the flexibility to modify milestones to fit our different types of sales.

Salesperson: What is your organization hoping to accomplish with a CRM system?

Buyer: At this stage, I'm not prepared to get into a detailed discussion. What I really want is pricing information to determine if you should be placed on our short list of CRM vendors.

Salesperson: In order to make a recommendation and provide pricing, l would need to get a better understanding of your requirements. Other companies I've worked with were considering CRM because they wanted to improve in at least one or more of the following areas:

- Reduce the cost of sales
- Lower IT costs for providing a single view of customers
- Improve forecasting accuracy
- Drive higher revenues

Are any of these objectives driving your company's evaluation of CRM?

Buyer: Our major objective is improving forecasting accuracy, but as I've said, I don't have time to have a detailed discussion.

Please note that this is an inbound call. The buyer started by asking for a demonstration, pricing, and a proposal, so the seller can assume another vendor is driving the evaluation. Upon learning the buyer's title, it is clear she is not a key player, so instead of asking what she hopes to accomplish, the question asked was what her organization was hoping to accomplish. This is an attempt to elevate the conversation and do solution development by proxy. This means using a key player prompter to have the discussion. If the buyer doesn't know the business drivers or can't answer some of the diagnostic questions, the seller can ask for access (with or without the initial caller) to higher levels.

Asking what requirements have already been determined allows the buyer to share whatever research has been done and begins to allow the seller to determine the potential fit. If, for example, the seller's offering isn't hosted, there would have to be a quick determination of whether that requirement was an absolute. If it were, there would be no reason to continue on. Not asking the question about requirements and trying to jump into a diagnosis would be frustrating for a knowledgeable buyer.

This buyer's attitude is significantly different from that in the call we first described on the CFO. This buyer already has an idea of what she wants. It's possible that she's already settled on one of your competitors and is feigning interest, either to satisfy her company's bid procedures or with the intent of using your price as a lever to negotiate the best deal from Column A.

At this point, rather than ask "How does your organization forecast today?" a better alternative would be to ask "As relates to forecasting, what specific CRM capabilities is your organization looking for?" This is a further attempt to respect the research that has been done as well as to have the buyer consider which requirements directly map to improving forecasting accuracy, a step that may not have been considered. After the buyer answers, the hope is that sufficient credibility has been established so the question "Can you describe the way your organization forecasts today?" will allow a diagnosis to begin and the seller can work down the left side of the SDP. This approach is consistent with the core concept of making yourself equal before you make yourself different.

The third type of interaction is with a buyer that has done extensive research but whose requirements are an aggregate of research done without having spoken with a salesperson. Let's assume this buyer has identified a short list of vendors based upon that research, but rather than Columns A, B, and C, the list is Vendors 1, 2, and 3. The seller that most closely aligns with the buyer will most likely become Column A.

Let's assume this is an inbound found call from the buyer. As you'll see, this time the buyer will not readily share a goal with the seller.

Buyer: Hi. This is Allan Campbell with the XYZ Company. We're considering CRM software and I'd like to learn more about your offerings.

Salesperson: I'm happy to try to address any questions you have. How did you happen to contact us?

Buyer: I've visited several Web sites, felt your offering might be a fit for us, and wanted to determine if you should be one of the vendors we consider.

Salesperson: What type of organization is ABC Company?

Buyer: We offer process consulting to manufacturing companies.

Salesperson: What is your role at XYZ Company?

Buyer: I'm the sales operations manager.

Salesperson: Based upon your research so far, what requirements for CRM have you established?

Buyer: We definitely want a hosted solution and want to choose a vendor that has worked with professional services organizations.

Salesperson: As you may have seen on our Web site, we do have clients in your space. What is your organization hoping to accomplish with a CRM system?

Buyer: We feel we'd benefit from automating the pipeline.

Salesperson: How do sales managers review sellers' pipelines today?

Buyer: Most managers receive a spreadsheet the last week of the month that will be used to create the forecast.

Salesperson: How do managers assess opportunities prior to receiving the spreadsheets?

Buyer: There is no standard. Most managers monitor larger opportunities and will talk with salespeople if they need an updated status. It's not ideal, but hasn't caused any major issues.

Salesperson: You mentioned forecasting and spreadsheets. How are forecasts created?

Buyer: There is no standard, but we have three regional managers, each with six first-line managers reporting to them. On the 25th of the month, first-level managers ask for updates on the pipeline in Excel spreadsheets that are e-mailed. The managers review them and call salespeople with questions on selected opportunities. The first-level managers send the forecast to the regional managers, who massage the numbers and give them to me. I review them with the VP of sales, and she gives the CFO the final forecast.

Salesperson: This has been helpful in allowing me to better understand your current situation. Organizations we work with have the following goals when evaluating CRM:

- Drive higher revenues
- Shorten sales cycles
- Improve forecasting accuracy
- Reduce start-up times for new hires
- Increase close rates by tracking leads

Do any of these issues align with your objectives for CRM?

Buyer: Driving higher revenue and improving forecast accuracy are important to us.

Salesperson: Which do you consider a higher priority?

Buyer: Our CFO wants to see a better forecast.

Salesperson: We can discuss driving higher revenue later. Based upon what you've seen so far, what capabilities from a CRM system will help you improve forecasting accuracy?

Buyer: Standard milestones across all regions would help as well as updating a central database rather than using spreadsheets as we do.

Salesperson: Let's make sure we're on the same page as to how you would use standard milestones. After making calls, would you want salespeople to be prompted to report progress against a standard set of milestones for that opportunity?

Buyer: Yes, and I think it would be helpful to get all three regions using the same milestones.

Salesperson: I'd like to drill down further on how you forecast and see what other capabilities would be needed.

As you can see, the most important goal of achieving a more accurate forecast is the one that would be discussed first. The buyer's initial response to what he wanted to accomplish with CRM was fairly nebulous. Automating the pipeline is not a business issue many executives would pay money to achieve, as it is difficult to assign a value to being able to do so. For that reason, the seller asked environmental framing questions to get the buyer talking and learn more about their company's current situation.

After asking those questions, a goal had not been shared, so the seller offered the list of goals. Buying cycles begin when a buyer shares a goal that the seller's offering can help the buyer achieve. Once the goal has been shared, the seller asks what capabilities the buyer believes his or her company needs. In this case, a feature (standard milestones) was given. To be sure there was common agreement on what that meant, the seller offered a usage scenario that the buyer agreed was something he wanted. From there, the seller would proceed down the left side of the SDP and, with the buyer's help via responses, attempt to build a solution.

Vision Building around a Commodity

Solution Development Prompters can be used to facilitate virtually any sales discussion that can be distilled to a buyer and business issue. We have worked with companies that sell what is perceived as a commodity, and—with some modifications—the vision-building model still works.

Let's say, for example, that you are a regional overnight delivery service and you have the following differentiators when compared to national carriers:

- You can accept bundles.
- Your weight limits on packages are higher.
- Pickups can be made as late as 8:00 p.m.
- Deliveries can be as early as 7:30 a.m.
- All shipments are ground-based and within a 300-mile radius.
- You can deliver to a construction site without an address.
- You can offer a 20 percent savings over national carriers.

In this case, nearly every prospect on which you're calling is already using and familiar with one or more overnight delivery services. Many traditional salespeople would lead with price in this situation, but this is a dangerous approach. Many customers would conclude that they would receive inferior service from a previously unknown carrier who initiates a discussion based on lower price. Another problem with this approach is that it creates a commodity sale mentality. Even if successful in generating interest, the buyer is likely to invite other carriers in to have them compete on price.

In selling situations such as this, it is important to give the buyer a reason to be unhappy with the current service. This can be done by selecting a Success Story that highlights one of your strengths and/or one of a national carrier's potential weaknesses.

The question that follows a Success Story can't be too obvious. For example, "How do you handle your overnight deliveries today?" is so basic as to be insulting. Since most people understand how to use an overnight delivery service, a more appropriate question would be, "What would it take for you to consider switching overnight delivery companies?"

After getting the buyer's response, you can then start by asking usage scenario questions on the right side of the SDP, with each of them being a potential differentiator. The seven differentiators listed previously would have to be chosen judiciously, based on the title and industry the salesperson is calling on. A manufacturing company may be interested in shipping pallets, but a law firm or a bank would not be. Do your homework, here. A company billing its clients on a cost-plus basis might not find a lower price attractive.

Let's assume that you (again, a representative for the regional overnight delivery service described previously) are calling on the office manger of a law firm. After a brief introduction and Success Story about another law firm that elected to use your service, the conversation might go as follows, using the SDP shown in Figure 13.1.

Salesperson: What would it take for you to consider switching overnight delivery companies?

Buyer: We're pretty satisfied with FBN Overnight Delivery's service.

Salesperson: Most people are satisfied with FBN, but let me ask: When attorneys are faced with a deadline, would it be helpful if you could arrange on-site pickups as late as 8:00 p.m.?

Buyer: We usually have to get things done by 5:00, but 8:00 would be helpful to us.

Salesperson: When clients need quick turnaround, would you like to be able to have deliveries to them made as early as 7:30 the next morning?

Buyer: Some of our clients would want contracts or documents that early.

Salesperson: When shipping critical documents within a 300-mile radius, would you feel more comfortable having your deliveries be ground-based, and thereby bypass delays due to airport closings and similar problems?

Buyer: We really haven't had many issues related to weather delays in deliveries.

Salesperson: When shipping documents within 300 miles, would you like the ability to lower overall costs by using ground-based delivery?

Title: Business Manager, Law Firm **Goal:** Improve customer service for document deliveries
Product/Service: Overnight Delivery Service

What has your experience with your current carrier been?

Frame · Confirm · Diagnose

What would it take for you to consider switching your overnight delivery service?

Usage Scenarios

Event: When attorneys face tight deadlines
Question: Could mistakes be minimized if
Player: You
Action: Could arrange on-site pickups as late as 8:00 p.m.?

Event: When clients require quick turnaround on documents
Question: Could responsiveness be improved if
Player: Your firm
Action: Had the ability to make deliveries as early as 7:30 a.m.?

Event: When shipping critical documents within a 300-mile radius
Question: Could late deliveries be avoided if
Player: You
Action: Used a ground-based delivery service and could avoid delays due to flight delays or cancellations?

Event: When shipping documents within a 300-mile radius
Question: Could costs be reduced if
Player: You
Action: Had the option to take advantage of ground-based deliveries?

Diagnostic Questions

1. If your attorneys are pressed to meet a deadline, what options do you have with your current service? How often has this become an issue? Has the quality of the firm's work ever been compromised by having to meet a deadline? What problems did that cause?

2. How often do clients want documents prior to 10:30 a.m. and how do you handle these requests? Have you incurred expediting charges? How many of your clients would find getting documents three hours earlier beneficial?

3. How often have airport logistical issues caused documents to be late? How understanding were clients of these delays? For clients within a 300-mile radius, was it strange to realize flight cancellations caused the delay?

4. For documents being shipped in the tri-state area, do you feel air-based transport to be overkill? Would you agree ground-based transportation would be less costly to your delivery service?

Figure 13.1 Solution Development Prompter: Selling Overnight Delivery Services to a Law Firm

Buyer: Our clients have become very cost-conscious, so we would be interested in reduced shipping costs. In fact, now that I think of it, most of our clients are local.

What's happened here? You've gotten a lukewarm response to the third usage scenario, but the buyer has responded well to the other three. After framing a question—such as, "What has been your experience with FBN's services?"—to bring the conversation to the left side of the SDP, you would do the diagnosis for reasons 1, 2, and 4 to obtain details and quantification on how not having the corresponding capabilities is affecting the business manager and the law firm. After summarizing the diagnosis, you would then summarize the buyer vision and seek the buyer's agreement:

Salesperson: To summarize, if you could have the abilities to arrange pickups as late as 8:00 p.m., arrange deliveries as early as 7:30 a.m., and reduce the cost of next-day deliveries, then would you consider trying our service?

Buyer: Certainly I would be interested. First I want to take a further look at your company. If things check out, I would be willing to give you a try.

For noncommodity offerings, sellers should diagnose by starting with the left side of the prompter. In the same way sellers should not lead with product, they should avoid leading with usage scenarios as well. For offerings whose use is obvious to buyers, we suggest sellers start on the right side of the prompters.

The purpose of the SDP is to arm sellers with artificial patience and artificial intelligence to determine which usage scenarios the buyer is likely to need, simply by asking questions. These usage scenarios become capabilities when the buyer agrees they would be useful. The final step is to see if by using all the capabilities, the buyer would be empowered to achieve the desired goal. This is accomplished by asking, "If you had (summarize the capabilities), then could you achieve (buyer goal)?"

Once a buyer vision has been created, you should see if the buyer will share any additional goals, so you can create further visions and develop associated value. After developing shared buyer goals, the next step is to begin qualifying the buyer—a critical requirement for successful selling, which we'll cover in the next chapter.

Chapter 14

QUALIFYING BUYERS

Many organizations have great difficulty forecasting top-line revenues. We believe that this reflects an underlying problem: Pipelines contain unqualified opportunities. Most organizations have no standard way of accurately assessing which prospects are likely to buy and, therefore, rely upon the opinion of their salespeople.

Our strong sense—as will become clear in this chapter—is that the sales manager should disqualify buyers, based on the best available correspondence between the salesperson and the prospect. The alternative is to give this responsibility to individual salespeople, which almost inevitably leads to unqualified buyers being in the pipeline, resulting in inflated top-line revenue estimates. So how do the sales manager and the salesperson work together to qualify buyers, build pipeline, and develop more accurate forecasts?

A prerequisite is to agree to apply a standard set of terms describing the key players involved in making buying decisions. This facilitates qualifying multiple key players who play different roles in a given opportunity. A prospect with all roles filled is a better bet at forecasting time.

We define key players as being those individuals whom a seller must access in order to sell, fund, and implement an offering. As you would expect, the number of key players is proportional to the size and complexity of what is being sold. Here are our definitions of the key players:

- *Coaches* want the seller to win the business, and are willing to provide information and do inside selling. They have only limited authority within the organization, but they can serve as the eyes and ears for a salesperson as an opportunity develops.
- *Champions* provide access to key players, as requested by the salesperson, and can be found at any level within the prospect organization. Generally speaking, the higher within the organization your champion is, the better your chances of success and the shorter the sales cycle. The ideal situation is to have your champion also be the decision maker (see next item). In such cases, the buyer will often volunteer access to other key players even before the salesperson asks for that access, and this access will be to people *below* him or her in the organization—a good thing. While bottom-up access is necessary at times, the first choice is top-down.
- *Decision makers* can make the vendor selection and cause unbudgeted funds to be spent, which (as explained in earlier chapters) is critical if a seller initiates a buying cycle in an organization that wasn't looking to change, and therefore has no budget for change. In addition, a decision maker can commit internal resources to evaluate a salesperson's offerings. In the case of purchases by committees, there can be multiple decision makers.
- *Financial approvers* are the people who must sign off on expenditures. Their role can range from being passive (rubber stamp) to being an active and involved player in the decision process. Gaining financial approval is easier when this person understands the value of addressing the goals the organization wants to achieve as well as how the offering is going to be used.
- *Users* and *managers of users* are people involved in using the offering. For implementations affecting a wide group of people within an organization, supportive and enthusiastic users can be critical to a seller's success. Users can help sales campaigns by providing a groundswell of support. (Conversely, their reluctance or skepticism can scuttle an otherwise viable opportunity.) Users don't usually have business goals. Their concerns are more personal. They want to decide if the offering will improve their stock in their company and simplify or complicate their lives. It's rarely possible for a seller to interface with all potential users, but getting (at least) some opinion leaders on board—including, for example, managers of users—can be a critical step in making the sale. Users also prefer to do business with recognized industry leaders because there will be more demand and job opportunities.

- *Implementers* are the people responsible for migrating from the current method to the new offering. Often their major concern is not a corporate objective. They will be measured on their ability to integrate the new offering on schedule and under budget. They prefer doing business with vendors that offer professional services and ongoing support.
- *Adversaries* are individuals who don't want to change, want to control change internally, or want to do business with a competitor. They can include, for example, champions for a competitor, individuals whose power is derived from the current method of doing things, IT staff members who want to develop the desired capability internally, and so on.

In our experience, salespeople try to avoid talking with their adversaries, which can be a mistake. A salesperson's objective should be to convert, neutralize, or eliminate adversaries. Of course, this needs to be done carefully. For example, a one-on-one meeting can be confrontational and can further polarize opposing positions. Instead, we suggest including people who are on your side when you meet with adversaries—preferably, a proponent who outranks your adversary. This can allow a more reasonable discussion of requirements, strengths, and weaknesses of offerings.

These definitions of members of the buying committee become the basis for discussing and developing strategies for specific opportunities. Look at Figures 14.1, 14.2, and 14.3. In these charts, we've laid out three different sized opportunities and identified the key players and their associated titles and goals. (Note that there are occasions where a key player plays more than one role.) Also note the emphasis on goals: the starting point of all CustomerCentric Selling.

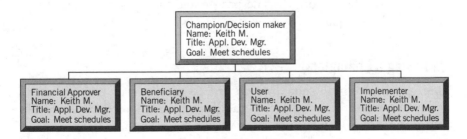

Figure 14.1 Opportunity Organization Chart: Middleware Opportunity—
$35,000

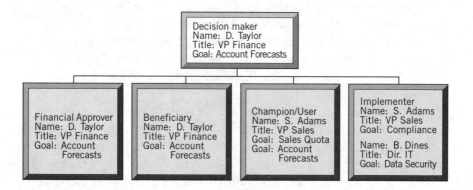

Figure 14.2 Opportunity Organization Chart: Sales Process Automation— $250,000

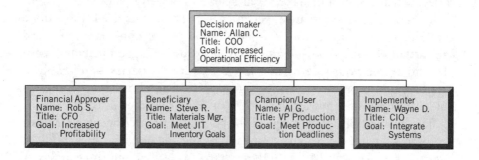

Figure 14.3 Opportunity Organization Chart: ERP Deployment—$2 Million

This may look like a lot of extra work. But given a simple organizational chart software package and a little practice, it should prove relatively easy. And in our experience, understanding, preparing, and updating simple charts like this helps both the salesperson and the sales manager, as they work together to qualify opportunities.

Qualifying a Champion

One key element in the qualification process is to identify and reinforce a champion. When the salesperson is calling high, the champion will often be self-nominating. He or she will often volunteer access to key players. More often, of course, he or she has to be asked through the kinds of Customer-Centric Selling correspondence with buyers. After a call on a potential champion, the salesperson should be required to answer the debriefing questions in Figure 14.4.

> *Opportunity source?*
> *Name, title, and company?*
> *Buyer's goal(s)?*
> *Current situation?*
> *Whom else do we want involved?*
> *Buyer's vision(s)?*
> *Personal/dollar value to person/organization?*
> *Roles of buyer?*
> *Next step(s)?*

Figure 14.4 Sales Call Debriefing Questions

Once the answers to the debriefing questions have been edited and approved, the seller now composes a champion letter. The champion letter, fax, or e-mail serves many important roles:

- It provides a sanity check for salespeople to verify that they have articulated the buyer's goal, current situation, potential value, and vision.
- After sellers demonstrate mastery of this process, sales managers can allow the champion letter to be sent without being edited. In such cases, it allows the manager to audit a salesperson's achievement of milestones to see if a prospect is worthy of being in the pipeline. Any process must have an audit trail, and assuming that salespeople create visions using Solution Development Prompters, all of the debriefing questions contained in the champion letter can be answered by executing the prompters.
- It serves as a reminder to the buyer of the conversation with the salesperson. Unlike vendor brochures, this letter minimizes the chance of the buyer becoming confused when evaluating offerings from other competitors.
- It facilitates internal selling by providing prospect-ready messaging (the words for your champion to use to explain or defend his or her interest). For this reason, many salespeople prefer to e-mail the champion letter on the day of the call, and follow up via snail mail. Our preference is e-mail, which can be forwarded easily to other key players, thus becoming an internal selling document.
- It communicates that the salesperson is, in fact, a sales professional, someone who took the time to listen, took notes, and documented the discussion back in a professional manner. As we've discussed ear-

lier, our belief, one that is being validated by the market, is that a salesperson can use *how* they sell as a competitive differentiator. It is our experience that very few salespeople take the time to follow up in writing after a meeting with a prospect. If they do, it's usually something pretty lightweight, such as "Great meeting. I'm looking forward to scheduling a Web demo for you next week." The salesperson who can put down in writing what he or she believes the prospects' goals and objectives are, a concise summary of how they operate currently, the capabilities they feel they need moving forward, and so forth will enjoy differentiation from most competitors beginning with that initial interaction.

We include a sample champion letter in Figure 14.5. We believe that the sales manager should be involved in writing, or at least editing, champion letters until he or she is confident that the salesperson can accomplish this without help. Having a half dozen good examples should build that confidence in both parties.

Take a minute to read the first three paragraphs of our sample letter. Here's where the goals, current situation, vision, and value for the champion are summarized. (The insert in the upper right-hand corner is not included in a real champion letter.) Please note that all answers to the debriefing questions come from executing the CustomerCentric Selling process. Traditional salespeople need both a map (milestones) and explicit directions (a defined sales process plus Sales-Ready Messaging).

In previous chapters, we stressed the importance of consistency in messaging. What many organizations fail to realize is that a great deal of selling occurs while the salesperson is not present at the prospect organization. How? After a successful sales call, many buyers attempt to share their excitement with other people within the organization. In fact, the better the call, the more likely this is to happen.

But how confident are you that your message will get across accurately? Consider how long it takes a salesperson to become proficient at relating the offerings in a way that makes sense to the many different buyers he or she calls on. Most likely, this is an intensive, full-time effort over several months. How well prepared is a buyer who spent 45 minutes with a salesperson to re-create the excitement the buyer felt about a vision of using the offering to finally achieve a goal or solve a problem?

Take an example from everyday life. You attend a professional meeting, and the after-dinner attraction is an inspirational speaker (who most likely has practiced and delivered this same talk many, many times over the previous months or years). You are carried away by the speaker and the subject, and—on returning home—you attempt to convey your excitement

Qualification Milestones

1. Goal(s)
2. Current situation
3. Vision(s)
4. Value
5. Access to Key Players

To: Wendy Komac@xyzsoftware.com
From: DBranfman@spa.com
Subj: Follow-up to our conversation

Dear Wendy,

Thank you for your interest in SPA.com. The purpose of this letter is to summarize my understanding of our discussion. You told me your primary goal is improving revenue projections with a more accurate sales forecast.

Today's forecasting metrics vary by office, many unqualified or stalled opportunities are in the pipeline, close rates vary widely by salesperson, and earnings have been impacted when major opportunities don't close when forecasted. You said missing earnings for another quarter could affect valuation by as much as 20 percent. You believe you could improve forecasting accuracy if you had the following capabilities:

- After every sales call, your salespeople would be prompted to report progress against standard companywide milestones.
- When reviewing pipelines, your sales managers could evaluate progress and e-mail suggestions regardless of their location.
- On an ongoing basis, the system could track the close rates of every salesperson and apply them to predict revenue.
- When a quarter hinges on a make-or-break opportunity, you and other senior executives want the ability to inspect progress against company milestones before finalizing your projections.

You indicated that you are interested in further investigating SPA.com. Based on my experience, I suggest our next logical steps are

1. Confirm you are in agreement with my summary of our discussion.
2. Arrange telephone or in-person interviews with your VP Sales, Sales Operations Manager, and CIO, who would all be involved in the implementation of Sales Force Automation.
3. Summarize our findings to the group and determine if a further evaluation is appropriate.

I will call you on Tuesday, January 7, at 9 a.m. to review this letter and discuss our next steps. If that time is not convenient for you, please let me know an alternative. I look forward to working with you and your organization.

Sincerely,

Dave Branfman
Senior Account Executive
SPA.com

Figure 14.5 Sell Cycle Control Champion Letter (E-mail): Qualifying the Buyer

to your spouse. Hard to do, right? Most likely, it's one of those "you had to be there" situations, and you may find that your enthusiasm is now muted. Maybe that speaker wasn't that good, after all. . . .

So messaging is important in your correspondence from the very first encounter with a potential champion. Give the champion the script he or she needs in order to serve as your backup.

Now look at the fourth paragraph of our sample letter, which begins, "You indicated that you are interested. . . ." One of the trickier and more important building blocks of the champion letter comes toward the end, where the salesperson attempts to shape the further investigation of the opportunity. This is where the salesperson attempts to get the champion to agree to provide the salesperson with access to key players. Which key players? The titles will vary, depending on the complexity of the offering, how many people will be affected during the implementation, the size of the proposed expenditure, and the size of the target organization. Another variable may be the state of the economy. During difficult financial conditions, even add-on business with existing customers may require more sign-offs, and at higher levels, than previous orders. A rule of thumb is to review your Targeted Conversations List.

For these reasons, the sales manager should be involved in these decisions, at least until the salesperson has demonstrated the ability to make these kinds of determinations. The sales manager should not hesitate to get involved in these decisions again, if circumstances change, either on the seller's end or on the buyer's end.

This approach—requesting access to key players in the champion letter—relieves the seller of the burden of having to request access during a sales call. At the same time, though, it ensures that this critical step is actually taken. Some traditional salespeople are primarily concerned about getting and keeping opportunities in their pipelines, and are therefore hesitant to ask tough qualification questions. This isn't acceptable. An opportunity isn't real until access to the entire buying committee has been granted and documented, which leads us to the next step.

Following Up on the Champion Letter

Once the champion letter has been sent, the salesperson needs to follow up on that communication in order to get the buyer's agreement to the following points:

- The letter accurately summarizes the conversation(s).
- The buyer is willing and able to provide access to the requested titles.
- After interviewing all key players, there will be a chance to gain consensus that further evaluation is warranted.

Once the salesperson has verified these points and can produce the champion letter, the sales manager can now grade this prospect as a C. As we'll emphasize again later, sales management should perform grading of pipeline—and forecasting in general. It should *not* be the responsibility of salespeople, who historically are optimistic and motivated by their desire to have their managers believe that everything is OK within their pipelines, regardless of their actual condition.

There will be times when the follow-up call to verify the contents of the champion letter will not go according to plan. (If it always did, there would be less reason to write champion letters.) Buyer "push-back" or disagreement must be resolved if the prospect is to be considered viable.

The buyer may question or dispute the contents of the letter, in which case a discussion is necessary to clarify issues. If the discussion succeeds, the champion letter should be modified to reflect whatever changes are necessary. The seller qualifies a champion after obtaining the buyer's acceptance of the revised letter.

Sometimes the salesperson's request for access to key players may be challenged or denied. In the following paragraphs, we present the most common reasons why access is denied—at least initially—and suggest ways to handle them.

1. *The buyers indicate that they will sell it internally.* This reluctance may be an indicator that you are Column B (vying for a silver medal), especially if the buyer is the one who initiated the contact. The prospect may have been instructed to get pricing but not to grant access to others. Or, alternatively, buyers may simply want to maintain control and get all the credit for introducing the concept to others. In our experience, any one of these conditions dramatically reduces your chances of success in both selling and forecasting.
2. We suggest making it clear that your champion is welcome to accompany you on meetings with key players whenever he or she feels it is appropriate. This may help to address the issue of the person's wanting to maintain control and exposure. We have also found it effective to make the (accurate) point that you and the prospect have spent only a brief period discussing your offerings, and that it is unfair to place the burden of selling the offering internally on his or her shoulders.
3. *The buyers say that key players' involvement is unnecessary.* In these cases, the salesperson can and should point to potential implementation issues if everyone is not on board from the outset. Another option is to indicate that unless key players are aware of an evaluation, both the prospect and the salesperson may wind up spinning their wheels by undertaking an unsanctioned initiative.

4. *The buyer is skeptical and indicates that it is too early to involve other people.* Depending on the complexity of your offering, this may be a valid concern. Up to this point, you (most likely) have had only a conversation or two with the potential champion about your offerings. Perhaps this is the juncture to offer a proof session or demonstration with a fairly straightforward quid pro quo: "If the proof satisfies you, then will you get me access to the specified key players?"

When attempting to get access to key players, the salesperson should be politely persistent. This is important. It simply can't be sidestepped. Failure to have conversations with these people leaves the salesperson and company vulnerable to long sales cycles, no decision, silver medal competitions, and other bad things. Ultimately whether a seller wins or loses, a commitment to a sell cycle of any length is an expensive proposition. The best way to qualify opportunities is to have the buyer agree to measureable events, such as gaining access to people involved in making the decision.

If access is not forthcoming, it is important to figure out what's really going on: Is the champion unable to provide access, or unwilling? If a prospect is unable to obtain access to decision makers, the salesperson needs to ask who could provide that access. If a prospect persists in being unwilling to grant access, the sales manager should be involved in making the decision as to whether to keep competing for the sale. Part of that decision can include doing a "competitive sanity check" (Figure 14.6). The competitive sanity check, much like the call debriefing questions, provides a way to objectively begin to assess if you should, in fact, compete.

Opportunity source?
Name, title, and company?
Buyer's goal(s)?
Current situation?
Whom else do we want involved?
Buyer's vision(s)?
Personal/dollar value to person/organization?
Roles of buyer?
Next step(s)?

Figure 14.6 Competitive Sanity Check Questions

Qualifying Key Players

Once a champion agrees to provide access to key players, phone conversations or face-to-face sales calls should be scheduled. Ideally, the champion and the seller together should strategize the sequence of these calls. Often a champion can prepare a key player for a call, and—in some cases—the champion may want to accompany the seller on certain calls. These meetings tend to yield more favorable outcomes if your champion has copied key players on your correspondence. When a champion identifies a potential adversary, we suggest calling on that person last and asking the champion to participate.

The good news is that calls on key players may be less challenging than initial calls on potential champions, because a few hurdles have already been surmounted. Key players may have a sense that incompetent or insincere salespeople would not have been granted access. In fact, the chances of successful key player calls are often influenced by the power your champion wields within the organization.

The objective in decision maker and key players calls is to briefly introduce yourself and your organization, summarize the previous calls made within the account, give the buyer an opportunity to share his or her goals, diagnose each, create visions, and establish value. For these reasons, preparation is vitally important. Great preparation will keep you out of a number of traps. For example, there are some stereotypical "salesy" behaviors that can lead buyers to draw unfavorable conclusions about a salesperson they are meeting for the first time. Part of your job, therefore, is to demonstrate to the buyer that you don't conform to the stereotype of traditional salespeople.

Again, great preparation helps. We suggest that you arrive prepared with a "call introduction," a summary of the meetings within the account to date (goals, current situation, visions), and a list of potential goals, Success Stories, and corresponding Solution Development Prompters for each potential goal of the title that is being called on.

Salespeople must develop the call introduction in their own words, but it should be concise and fact-based (rather than opinion-based). Here is an example of a call introduction—typically delivered after introductions have been made and a certain level of rapport has been established:

> Today I'd like to briefly introduce XYZ Company, summarize meetings I've had with other members of your organization, discuss your objectives, and mutually determine if there are areas where our offering would have value for you. Are there any other items you would like to cover today?
>
> XYZ Company enables organizations to use our offerings to reduce engineering design cycles, thereby shortening time to market.

We were founded in 1995, and last year achieved $95 million in revenue. Some of our clients include Boeing, Hewlett-Packard, and IBM.

I was introduced to your company by George Agnew, your VP of production. He would like to reduce scrap (goal) by having the number of late engineering changes reduced. I also met with Ken Filosi, your VP of engineering, who indicated that he wants to reduce engineering design cycles and reduce recalls due to product defects (goals). That gets you up-to-date with the meetings I've had so far. Perhaps you can tell me, in your role as CFO, what are you hoping to accomplish?

At this point, as in the conclusion of the telephone-prospecting script, your objective is to have the buyer share at least one specific business goal for which you have a prompter. (To get a sense of how to handle the possible responses, review the previous chapter.) In calling on a key player, however, keep in mind that another situation may arise. Sometimes senior executives merely want to meet the salesperson and understand the conversations that have gone on to date. Since they are able to connect the dots on their own, they may not necessarily need to share a goal during the meeting.

In the example cited, once the CFO understands that his staff believes they can reduce scrap, shorten engineering design cycles, and minimize recalls, that may be sufficient for the salesperson to win the CFO's support for the project. It's almost always worth asking, "What are you hoping to accomplish?" But if the question doesn't elicit a goal, don't push it. A sensible next step is to tell a Success Story and/or offer a list of goals for the CFO. If there still is no positive response, the salesperson should engineer a polite exit. This entails thanking the CFO for the opportunity to apprise him or her of progress to date, informing the CFO that a meeting will be held after all key players have been interviewed to gain consensus to proceed with the evaluation of the offering, and inviting the CFO to participate in that meeting.

As early as possible in the buying cycle, as implied in the preceding scenario, the salesperson should conduct meetings with all key players. This accomplishes several objectives:

- Everyone understands the potential benefit to him- or herself and the organization.
- Getting everyone involved can often result in larger payback and therefore justify potentially larger transactions.
- Having multiple points of contact in the organization means that you may not have to start all over if one person gets fired, is promoted, leaves the company, or dies.

- If there is a strong adversary, he or she will be identified fairly early. If the adversary is powerful and can't be neutralized, the salesperson (in concert with the sales manager) may decide to withdraw rather than go the distance and lose, bringing only a silver medal back to the office.
- Again, this is a reality check. It is highly unlikely that a prospect will grant these interviews to anyone who doesn't represent Column A.

Like the champion call, these calls on key players should be documented. Whenever a new goal is shared, the equivalent of a champion letter should be generated, although the request for access to key players should be eliminated as that only applies when you are trying to qualify a champion.

Qualifying RFPs

We touched on the subject of RFPs (requests for proposal) in Chapter 5. Sellers also receive RFQs (requests for quotation) and RFIs (requests for information). We'll refer to them collectively here as RFPs.

RFPs represent a particular challenge when it comes to qualifying buyers. As also noted, they tend to come in two flavors:

- Those that you "wired" because you were Column A
- Those that someone else occupying Column A wired, and for which you are being asked to serve as a silver medalist

Yes, there will be an occasional "stray bullet" where the sender of the RFP doesn't know the requirements, and therefore has not established a favored vendor. We find these to be rare, and they most often turn out to be fishing expeditions—either for companies to discover what is available out in the market or for their IT department to receive free education in order to generate specifications for in-house projects. We have found that many of these situations turn into long sales cycles, with a high probability of no decision being made.

By their nature, RFPs slow down the buying process. They are more common among mainstream-market buyers. Companies use several justifications to defend the time and effort involved in issuing RFPs:

- Companies find out what offerings are available.
- Vendors talk about one another, allowing a more informed choice.
- Companies meet due diligence requirements.
- Companies get free advice/consulting.

- Companies can make an assessment of vendor submissiveness.
- Vendors bid against one another.
- Companies give the appearance of being fair to all vendors.

As an aside, many organizations talk long and loud about their cost of sales. Amazingly, though, few calculate what it actually costs to generate and monitor RFPs with multiple vendors. Consider an organization that issues an RFP to six vendors, with the intent of stirring up a price war, for a $75,000 transaction that has the potential to allow them to save $5,000 per month. Conservatively speaking, the time to generate, publish, distribute, and provide adequate time for vendors to respond to the RFP will add 90 days to the process. Let's also assume a cost in labor-hours of $3,000 for the resources required to interact with six vendors (again, that's conservative). Without regard for the time and effort needed to actually write the RFP, which may involve expensive talent, here is an estimate of the imbedded costs:

$$
\begin{aligned}
(3\text{-month delay}) \times (\$5,000/\text{month potential savings}) &= \$15,000 \\
(6 \text{ vendors}) \times (\$3,000 \text{ cost/vendor}) &= \$18,000 \\
\textbf{Total cost of RFP process} &= \mathbf{\$33,000}
\end{aligned}
$$

Based on these figures, the RFP must enable the issuing company to negotiate a $42,000 ($75,000 − $33,000) price with the gold medalist just to break even.

Having looked at this from the side of issuing organizations, let's consider a vendor's perspective. Over the past 12 months, how many RFPs has your company responded to where you were reactive rather than proactive (meaning you were surprised when you received the document)? Now estimate your win rate on those "opportunities." If that figure is acceptable, feel free to skip the next few paragraphs.

We worked with a client that had an entire department whose sole responsibility was responding to RFPs. The average response took 80 labor-hours—and the company's 145 responses to unsolicited RFPs over the previous 12 months had resulted in precisely three wins. Perhaps your win rate on unsolicited RFPs is better than 2 percent. (We hope so.) But it's probably not satisfactory. The hard fact is that if you play by rules that have been prewired by your competitor, more often than not you will be receiving a silver medal. On analysis, most companies discover that responding to RFPs wired by other vendors is an unprofitable practice.

So let us propose a qualifying alternative.

When issuing an RFP, organizations want something from vendors: namely, a column (either A or—more likely—something east of A) on the spreadsheet. We suggest that you offer a column in exchange for access to a key player. If the organization issuing the RFP won't give you access, this is a clear signal that the relationship will end unhappily for you.

The difficult reality of RFPs is the realization that the prospect is going to spend money with someone. It's not going to be you, but someone is going to get that business. The challenge is to resist the temptation of chasing an opportunity that is very likely to be unwinnable.

We worked with a financial EDI software company in New England a number of years ago. Over the course of delivering the CustomerCentric Selling workshop to one of their groups, we had the VP of Sales act as one of the coaches. When we got to our recommendations regarding unsolicited RFPs and how they are a losing proposition, the VP of Sales' hand shot up in the back of the room. He then proceeded to inform us, and all of the students, that their company had just exactly the *opposite* experience. They had recently responded to an unsolicited RFP and won the business. Our position was that that was the worst thing that could have happened to them. When he asked "Why?," we first asked him if he would agree that this was the exception not the rule. He agreed. We then explained to him that this one exception would be the one that everyone points to in order to justify investing the time and resources filling out the next 99 unsolicited RFPs that he didn't have a chance of winning.

The message, whether an opportunity is discovered proactively or reactively, is to scrub the input into your pipeline. Sales managers (unless they choose to make an exception) should require documented access to key players before authorizing the resources needed to compete. Would you prefer gold or silver?

In the next chapter, we look at the challenge of managing a sequence of events across the life span of a sale—the selling organization's equivalent of project management.

Chapter 15

NEGOTIATING AND MANAGING A SEQUENCE OF EVENTS

In this chapter, we look at the challenge of transforming the sell cycle from a realm of mystery—which is how some buyers and sellers view it—into a rational and orderly process that both the buyer's organization and the vendor agree on.

But first, to introduce the subject, let's imagine that a salesperson has worked on a major opportunity for four months. Imagine further that a CustomerCentric Selling sales consultant is hired to analyze each opportunity in the pipeline, and the consultant asks the salesperson to estimate when this particular opportunity will close. For the purposes of this example, let's assume the CustomerCentric Selling sales consultant knows the decision maker on this transaction, and can ask him or her to provide a date when the sale can be made. What is the likelihood that the buyer's date will be later than the seller's date?

A few observations:

- Most closing is driven by the agenda of the sales organization, with little or no regard for the buyer. Many organizations that are under pressure to meet monthly, quarterly, or annual targets resort to "blitzes" to bring in business, based on those internal pressures.

- The vast majority of closing occurs before the salesperson has earned the right to ask for the business. When salespeople attempt to close orders before buyers are ready, they run the risk of being perceived as a traditional pushy salesperson—or, worse, of scaring the buyer off entirely.

Many companies that have taken the time to document their sales process often include a step or a stage called "Qualified." This is usually a fairly subjective assessment based on when other prospects have been deemed ready to buy rather than the specific requirements of each unique prospect. While it is true that many of the steps do remain consistent, the problem is that the salesperson never gains that agreement from each subsequent prospect. Additionally, this also gives the impression to the salesperson that once an opportunity is "Qualified," it's appropriate to close them at any point after. The reality is that the companies with the highest degrees of forecast accuracy are those that view "qualification" as a continuous exercise, not a binary step.

If a salesperson closes before a buyer is ready, discounting is the most common method of giving the buyer an incentive to sign early. In these premature efforts to close, a great deal of negotiating is done with nondecision makers. This can be demeaning for buyers who can't commit. In some instances, the discount offered to non-decision makers becomes the starting point for the real negotiations.

In our workshops, we sometimes ask participants, "How can you know when a transaction is closable?" There is almost always a prolonged silence, as people realize that this question is not readily answerable with their current approach.

In fact, many organizations (buyers and sellers) view sell cycles as random series of events that sometimes result in orders. Salespeople push buyers to go through sales cycles without gaining consensus or commitment. Many salespeople do not ask for, and therefore fail to get, access to the people within the prospect organization who will be required to sell, fund, and implement the recommended solution. How many "opportunities" in your current pipeline have at least one documented buyer goal?

Just as a competent chess player thinks several moves ahead, salespeople should do the same as they attempt to facilitate the buying process. Despite the fact that every sale appears to be unique, based on the size of the transaction and the size of the prospect organization, there are many common steps in the buying process that have a high probability of recurring. The key is getting each individual buyer to overtly agree to what those steps should be.

By agreeing to and adhering to a clear sequence of events, the salesperson provides documentation that allows sales management to continue auditing and grading opportunities. Like the qualifying efforts described in the previous chapter, this removes overoptimistic opinions from the forecast and minimizes the phenomenon of salespeople "selling" their managers on how good their pipeline is. When they make their forecasts, sales managers should have the benefit of a piece of paper that shows a planned sequence of events for each potential sale, and what progress has been made in that sequence.

By documenting sales efforts and gaining commitment to sequences of events, sales managers can play a vital role in deciding what deserves to be in each pipeline. As soon as an opportunity does not look winnable, the sales manager should brainstorm with the salesperson as to how to change the landscape of the decision. If the two of them together are unable to figure out a way to do this, they should withdraw from the opportunity. The alternative is hanging in there with a high probability of being one of several silver medalists.

When documented by means of a clearly stated sequence of events, the process of controlling a sales cycle begins to resemble project management. The decision process embedded in a sales cycle has a defined beginning and end, and—as noted previously—the selling organization has the ability to assess progress and probabilities of success throughout.

There's also an ancillary benefit. When the seller handles sales cycles in a highly professional manner, buyers are likely to conclude that the selling organization's implementation will be professional as well. This perception can allow buyers to feel more comfortable with a given company, and especially with a relatively untested company selling complex offerings. We believe salespeople and the companies they represent can make the *way* they sell a competitive advantage and a differentiator.

Gaining the Commitment

The first step, of course, is gaining the commitment from the buying organization to move forward with the evaluation of the offering.

As noted in the previous chapter, we believe that prior to committing to a buying cycle, salespeople should meet with all key players to understand their issues, determine if their offering represents a fit for the buyer's environment, establish potential value, and gain consensus that a formal evaluation makes sense. Key players should understand what's in it for them. They should then come to some consensus and agreement on (1) the steps needed to reach a decision and (2) the time frame for the overall evaluation.

Now it's time to move the process forward. To do so, the salesperson has to orchestrate getting all the key people together. This is the meeting that, in the previous chapter, you invited the CFO to attend. The seller has to summarize progress to date and verify that the buyers feel there is enough potential benefit that further investigation is warranted. Finally, and most important, the seller has to obtain a commitment to proceed.

At some point in this process, the seller may attempt to push toward a commitment by pointing out a fact that should be obvious, but often isn't. By taking the time to evaluate this particular offering, the buyer is making a serious commitment of time, resources, and effort. Yes, the seller has a lot at stake, but the buyer, too, has money on the table, and that pile of chips is only growing. (Of course, the seller can be prepared to point out the cost to the buyer of *not* moving forward if value has been established.)

Asking for a commitment benefits the selling organization in several ways. First, it continues the qualification process. (If this opportunity is going to fizzle, let's find out sooner, rather than later.) Second, the selling organization wants to shape the sales cycle as much as possible. Third, the seller can incorporate steps in the buyer's process so that the sequence of events actually merges the buying and selling process into one.

Looking for a commitment will not always succeed. A salesperson selling enterprise software recently told us about his attempts to obtain agreement on a $100,000 opportunity that he was working on. The VP of engineering and the CIO were in favor of committing the resources necessary to work with the vendor. The VP of manufacturing, though, had a track record of having difficulty with implementing technology and was known to be a potential adversary. Sure enough, during the meeting designed to gain consensus, the whole deal came unraveled, as the VP of manufacturing argued passionately and ultimately succeeded in convincing everyone that it was "not the right time" to consider new software. When asked, the seller felt had it gone the distance, the VP of manufacturing would have killed it at the end.

So is our recommendation—scheduling a meeting to extract a commitment from the organization—a bad idea? We don't think so, because we believe that in sales, bad news early is actually good news. Would you rather learn that the "opportunity" is a pipe(line) dream in month 1 or in month 6, after you have expended a great deal of time and resources and have been carrying it on your forecast as having a high probability of closing?

Our experience is that salespeople make two fundamental mistakes when they attempt to implement this concept of a mutually agreed-upon sequence of events.

Mistake 1: The first three or four prospects that the salesperson attempts to put a sequence of events in place will balk at the concept. The salesperson hears things such as "Thanks for the thought, but we have our own process. We'll let you know what we need and when we need it." As a result, the salesperson makes the mistaken determination that the sequence of events doesn't work. Is that the case? Or could it be that the salesperson is really finding out that the prospect is not as serious as he would have hoped and the salesperson just doesn't want to face that reality?

A buyer's willingness or unwillingness to commit to a mutually agreed-to plan moving forward is the watershed qualification event in the entire process. If they are agreeable, you've likely positioned yourself as Column A. If they are unwilling (or unable), you are likely finding out, whether you want to recognize it or not, that something just isn't right.

Mistake 2: When the salesperson does get a mutually agreed-to plan in place but fails to keep it current. We'll discuss Mistake 2 in detail later in this chapter.

Keeping Committees on Track

After obtaining consensus from the committee that the value of the potential solution warrants further investigation, there is a great chance to begin qualifying the opportunity. The first thing the salesperson should ask the committee is to describe their buying process. Often this is the first time a buying committee has ever been asked that question, and they are unsure how to answer it. If that is the case, we suggest the seller should ask some questions to draw the buyers out. Typical questions would be as follows:

- Will procurement be involved? If so, how and when?
- Will we need to get on a preferred vendor list?
- What is your time frame for making a decision?
- What is your budgeting process?
- How will IT determine strategy/platform compatibility?
- What is your policy on issuing RFPs?

The seller must decide which questions are appropriate, but the desired result is to uncover steps the buyer will need to go through to evaluate your offerings and if they want to move ahead, how the purchase will be done. This is an important step if a vendor is going to be customercentric and is consistent with our feeling that buyers want to buy rather than be sold.

When we reach this point in the CustomerCentric Selling training, many salespeople push back on the idea of introducing things like RFPs if the buyer doesn't. Why would you introduce something that could potentially extend your sell cycle and introduce competitive pricing into the mix? Well, if a company has a policy that all proposed expenditures over *x* amount of dollars require three bids, and so on, when do you want to find that out? Now? Or six months from now when you think the opportunity is ready to close only then to find out that an RFP must first be issued?

Sometimes asking how they buy and what they would like to see can elicit requests for demonstrations, site surveys, proposals, and so on. These are things that will take a sales organization a great deal of time and effort. Conservative mainstream-market buyers are also apt to ask for things a salesperson does not want (or lacks the authority) to commit to doing. Examples would be a money-back guarantee, a lengthy free trial with no exposure, and the like. While early in a company's history salespeople may have to make concessions, as the offering matures and an installed base has been established, these requests become unreasonable. How does a salesperson respond?

One option is to take them head on, potentially responding, "We would never be willing to do that for you." In light of the fact that you've just gotten consensus to continue with considering your offerings, this represents an inopportune time to take such a hard stance. Keep in mind that you have a decision maker or makers with their subordinates in a meeting. It is likely that the senior executive wants to flex his or her muscles on a salesperson. An alternative is to merely acknowledge you've heard the request without agreeing or disagreeing.

Once the prospect has had an opportunity to respond to what the management would like to see in order to evaluate your offerings, the salesperson now has a chance to share an example of a Sequence of Events template showing typical steps previous buyers have taken on the way to making a decision on the offerings. Hopefully, this can serve as an outline for a final agreement on the steps and an approximate time frame for the buyer's arriving at a decision. A sample is shown in Table 15.1.

The salesperson can end the meeting by disarming any misconceptions in the event the committee has asked for things that he or she cannot commit to by thanking everyone for their time and indicating he or she will take the list back to the office and propose what he or she feels is the best way to proceed. If it is clear there is a single decision maker, the suggestion would be to commit to sending a draft copy to that person for review. After that step, any necessary changes could be made prior to copying the other members of the buying committee.

After negotiating the internal resources the company is willing to commit, the salesperson can send a cover letter and draft copy of the sequence of events. A phone call or meeting to follow up should be scheduled with the decision maker, to ensure that the person has had a chance to review the document. The salesperson will then ask what, if any, changes are necessary. At this stage, any unreasonable requests (i.e., a money-back guar-

Week of	Checkpoint	Event	Billable	Responsibility
May 25	✓	Prove capabilities to committee members	$20,000	SPA.com
June 1		Survey current system		SPA.com
June 18	✓	Develop implementation plan with IT		Both
June 18		Share survey results and provide estimated cos		SPA.com
June 18	✓	Facilitate cost versus benefit analysis		Both
June 18		Provide contracts to legal		Both
June 18		Define success metrics		SPA.com
July 6	✓	Gain legal approval of contracts		Both
July 13		Make corporate visit		Both
July 20	✓	Deliver proposal		SPA.com
July 27		Begin implementation		Both

Table 15.1 XYZ Software Sequence of Events

antee) would be notable by their absence in the draft of the sequence of events. This means one of two things will happen. One possibility is that the buyer will not raise that point, in which case you can proceed. The other would be for the decision maker to challenge the fact that the money-back guarantee was not offered.

The salesperson could then ask the reason for wanting a guarantee. It is likely that the buyer will explain that it is to mitigate risks associated with the decision. At this stage, the salesperson (if this is not one of your very first customers) could respond that because 53 other companies have already implemented this application, the company would not be in a position to offer a guarantee, but the prospect can visit or talk with one of the company's customers who has already successfully implemented. If the buyer insists on a guarantee, the salesperson may have to determine if this is a showstopper, in which case the buying cycle may come to a grinding halt. While this is not the desired result, most would agree that it is better to find out now rather than at the end of the sales cycle. Bad news early is good news.

When the salesperson calls to follow up, it is a bad sign for a decision maker to agree to the sequence of events without requesting changes. This could be an indication that either the document hadn't been reviewed or the prospect was taking the commitment lightly. The correct response is to change dates or challenge some items. Your objective is to be able to remove the word *DRAFT* from the document, but it is most effective if the buyer makes changes because then he or she takes some ownership in the buying cycle. Some of our clients purposely leave some dates blank so their buyers are required to make changes.

Gaining Visibility and Control of Sales Cycles

In any event, if and when the sequence of events has been successfully negotiated with the decision maker, we suggest that at that point all committee members should be copied with the sequence of events. Both buyer and seller now have an agreed-upon approach to making a buying decision. Buyers find it comforting (and unusual) to be working with a salesperson who has already thought to ask about and negotiate the steps leading to a buying decision. At this point, the seller has gotten agreement from the committee for the approximate duration of the sales cycle. Now the salesperson has a far more realistic view of when, from the perspective of the buyer, the opportunity may be ready to close.

As for controlling the buying cycle, both the buyer and seller share veto power at each checkpoint. That is to say, each of these steps represents an opportunity for either party to withdraw from the evaluation.

Why Would Either Party Withdraw?

Consider for a moment the potential reasons a buying committee would elect to withdraw from a negotiated evaluation: a change in priorities, an economic meltdown, an acquisition, a reorganization, insufficient payback on the proposed project, references don't check out, investigation shows the offering not to be a good fit, and so on.

Now brace yourself as we begin to list reasons for a vendor to elect to withdraw from an ongoing sequence of events. Some traditional salespeople cannot begin to fathom any circumstances that would make them remove an opportunity from their pipeline. Here are some potential reasons for a vendor to withdraw: customer expectations may be unreasonable, the offering may not be a good fit, the transaction may not be profitable, a review may show that the prospect is not creditworthy, and so on.

While all these reasons are valid, the most compelling reason to withdraw is when you realize the opportunity is not winnable. The manager who wants the sales staff to compete to win, not just to keep busy, usually must make this decision. As soon as you believe you are not Column A and you cannot change the requirements list, it's time to find a different opportunity to work on. Traditional salespeople, wanting to hang in until the end (and keep their pipelines inflated), sometimes have to be forcibly removed from the "prospect."

Most sequences of events serve as a road map but will not be static documents. Earlier in this chapter we mentioned that salespeople typically make two mistakes when implementing this approach. Mistake 1 is when they misinterpret a buyer's willingness to commit to a mutually agreed-to sequence of events. Mistake 2 is the worst of the two. Mistake 2 is when the salesperson does get a mutually agreed-to plan in place but fails to keep it current. In other words, whenever something changes in the sequence of events (a rescheduled meeting, another proof session is added, etc.), it is incumbent upon the salesperson to *republish* the plan reflecting those changes. Doing so keeps it a living document. In fact, the first time something changes and the salesperson *doesn't* update the plan, the document is outdated and so loses all of its value.

Once this process is in place, sales managers enjoy several potential benefits:

1. They can coach salespeople (especially new hires) through the process step-by-step.
2. Planning for allocation of resources can be done.
3. Each checkpoint the buyer agrees to further validates the buyer's commitment and increases the likelihood of a successful comple-

tion. A buyer's agreement to continue in the evaluation is a measurable event.

4. Sales managers have the ability to assess (disqualify) opportunities if they do not appear to be winnable.

5. It is unlikely that buyers looking for Column B, C, or D would commit to a sequence of events with a silver medalist. Even if they do, it usually dies after the first few steps.

6. It is far easier to forecast close dates because buyers have agreed to tentative dates for delivery of a proposal and a decision. This helps take vendors away from the tendency to close based on their agendas.

7. Most executives prefer to be involved early and late in the buying process. The sequence approach supports this. In most cases, the defined steps will be executed with lower levels within the organization, so it is important to merely keep Key Players apprised via letter or e-mail when the steps are completed. Gaining access to the Key Players before issuing the proposal allows their involvement near the end of the buying process.

Negotiating the sales cycle also addresses a problem that virtually all salespeople face: not knowing when an opportunity is closable. Our belief is that the right time to close is when a sequence of events has been completed to the buyer's satisfaction and the seller's satisfaction. Our clients learn that each step in the sequence of events is a miniature close and that asking for or getting the order becomes a logical conclusion.

While we are on the subject of buying cycles, one of the most frightening situations occurs when a mainstream-market buyer is being asked to commit to a large expenditure (let's say, $500,000) for an application that has never been implemented before. Many key players consider the potential impact on their careers if the anticipated results aren't achieved. The sequence of events can be used to mitigate risk by providing a "pay as we progress" approach. By this we mean that the $500,000 expenditure can be broken into smaller pieces (feasibility study, preliminary design, prototype, and so on) that are billable events. After each, both the buyer and seller assess where they stand and make a determination as to whether to proceed.

Reframing the Concept of Selling

Earlier in the book, we articulated our desire to reframe the concept of selling as helping buyers achieve goals, solve problems, or satisfy needs. This definition applies to the buyer-seller relationship. At a higher level, we believe that the sequence-of-events approach empowers our clients to extend this philosophy to a company-to-company perspective. Negotiating the steps in the buying cycle enables all committee members (the prospect organization) and all members of the selling organization to be on board with the stated objective of determining if the offerings can satisfy the overall needs of the prospect. As soon as this doesn't appear to be possible, either party can opt out of expending further resources.

Mainstream-Market Buyers

In previous chapters, we described the phenomenon of mainstream-market buyers. Sales cycles with these buyers most often move at a slower pace than those involving early-market buyers. These mainstream-market decisions are almost invariably made by committees consisting of several people, with the majority of them having the ability to scuttle the project by saying no, but lacking the authority to say yes. Mainstream-market buyers are often governed by one or both of the following principles:

1. They are looking, but they lack a strong commitment to buy. Salespeople in these situations may begin throwing resources at the opportunity, hoping that the right thing will happen. In these cases, they run the risk of providing free information. These can be relatively easy situations for mainstream-market buyers to be involved in because the vendors do virtually all of the work as the buyer is getting exposure to new approaches. Unless compelling reasons to act can be uncovered by the salesperson, the result may well be no decision. The most common reasons for this result are as follows:

   - The salesperson never negotiated a sequence of events with all key players.
   - Business goals or problems were never identified.
   - The buyer did not fully understand what he or she was buying or how it would be used.
   - There was no compelling cost versus benefit.
   - The buying committee was concerned about the staff's ability to implement the recommendation.

2. If, for some reason, a mainstream-market buyer gets serious about making a decision, it is a virtual guarantee that the buyer will shop the transaction around by talking with other companies that offer similar products. In some cases, if there are no comparable offerings in the market, the buying decision will come to a screeching halt. Mainstream-market buyers want to compare offerings from at least two or three different companies. Doing so may verify in their minds that it is too early to risk going ahead with the project. They are

likely to postpone a decision unless the offering gets to a point where multiple companies are in that space and the offering shows the potential to become the de facto standard.

Assuming that there are alternatives, mainstream-market buyers will feel compelled to invite at least three companies to assess their needs and make a recommendation. We refer to this process as "running a beauty contest." While it is an advantage to have been the vendor that caused the sales cycle to begin (Column A), many unfavorable things can begin to take place. Despite the fact that a start-up company has a superior offering, mainstream-market buyers are apt to evaluate more established companies. Even if the seller has inferior offerings, doing business with a known corporate entity potentially lowers exposure to risk and second guessing if the project fails to meet expectations. Within the technology sector, for years IBM was seldom thought to have the latest or least expensive offerings. IBM did, however, represent the safest choice. Many transactions were won by appearing to be the safer alternative. At times, inviting two or three different companies to present their offerings will confuse mainstream-market buyers, which always have "no decision" lurking behind the scenes if things get overwhelming.

Chapter 16

NEGOTIATION:
THE FINAL HURDLE

The negotiations covered in this chapter center on the conversations that (1) follow the evaluation process and (2) precede the formal customer agreement to move forward. Many of the ideas in this chapter, however, have their roots in the concept of quid pro quo, a technique that customercentric sellers use throughout the sales cycle.

Unfortunately, when it comes to negotiating, there are no magic bullets. The salesperson has to be prepared and has to stick to the game plan. A misstep can cause significant damage. If salespeople fail to establish value and earn the respect of key players as peers, for example, the buyer has the upper hand when it becomes time to negotiate. If the seller has been subordinate throughout the sales cycle, giving whatever the buyer requests and getting nothing in return, who do you think has the upper hand when the subject of price arises?

Sticking with the disciplines outlined in this book is not always easy, and the stress of negotiating can cause a seller to revert to traditional behavior. But this can be doubly damaging. If during the sales cycle a seller has taken the approach of helping the buyer achieve a goal, solve a problem, or satisfy a need, and then suddenly shifts to persuading, convincing, and "hard closing," the buyer is likely to feel manipulated and begin to lump the seller into the pervasive negative stereotype.

Traditional Buyers and Sellers

Let's consider the positions, expectations, and relationship of buyers and sellers in a traditional negotiation, beginning with the position of both parties at the start of negotiations.

Home teams, as most sports fans know, enjoy a decided advantage. Negotiations are usually carried out at prospects' locations, so these encounters are "away games" for sellers. The seller is therefore at a disadvantage from the beginning. Most of the circumstances surrounding the negotiation favor the buyer. The buyer sits in his or her leather chair, for example, which tends to be slightly higher than the cloth chair the salesperson occupies. The buyer is the host, providing all creature comforts; the seller can only accept or decline those comforts.

Buyers are perfectly willing to conclude a potential closing meeting without consummating the transaction. In fact, sometimes they prefer it that way. People buying cars in the traditional fashion understand that sometimes the best way to determine if they have gotten the best offer is to leave the showroom. (Note that car salespeople work on their home turf, which changes some of the dynamics.) If the car salesperson sees the buyer walking out the door, he or she may also see the sale slipping away—and hurriedly start negotiating downward.

Given this phenomenon, many buyers orchestrate negotiations over the course of multiple meetings. The starting point for each meeting is the last (lowered) price from the previous meeting. Experienced buyers are fully aware of the quarterly pressures that selling organizations face and may time the real closing meeting to coincide with that cycle.

Buyers have the luxury of knowing that regardless of how adversarial or personal a negotiation gets, forgiveness is only a phone call away—if, that is, they award the gold medal to the seller they've been battling with. Buyers don't usually have a great deal personally at stake. Sellers, by contrast, have commissions, pride, and career paths on the line—stakes that are heightened in the case of large transactions toward the end of a quarter. The buyer can be patient, comfortable in the fact that it makes little difference to him or her whether the contract is awarded on December 28 or January 10. The buyer can sit back and see how badly the seller or vendor wants this deal to happen now.

Experienced buyers know what they want to pay and have a proactive plan for getting to or below that figure. Sellers—wanting to get the deal, and assuming that the negotiated price will be less than the initial asking price—ad lib responses to the buyer's implicit strategies and explicit comments. Smart buyers have at least three vendors competing, know their vendor of choice, and rarely show their hand. Buyers try to keep all vendors paranoid and convinced that price will drive the ultimate decision. Sellers can seldom be certain that they are Column A, which is exactly what the buyer wants.

As emphasized in previous chapters, the essence of CustomerCentric Selling is shaping conversations between buyers and sellers. Not surprisingly, we view negotiations in exactly the same way. Of course, conversations about business issues (framed by title/vertical industry/goal) are very different from negotiation conversations. But the good news is that this latter kind of conversation is easier to predict and script. You have a buyer attempting to get the best possible deal and a seller trying to close the transaction and (in theory) get the highest possible price.

So let's look at negotiation as a conversation the seller has earned the right to have, because he or she has executed all the necessary steps in the sales cycle and has otherwise behaved in a consistently professional manner. While you can seldom be sure you are the gold medalist, customer-centric sellers can take heart in knowing that the buyer has already said yes in making commitments at each checkpoint in the sequence of events.

The Six Most Expensive Words: "Where Do We Need to Be?"

Buyers expect discounts. Sellers expect to discount to get the business. Buyers squeeze sellers on price. Sellers expect to get squeezed. It is a generally accepted barbaric ritual of buying. That is the reason that sellers start with prices that leave them a little room to discount.

So it never should come as a surprise when, early in the negotiations, the buyer asks the seller for the "best possible price," or words to that effect. One of the most common, least appropriate, and most expensive responses a salesperson can make to such a request is, "Where do we need to be?" These six words allow the buyer to make the following conclusions:

- The seller is not controlling the discussion.
- The seller has already acknowledged that discounting is necessary and appropriate.
- The seller has wide latitude and authority to discount.
- Negotiation is not the seller's strength, given this weak opening response to the request for a better price.

Lawyers cross-examining hostile witnesses are taught never to ask a question to which they don't know the answer. The same is true for salespeople starting negotiations. Whether a buyer's answer to those six words is reasonable or not, the question allows them to put a stake in the ground that the seller is forced to address. Smart buyers will cite a figure well below what they are willing to pay. At this point, the buyer is now in Phase 3 of the buying cycle where the cost shifts to a price. You wouldn't be at this meeting if the buyer couldn't afford your offering. The objective of negotiations for buyers at this point is to be sure they are getting the best possible deal.

Here are some common errors made by salespeople (often with the support and direction of senior management of the companies they represent) during the negotiation process. Some will be familiar from previous chapters, while others are new.

- In the absence of an agreed-on sequence of events, the attempted closing is timed to serve the salesperson's agenda, rather than the buyer's. The most common way to get buyers to sign earlier than they want is by enticing them with discounts.
- Salespeople attempt to close non-decision makers. This can be demeaning to a "buyer" who in fact is merely a messenger. Beyond that, whatever discount is offered can become the starting point for further negotiations, if and when the decision maker gets involved.
- Salespeople selling non-commodity offerings mistakenly believe they can negotiate their way into Column A by treating price as the only variable. Ideally, negotiating should take place *after* the buyer makes the decision to buy from a particular salesperson.
- Many salespeople have difficulty tolerating silence while negotiating. Smart buyers remain quiet for a few seconds after asking the salesperson the price, or after being asked to buy. In the closing process, many sellers experience a marked loss in their ability to listen, understand, and respond (a phenomenon we call *vapor lock*). In fact, as a general rule of thumb, the more a salesperson talks during a negotiation, the more likely they are to offer concessions. There is great power in politely saying "no" when a buyer asks for a discount and then waiting to see how they respond.
- Many salespeople get (unnecessarily) defensive. Defending or explaining the price during negotiation is generally counterproductive. At this stage, the buyer is merely doing his or her job. He or she simply wants the best deal and really isn't interested in whether the pricing leaves your company sufficient profit.
- Salespeople compromise their power by saying things like, "That's the best I can do for you." This statement alone can make it impossible to close that day. Smart buyers ask who within the organization can do better—and pointedly instruct the seller to bring that person to the next meeting.
- Sellers who are behind quota should not negotiate large transactions without the involvement of their manager. The good cop (seller)/bad

cop (manager) game can be played to the seller's advantage. However, if the manager is not at or above his or her quota, this can be a problem as well. Over the years we've seen many salespeople coerced into bad negotiating behavior by managers who are eager to get deals done. As we'll discuss later, preparation is the key. Knowing what is a win-win versus just what you're willing to give and then having all parties, seller and manager, agree to the rules of the road in advance is critical.

We were teaching a workshop recently, and one of the attendees—let's call him Bill—seemed distracted for the first day and a half. At one of the breaks, we asked him if everything was all right. He told us that a buyer's decision on a major transaction was being made that Friday. He had quoted $960,000, but his coach inside the account had let him know that the organization had budgeted $850,000—a price that Bill was ready to meet. The CIO was the decision maker and had requested a new quote. Bill's manager happened to be a role-play coach at the workshop, so at lunch, we took the opportunity to brainstorm about how Bill and his manager should proceed.

During the workshop, Bill had realized that he was Column A in this transaction, having initiated the opportunity with a cold call. He was concerned, though, because Column B had been called in, and was the acknowledged industry leader in that market space. Based on our discussion, Bill and his manager agreed on a course of action, which Bill then set in motion before the lunch break was over. First, he called the CIO and said that he was not going to provide a revised quotation. He also asked for a meeting with his manager and the CIO on Friday afternoon at 4:00 p.m., and this request was granted.

This was good news. Our sense was that if they were not going to get the business, it was unlikely that the CIO would give them an appointment late in the afternoon on the day the decision was supposed to be made. After making the phone call, Bill looked as though the weight of the world had been lifted from his shoulders on his return to the workshop. He and his manager had agreed on the proper course of action and were now pursuing it—something that they evidently had not done much of in the past.

The workshop ended Thursday, and we asked Bill to get back in touch with us and let us know how the situation played out. On Monday, Bill called and told us that he had closed the order on Friday for $960,000. He admitted again that he had been ready, and even anxious, to drop $110,000 from the price, and probably would have gone even lower if it had looked like he had to. The result was a windfall of $110,000 that went straight to the bottom line of Bill's company. Given that's the case, why would Bill have been so willing to drop the $110,000? Probably because it was only a much smaller "pain" for Bill in the short term.

Most salespeople are paid a base salary plus a commission based on the gross amount of the transaction. For Bill, dropping $110,000 off the price was probably only a $3,000 to $5,000 decision on his part. In other words, at a 3 percent commission rate, instead of a commission of $28,800 on the full $960,000 contract, Bill would still get $25,500 on an $850,000 contract. The reality is that his company would have borne 97 percent of the discount.

So, how do you communicate the importance of reducing discounting to a salesperson if the real financial impact to him or her is marginal? We would suggest that you position it as a time impact instead.

In Bill's case, reducing the price from $960,000 to $850,000 was going to have a fairly insignificant impact on what he was personally going to take away from the deal at a financial level. But what was the iceberg effect? By the "iceberg effect," we mean that the impact that is readily apparent, in Bill's case a slightly reduced commission, often masks the true impact. What was the true impact in Bill's case? A 5 to 10 times increase in the activity required to make his quota for the year. In other words, just because Bill would have given away $110,000 to get the deal, that does not mean his quota for the year goes down by $110,000. What it really means is that now he has to put some number of new opportunities into the top of his funnel in order to eventually find one that will replace the revenue he just gave away.

While "always" and "never" seldom apply to sales, this situation (and others like it) leads us to conclude that sellers should always negotiate as though they are Column A. Why do we feel this way? In the situation just described, what if Bill was Column B and had rebid $850,000? That number would have been used to negotiate a better price from Column A, the preferred vendor. When he refused to rebid, one of two things was going to happen: Column A would get the business anyway, or the buyer would come back to Bill because he was the vendor of choice. Therefore, when you are asked for a best and final price, we suggest asking the buyer if (1) you are the vendor of choice and (2) price is the only remaining obstacle to doing business. If the answers are not yes and yes, we suggest that you ask the buyer to get back to you if and when you become the vendor of choice, at which point the negotiation can take place.

Traditional selling behavior dictates that if you are losing, you should discount as much as possible. You will either get the business yourself—by discounting yourself into becoming Column A—or force your competitor into significantly dropping the price. We disagree with both aspects of this tactic. Desperation discounting late in the buying cycle seldom secures the business. And since all vendors drink from a common well of pricing, irresponsible lowball prices are bad for all vendors.

There is another reason not to offer "fire sale" discounting, if you are losing late in the buying cycle. Assume Column B offers ridiculous pricing but still loses to LMN Company. The following month, the roles are reversed. As Column B this time, the salesperson from LMN Company gets the bad news from the prospect that Column A has been chosen. What is the LMN representative likely to say? How about something like:

> I appreciated the opportunity to compete for your business and gave it my best shot. While I don't agree with your decision, I understand that you are doing what you believe is best for your company. And, hey—just so you know—last month we were awarded a bid competing against Column A at MNO, Inc., but not before they offered an unbelievably low price. If you want to do business with Column A, you may want to contact Joe Jones at MNO to get details on the pricing that he was offered. In any event, I wish you well. Please contact me if I can be of service in the future.

In other words, the aggressive discount offered in a losing situation now comes back to haunt the vendor who has moved from Column B to Column A. Assume that one way or another, the word will get out as to how your company is selling. If it does get out, will you be happy? Will you be well positioned for your next negotiations? What happens to the perceived value of all the vendors' capabilities in your target markets?

Three Questions You Should Ask

Prior to attempting to close and potentially have to negotiate, it is our suggestion that the salesperson reconfirm that it's appropriate to do so by taking a step back and asking three questions that are designed to verify that this is the right path to follow at this point in time. The buyer is asking for a concession, and the seller is politely saying "no". Our belief is that when the buyer "squeezes" the salesperson three times and the salesperson politely says "no" each time, if the buyer continues to squeeze, now it is time to transition into negotiation mode. However, prior to doing so, it is our suggestion that the salesperson reconfirm that it's appropriate to do so by taking a step back and asking three questions that are designed to verify that negotiation is the right path to follow at this point in time.

Question 1: "Assuming we reach agreement, are we the vendor of choice?"

If you are not the vendor of choice, why would you be negotiating price? Remember, it is usually Column B that believes price will help them become Column A, not the other way around.

Question 2: "Is price (or terms, or whatever they are squeezing you on) the only issue?"

Prior to proceeding toward the actual negotiation, let's first get everything out on the table. Smart buyers will lead a salesperson down one rabbit hole—price—get the concession they were looking for, and then throw an entirely different issue at the seller in order to get additional concessions. By asking up front what all of the issues are, the salesperson is in a better position to navigate the negotiation.

Question 3: "Again, assuming we reach agreement, can you personally get this done today?"

How frustrating is it as a salesperson when you reach what you believe to be a final agreement, only to then find out that other signatures are required?

Asking these three questions, after politely saying no to their request for a concession, puts you in a stronger position for the actual negotiation. Only when you get what you consider to be an affirmative response to these qualifying questions should you proceed forward.

The Power of Posturing

Sometimes the best negotiating stance is not to negotiate—as long as you're in a strong position and you strike a pose that is informed and reasonable. We call this *posturing* (without the negative connotation normally associated with that word).

Let's say a coach asks the seller's best and final price. Wisely, the seller—call him Bob—asks if his company has been selected and if price is the only remaining open item. The coach says yes. Now Bob asks, "Doesn't Sherry have final signing authority?" The buyer agrees and sets up a meeting for Bob and Sherry. Not surprisingly, Sherry begins the meeting by squeezing Bob on price:

> Sherry: Bob, thanks for coming in today. Our organizations have spent a great deal of time on this project, and we believe that you have earned our business. I compliment you on understanding our business issues and defining exactly what we need to do

to improve our results. My staff is comfortable with your recommendation. Having said that, one of the reasons we are even considering your offer is that our margins have taken a beating, and we believe your offering can help. But in this climate, $250,000 is a significant expenditure, and I would like you to sharpen your pencil so we can see if we want to get started.

Sherry has been through negotiations numerous times. Given the size of the expenditure, she already has an idea of what type of discounting should be possible. The vendor decision has been made, and now it is a matter of getting the best possible deal. Bob knows the pricing was presented as a step in the sequence of events three months ago and in fact was a delineated checkpoint. By not challenging it back then, the buyer implicitly agreed they could afford it. Now that it is time to buy, though, they want to pay less.

Rather than responding with the deadly six words, Bob surprises Sherry:

Bob: I don't understand, Sherry. We presented pricing 3 months ago. If it was an issue, why wasn't it raised then?

Sherry is somewhat taken aback by Bob's assertive (but accurate) response. Quickly gathering her wits, she counters:

Sherry: Well, I felt the pricing was high when you presented it, but I was sure you left some room to negotiate.

Bob: The pricing is based on our volume purchase discount. Is there anything you want to take out?

Sherry: We need all the proposed capabilities. Frankly, I need you to take out about 10 percent of the cost.

Bob: As I recall it, your cost-benefit analysis shows a payback in five months. Doesn't it make sense to get started now?

Sherry: Well, yes. We want to get started, and that is why we scheduled this meeting. The cost-benefit analysis will look even better if you lower your price.

Note that in this dialogue, Bob was pressured for a better price no less than three times. Each time, he postured, using questions that politely said no to each of Sherry's requests. Each "no" was unemotional and virtually impossible for her to challenge or disagree with. The buyer has already made the decision to buy but has the emotional hurdle of needing to believe she is getting the best possible deal. By saying no three times, Bob is actually helping Sherry make her decision.

Without getting too formulaic about it, posturing often consists of preparing three questions that politely decline the request for a better deal. These should be planned in advance and customized to each situation. Ending these polite no's with a question puts the ball back in the buyer's court. Our experience indicates that it is impossible to drop price while listening. Here are some examples of polite no questions:

- *Put it on the buyer's shoulders:* "Is there anything you would like to take out?"
- *Feign surprise:* "You've known the cost for two months. Why is this coming up now?"
- *Remind the buyer of the value:* "By your numbers, the savings are $36,000/month. Shouldn't we get started?"
- *Reference buyer goals:* "We've spent a lot of time together in the past four months because you want to improve forecasting accuracy by 30 percent. Has anything changed?"
- *Reference usage:* "Didn't you say that after calling on customers, you want your salespeople prompted to update pipeline milestones, so managers can help with qualification and you can improve the accuracy of your forecast?"

Some buyers will agree to go forward after one, two, or three of these polite "no's." If so, the seller receives an order for the full amount merely by posturing—that is, without negotiating. In the example so far, Bob has not yet reached the point where negotiation is appropriate. Posturing provides artificial patience during a stressful time and maximizes the possibility of a more profitable transaction.

Negotiating

In some cases, of course, buyers will continue to press for a better deal, and getting the order will require more than posturing—it will require real negotiation. In real negotiation, there are two key components: *get* and *give*. Note the nontraditional sequence of these two words, which is deliberate: get first, then give.

Throughout the buying cycle, as noted in previous chapters, the seller should be trying to establish an atmosphere of quid pro quo. This is sometimes hard to sustain, since the buyer has been conditioned to wield disproportionate power with traditional vendors and sellers. But when the seller is offering a way for the buyer to achieve a goal or solve a problem, he or she doesn't deserve to get run roughshod over. Prior to giving, therefore, the seller should first ask for something from the buyer. Why? Because of the following:

- If the seller offers a concession, the buyer will take it and still want a lower price.
- The psychology is to convince the buyer that he or she is getting the best possible deal. If the buyer first has to make a concession, the seller's concession will appear to have more value.
- If the buyer will not agree to a concession, the seller should leave without offering what he or she was willing to give, and without burning the bridge.
- Getting the buyer's commitment first allows a conditional "give." This empowers the seller either to get an order or to leave without setting a lower number that will become the basis for subsequent negotiating meetings.

There are many different things a seller can ask for. Our suggestion is that it be something that is of value to the seller. Following are some examples:

- A deposit up front, with the balance due in 30 days
- A larger transaction (accelerating the order of future requirements)
- A longer lease term or maintenance commitment
- A press release documenting results
- An introduction to another division or department

It should be noted that the seller cannot ask the buyer to commit to providing the "get" that is requested. The question is whether it would be possible for the buyer to do what is being asked. For example:

Seller: For me to consider a concession, I would need some help from you.

Buyer: What do you have in mind?

Seller: Would it be possible to extend the maintenance contract from one year to two, and for you to serve as a reference for four prospects over the next 12 months?

Buyer: I don't see a problem with extending the maintenance agreement. And, assuming our implementation is successful, I could serve as a reference for you.

Seller: If you can extend the maintenance agreement and agree to be a reference, I'm willing to include our forecasting module, which has a value of $10,000, at no additional cost. Would you like to move forward?

Buyer: Is that the best you can do?

Seller: It is. Can we move forward?

Buyer: Make the changes to the agreement, and let's go ahead.

In short, our approach to negotiating makes use of things the seller learned during the buying cycle and attempts to foster a spirit of quid pro quo in order to get to the actual closing under acceptable terms.

We also suggest that a seller should be prepared with two "gets" to ask for. The first one should be more aggressive than the second. That way if a buyer is unwilling to commit to the first "get," the seller can then ask for the second. The seller's hope is the buyer will say yes to a "get" because if he or she doesn't, there won't be an attempt to close and a subsequent negotiation discussion will have to take place.

We also suggest that sellers try to avoid giving a percentage discount of the whole price because this sets a precedent for all future transactions if the transaction closes. Remember from our story about Bill and the $110,000 discount earlier in this chapter that when you give away a percentage discount, you are giving away pure margin dollars. In the example given, a module is given as a concession but it still allows the pricing to remain intact. Another significant concession that doesn't cost vendors a great deal is to offer to accelerate the implementation (provided the resources are available). This is only effective when a solid cost versus benefit has been created, but if the buyer sees a potential $50,000/month savings, accelerating the implementation by two weeks amounts to a $25,000 concession.

The Conditional "Give" and Close

After the buyer agrees that the "get" is possible, the seller then conditionally offers the "give" and asks for the business: "Since you are willing to (summarize what the buyer said was possible), then I would be willing to (offer your "give"). Can we move forward?"

After asking this question, the seller must wait for the buyer to speak. Only one of two things can happen at this point. The seller will either get an order or have to walk. If the buyer does not close, we suggest leaving, because at this stage, any sweeteners put the seller back on the slippery slope of traditional negotiating. The seller should also take the concession off the table, out of play. We suggest ending the meeting in the following manner: "That's what I was prepared to offer. While it doesn't appear we can proceed today, this transaction makes sense for both of us. Why don't we give our positions some further thought? I'll call you Wednesday and see if we can try to reach agreement."

The seller's willingness to exit may persuade the buyer to move ahead. Whether it does or not, the intent is to avoid having the failed closing become adversarial, and to leave the two parties trying to move ahead with something that is a win-win. If the negotiating meeting is rescheduled, the seller needs to come prepared with a different set of "gets" and "gives" and see if the two parties can come to terms.

When sellers discount, they are giving away bottom-line dollars. If a salesperson averages a 15 percent discount, for example, he or she must close about six transactions to net the dollar equivalent of five undiscounted sales. By any measure, this is costly. If a seller is prepared, he or she can minimize these costs by coming out of the negotiation with a better price.

Apples and Oranges

One standard negotiating technique used by traditional buyers is comparing the price of a lesser offering to the seller's price. If the seller responds to this tactic by posturing, he or she somewhat weakens the position, because the discrepancy between the two offerings has not been addressed.

A more effective countermeasure is to be prepared to cite one of your major differentiators—that is, a capability that you provide that the lesser offering does not. As an example, assume that a sales force automation package from your competitor, the ABC Company, costs 30 percent less— a big difference—but, unlike your product, it does not dynamically track close rates by individual salespeople at each stage of the sell cycle. The discussion might go as follows:

Buyer: We like your system, but ABC's offering is 30 percent less than yours. What can you do for me on price?

Seller: You could choose to go with ABC, but have you considered that by having to use standard close rates for each step of the pipeline, a salesperson with a low close rate could inflate the gross forecast by entering two or three large opportunities? Can you see how that could cause you to miss your target?

Buyer: We would run that risk by using standard close rates.

Seller: One of the things we discussed was that when the forecast is being generated, our system can apply historical close rates for each rep at each milestone, so the final forecast will be adjusted.

One of your major issues is forecasting accuracy. Are you more comfortable with applying customized close rates by rep?

Buyer: I would have a higher level of confidence.

Seller: So comparing our offering and ABC's really isn't an apples-to-apples comparison, is it?

Buyer: Not exactly, but I would still like to see you sharpen your pencil.

At this point, after neutralizing the unfair comparison, the seller can now begin posturing with the prepared polite "no" questions.

Summary

Few salespeople admit that they are anything but outstanding negotiators—even if their approach is to discount until a buyer says yes. But if a sales cycle has been executed properly, the close should be a logical conclusion, rather than a fire sale or an arm-wrestling contest. Preparation is critical, and the seller should be prepared in advance to execute the following steps, as needed:

- Verify that you are the vendor of choice, and that price (or terms, etc.) is the only obstacle to doing business.
- Make sure that you are negotiating with a decision maker.
- Head off apples-and-oranges comparisons by having a differentiator and a situational question to highlight the buyer's need for it.
- Posture by using prepared polite "no" questions to respond (as many as three times) to requests for better pricing.
- Ask the buyer if the "get" you want is possible.
- Offer your conditional "give," and be prepared to walk if the order does not close at that point—leaving the door open, of course, for further rounds, but only after taking your concession off the table.

Chapter 17

Proactively Managing Sales Pipelines and Funnels

Many college students are procrastinators. The days before papers come due and exams arrive are stressful indeed as they scramble to catch up. While far from being optimal in terms of a learning experience, most procrastinators somehow manage to get by and complete their courses successfully.

Farmers can't work this way. A farm owner has to plan for the coming growing season. On a predetermined schedule, adjusted as necessary to reflect the prevailing weather conditions, a farmer has to turn over the soil, plant, fertilize, weed, and harvest. There is no way to stall, or to compress the steps needed to bring a crop to harvest.

Unfortunately, most salespeople act more like college students than like farmers. They approach their year-end quota in much the same way procrastinating students approach semesters: confident that they can cram as needed if they fall behind their year-to-date target. Is there a more optimistic person in the world than a salesperson sitting at 37 percent of quota going into the last quarter? (We have yet to meet such a person.) Most lagging salespeople convince themselves that somehow, the elusive numbers will be hit by the end of the year. The surge of hope stays alive until the last week or two, when they finally admit to themselves that the current year is a lost cause, and that it's time to "sandbag" orders so that they can hit the ground running the following year.

Salespeople simulate electricity: they follow the path of least resistance. Procrastination is an easy trap to fall into. And procrastination with respect to YTD quota position is reinforced by a salesperson's desire to have as many opportunities in the funnel as possible. Yes, if you add up all the items listed, the resulting figure may approach the gross domestic product of a small Central American country. But a closer look reveals that many of the "opportunities" listed in most pipelines have little chance of closing. This underscores the need for managers to grade funnels with an eye toward (1) setting appropriate activity levels and (2) disqualifying low-probability items.

As noted in a previous chapter, we distinguish between pipeline and funnel management. Pipeline milestones are graded and used by sales management for the purpose of forecasting, while sales funnel milestones are graded and used by sales management to assess the quantity of selling activity and the quality of selling skills at the individual salesperson level.

Left to their own devices, many salespeople compete to stay busy. In our view, the role of sales managers is to help them compete to win. But the prospect of putting a salesperson on an improvement plan—or, worse, firing an underperformer and recruiting and training a replacement—is enough to make a sales manager procrastinate like a college student.

The goal of managing pipeline is predicting what will close—forecasting—but these predictions are driven as much by personal agendas as by reality. A salesperson who is below quota has a specific agenda when forecasting: get my manager to believe that there is sufficient activity so that I can keep my job.

One major challenge in forecasting is that companies lack consistent qualification elements. Managers with experience at different companies bring along their own approach to grading opportunities. Even when companies attempt to impose standard milestones, an "80 percent probability" actually varies from salesperson to salesperson, and from district to district. The problem is that these milestones rely on a subjective judgment. Has the opportunity progressed to that level, or not? Well, tell a traditional salesperson who is behind quota that by the end of next week, she must have five opportunities at a certain milestone. By the end of next week, she will have six (thus allowing a margin for error, if one is successfully challenged by the manager). You can set your watch by it, but would you want to forecast these opportunities?

Predicting the date that an opportunity will close is a challenge for even the best salespeople. It's simply not their call. Forecasting can be as meaningless as pushing a few dates back by 30 days and tweaking a few numbers (especially when there is little or nothing that has been added in a given month). And these summaries tend to blow away in the first wind, in any case. If a salesperson forecasts a transaction to close in September and then forecasts it in October, and it finally happens in November, the accuracy is 33 percent—but what's remembered is that the salesperson got the business.

Salespeople despise forecasting because, in most cases, they are being asked to lie in writing. They know all too well that the exercise of forecasting is likely to bear little or no resemblance to reality. In fact, the major value of forecasting is that it has the potential to give salespeople with inadequate pipelines a wake-up call 12 times a year—that is, a message from on high that there are inadequate opportunities in their pipeline, and that they must increase their business development activities. Despite these wake-up calls, for many sellers procrastination is the preferred response.

So let's look at ways to improve forecasting, in part by removing salespeople from the process.

Milestones: Getting the Terms Straight

In order to break away from the insanity referred to euphemistically as forecasting, a number of complementary components are necessary:

1. Sales-Ready Messaging, designed to position offerings specific to title, vertical industry, and goal, which provides less subjective input into the pipeline. The key here is that these prompters define the outcomes of sales calls. A buyer's solution must be some subset of the usage scenarios on the right side of the Solution Development Prompter.
2. Auditable correspondence between the seller and the buyer.
3. Sequences of events containing estimated close dates, as negotiated with the buyer.
4. Companywide milestones, with defined ways to achieve and document them.
5. Sales managers (not salespeople) who are willing and able to audit milestones, grade pipeline, disqualify low-probability opportunities, and predict what will close.
6. Senior executive commitment to ride through potential "push-back" from salespeople and sales managers who prefer less visibility and accountability.

Items 1 through 3 have been described in previous chapters. So let's start with CustomerCentric Selling *milestones*, which most of our clients modify as needed and adopt as companywide standards. First, refer to Figure 17.1.

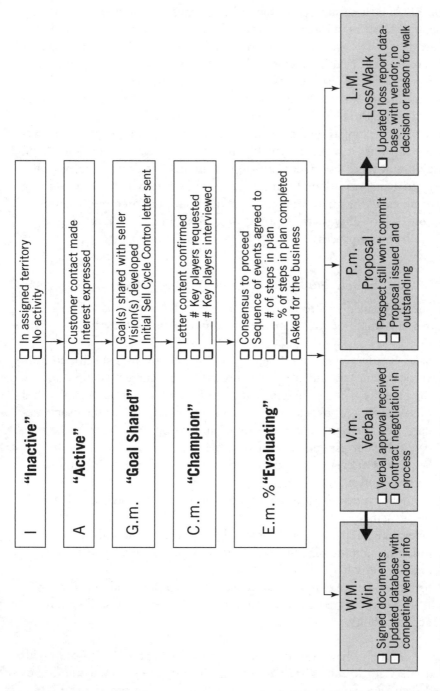

Figure 17.1 Grading Opportunities: Funnel Milestones (m = no. of months; M = total no. of months; % = % complete)

- *Inactive* means that an account fits a company's target market and is assigned to a salesperson, but there is no current activity. A salesperson's business development efforts should focus on getting a buying cycle to start by getting a targeted key player within the account to share a goal, which would advance it to the next milestone.
- *Active* indicates that contact has been made and some form of interest on the part of the customer or prospect has been expressed.
- *Goal Shared* is the initiation of a sales cycle in CustomerCentric Selling; it indicates that a targeted key player has shared a desire to achieve at least one goal that is on the list of business issues the seller can help them address.
- *Champion* status can be granted only by the sales manager. It happens only after all the qualification elements have been achieved: the letter, fax, or e-mail has been sent; the buyer has agreed to the content; and the buyer is willing to provide access to key players. The sales manager must have reviewed the customer document and graded it as a C, usually after a brief discussion with the salesperson.

  The opportunity remains a C while all key players are being interviewed, either in person or on the phone. All calls should be documented with each buyer, and there should be agreement that the content reflects the conversation that the seller had with them. After all key players have been qualified, there is an attempt to qualify the opportunity. Some of our clients like to not only track the number of months an opportunity is at this level but also get a sense for how many key players must be interviewed and how many have been called on. A greater number of key players most likely means that an opportunity will remain a C for a longer period of time.
- *Evaluating* status is determined by the sales manager, but only after the salesperson has gained consensus from key players that further investigation of the salesperson's offering is called for, and a sequence of events has been accepted by the buying committee. At the end of that month, the salesperson provides a copy of the cover letter and sequence of events, and the sales manager can change the status to E (and update the SFA/CRM system) if it is deemed a qualified opportunity.

Opportunities remain at this stage until one of three things happens:

1. The buyer withdraws (and the opportunity becomes a loss).
2. The seller withdraws (and the opportunity becomes a walk).
3. The seller asks for the business after the sequence of events has been completed.

Once the seller has asked for the business, the opportunity goes into one of four grades:

W (Win)	An order with all necessary documents signed.
L (Loss)	The buyer informs you that he or she will not be moving forward with you (a loss to either a competitor or no decision).
V (Verbal)	The buyer has given you a verbal commitment to go forward.
P (Proposal)	A proposal is provided to the prospect with a decision due.

A few notes about the chart in Figure 17.1. Many of our clients choose to assign probabilities to the G, C, and E grades. Until you accumulate your own historical data with your forecasting system, we suggest assigning initial probabilities of 10 percent for the Goal (G) level, 25 percent for the Champion (C) level, and 50 percent once the manager assigns the Evaluating (E) level to an opportunity. (Organizations with SFA or CRM systems may ultimately collect percentages for individual salespeople, enabling them to fine-tune forecasting accuracy.) For an E prospect, each agreed-to checkpoint increases the chances of getting an order.

Capturing the number of months (m) that a line item in the pipeline has been at a particular stage allows the sales manager to identify opportunities that are not progressing. For E status, adding a percentage to reflect the percentage of steps in the sequence of events that have been completed can also provide a meaningful point of reference for the manager. For the grades of W and L, it may similarly be useful to track the total number of months (M) that an opportunity was in the pipeline before you won or lost. After losses, data indicating whether the winner was a named competitor or there was no decision (meaning no gold medal was awarded) should be entered.

By implementing the system shown in Table 17.1, managers can detect early-warning signs that a given opportunity is stalled or in trouble. For each pipeline milestone shown, you'll see two examples: one that is on track, with normal parameters for a viable opportunity, and another that is beyond normal conditions. While there may be extenuating circumstances, the latter situation should prompt the manager to have a conversation with the salesperson. If necessary, both can agree on a course of corrective action to get the opportunity back on track. Alternatively, it may be appropriate for the manager to disqualify this line item from the pipeline, rather than allow the seller to toil with a low probability of getting the business. (Remember: Bad news early is good news.)

Grade	Example	Explanation
Grade G Goal	G.1/150,000 G.3/100,000	Buyer shared goal, less than 30 days old, $150,000 potential More than 60 days old, still no champion
Grade C Champion	C.1/300,000 C.3/100,000	Champion, less than 30 days old, still interviewing key players More than 60 days old, too small for large no. of key players—stuck?
Grade E Sequence of Events	E.5.50%/300,C00 E.1.25%/600,000	4 months old, 50 percent complete, low $—stuck? First month of plan, 25 percent complete, large account
Grade L Walk/Lose	L.2/300,000 L.11/600,000	Disqualified after less than two months—bad news early is good! Went the distance (11 months!) and lost
Grade P Proposal	P.1/100,000 P.4/600,000	Had to deliver proposal, less than 30 days old Responded to RFP over three months ago—need to take back
Grade V Verbal	V.1/400,000 V.2/200,000	Verbal less than 30 days old—still should be good Verbal over 30 days old—problem!
Grade W Win	W.5/400,000 W.8/200,000	Win—four-month sell cycle Win—seven months to close $200,000 order—did we make any money?

Table 17.1 Funnel Management Examples

Even without an SFA/CRM system, sales managers can now forecast by asking each salesperson to fax or e-mail the latest copy of the sequence of events for each opportunity. By reviewing these documents, the sales manager can assess each opportunity with a reasonable degree of objectivity and consistency (in an apples-to-apples sense).

In order to home in on forecasting accuracy, we suggest that sales managers maintain three pipeline categories for each salesperson:

1. Add-on business with existing customers, having the highest probability of closing.
2. New account business in which you were proactive and started as Column A.
3. New account business where you were reactive and started as Column B, C, and so on.

Forecasting is now a monthly review of pipeline, with sales managers choosing which opportunities are likely to close and the sequences of events providing lots of visibility and realistic close dates.

This monthly review also allows an opportunity to be proactive with salespeople who might be procrastinators. "Train wrecks" within a funnel do not happen overnight. Let's see how a manager can be proactive in anticipating a shortfall in a given funnel. A few variables are necessary to provide sales managers with visibility one sales cycle ahead, as shown in this example:

1. A salesperson's annual quota: $1.5 million
2. The average length of a sales cycle: 4 months
3. The probability that an E will close: 50 percent
4. Any shortfall in the salesperson's YTD quota attainment: 0

One way to reduce procrastination is to break down a quota to a monthly number—in this case, $125,000/month. Multiplying this by an average sales cycle tells you that in 4 months, a salesperson will be expected to close $500,000. If, however, the salesperson closes 50 percent of the sequences of events that were put in place, the funnel target would be twice that figure, or $1 million. This means that at any given time, when you take a snapshot of a salesperson's funnel, you would like to see at least $1 million at E status, as graded by the sales manager. If you were halfway through the year and the salesperson was $100,000 behind the YTD number, the target would be the standard of $1 million plus ($100,000/50 percent), or $1.2 million.

This may seem like a mouthful, so let's look at the activity balancing example that follows, where the per month quota is $125,000, the average sell cycle is 4 months, and there is a 50 percent probability of closing a Grade E prospect.

$$\frac{(\$125,000)\ (4\ \text{months})}{50\%} = \$1\ \text{million target "E" pipeline}$$

$$\$1\ \text{million} + (\text{YTD shortfall} \times 2) = \text{Target for the next 4 months}$$

By doing this calculation on a monthly basis, sales managers can help salespeople stay ahead of the curve. While managers should review changes to, and volumes of, A, G, and C entries, E opportunities provide the best sense of how things will look one sales cycle ahead. If the E funnel is below target, business development activity must be increased. The conversation could sound like this:

> Jane, you have been running on your numbers through April, but this month you only have $800,000 in E pipeline. Over the next month, I want you to make sure that you increase your business development activities. My suggestion would be to make a minimum of 10 new contacts per week. I'd also like to see you migrate two opportunities from C to E, and I will work with you on doing that. Hopefully, next month you'll have sufficient new opportunities in your funnel so that we'll both feel better about where you'll be YTD in September. We can then revisit how much of your time should be spent on business development.

This approach, in other words, emphasizes proactive rather than forensic sales management. If a salesperson competes for eight months and loses, it is no longer solely his or her responsibility. Each month (or more frequently), the sales manager should have made a qualify/disqualify decision at all checkpoints in the sequences of events that were approved. The sequences of events also allow a sales manager to get further upstream on opportunities, to coach new or struggling salespeople all along the way, and to have control and ownership of the forecast he or she provides.

When these kinds of analyses are performed on a monthly basis, corrections can be made to maximize the probability that salespeople will achieve their numbers—and thereby minimize turnover, either voluntary or involuntary. Involuntary turnover, as suggested, is difficult for all parties involved. From the company standpoint, there is a significant expense inherent in recruiting and training a replacement, lost continuity within the territory, ramp-up time for new hires, and management time spent on the territory during the interim period. By the time many managers (and salespeople) realize they are in trouble, it is often too late to save that year. An analysis on a monthly basis, therefore, is well worth the time it takes to perform.

In a previous chapter, we distinguished between "will not" and "cannot" attitudes in a salesperson. "Will not" is, in most cases, a management issue. "Cannot" is a skill issue, and will serve as the basis of the next chapter.

Chapter 18

ASSESSING AND DEVELOPING SALESPEOPLE

On at least an annual basis, most human resources departments require sales managers to formally assess members of their staff. And despite the fact that the sales manager should have reviewed 12 (or more) forecasts from each salesperson over the course of those 12 months, it can be a tough job to sit down and formally analyze what has transpired in a year.

Consider the following outstanding, average, and difficult performance reviews, which are composites from our experience working with salespeople over the years.

Salesperson A, Mary, consistently achieves 200-plus percent of quota. The manager invites Mary into his office, and begins:

> Mary, it is difficult to put into words what a pleasure it is to have you on my team. Thanks for your contributions over the past year. I've filled out your evaluation, so take a minute to review it and ask any questions you may have. (Mary spends two minutes reading the glowing evaluation and has no questions.) Well, then, this will go into your personnel file. I'm pleased to give you the maximum 5 percent raise on your base salary. Let me know if there is anything I can do to help you going forward. At this stage, my inclination is to just get out of your way and let you sell. Congratulations on a tremendous year!

Salesperson B, whom we'll call Joe, struggles to make his numbers. Two of the last three years he has made quota (as he did last year) by a few percentage points. He achieved 92 percent of quota two years ago. He enters the office and hears:

> Joe, let's review your performance evaluation. Take a few minutes to look at it, and then we can talk. (Joe sees several areas where he is considered average. There are a few areas showing his skills to be above average, balanced by areas needing improvement. It is a fair assessment that accurately points out his strengths and weaknesses.) Joe, I hope you agree with my assessment and comments. Overall, I'm glad to have you on the team, but I wish you could increase activity within your pipeline. If you were to increase prospecting activity, I think you could . . . (The discussion drones on for about 30 minutes, including comments about skill sets that must be "shored up," interspersed with compliments about strengths. The meeting grinds to a conclusion as Joe signs the evaluation.) Joe, I hope this session was worthwhile. I want you to strive to increase activity and make your numbers by the end of October. Wouldn't it be nice for us to be able to enjoy the holiday season at the end of this year by not having to scramble to close transactions? I've put in for a 2 percent raise in your base. Let's make this the year that you knock the fences down.

Keith, Salesperson C, finished the past year below 50 percent of quota, and is sitting at about 50 percent of quota year-to-date halfway through the year. This review promises to be difficult:

> Keith, why don't you come in and take a seat. (The manager rests his chin on both hands, effectively covering much of his face, and starts to talk.) Keith, Keith, Keith, this has been a rough couple of years for both of us. Do you see things getting any better? (Keith mumbles a vague, uninspiring answer.) Well, based on your performance over the past 18 months, we have two choices. One is for HR to get involved. We would put you on a performance improvement plan and give you a 90-day period to get year-to-date against your quota. It would necessitate weekly meetings and mounds of paperwork. If after 90 days you still weren't tracking to your numbers, I'd have to terminate you. Do you think that you can close that much business in the next three months? (Again, Keith's answer fails to inspire confidence.)
> Look, Keith, I know you have a family, and candidly, I'd hate to have to terminate you. Off the record, we could look at things another way. If you feel you can't make your numbers, the next 90 days could

be put to a different use. I won't be taking attendance, so you'd have time to explore other options. Most people find it is easier to find a job while they have one. Why don't you sleep on it, and let me know how you'd like to proceed. In the meantime, don't tell anyone we had this conversation. Maybe a fresh start at another company is just the thing you need to get your career on track. Let me know what you decide.

Sound familiar? Anyone who has managed salespeople has faced these situations. (And maybe you've even been Mary, Joe, or Keith at some point in your career.) Mary is a customercentric seller who neither wants nor needs to be managed, and will consistently produce. Joe is typical of traditional salespeople, who constitute the majority of sales forces. Every year, making quota is an adventure, and one that typically goes right to the end of the year. Keith's situation is a nightmare for everyone. He may be unskilled, unlucky, or lazy. Most likely, he'll be working for another company within the next few months, regardless of whether he opts for the performance improvement plan or immediately begins a job search.

The reviews presented above are typical of those received by salespeople who have not been supported by Sales-Ready Messaging and a sales process. The traditional sales manager knows what he or she is doing, in terms of traditional methods of motivating the sales force; he or she also seems to have a pretty good sense of the salespeople. But it's certainly fair to ask: Is this the first time that Joe has heard that he needs to improve? How long has Keith been bumping along on the bottom without intervention from above? Can either Mary or her manager articulate what makes her a customercentric superstar?

In this chapter, we want to introduce a sales management process to assess and develop salespeople.

Golf Is Easier

The title of sales manager is misleading. We believe a manager's primary responsibility is to develop people. The reality is that most traditional sales managers—including the one in our example above—are administrators attempting to drive numbers. They tell their direct reports what to do and in what quantity but are unable to teach them how to do it. This often results in a group of salespeople who are only capable of moving an opportunity forward to a certain point before the manager then has to put on his or her sales hat, parachute in, and take the deal the rest of the way. Put another way, they focus on the quantity of work but lack the ability to positively influence the quality of work of their salespeople. Sales managers have many different modes; they may try to motivate, intimidate, nurture, mentor, and so on. They finally admit defeat when their mode switches to counseling people out of the business.

But more often than not, the issue is not one of motivation. Most underperforming salespeople sincerely want to do better but lack the necessary skills. All the encouragement, incentive programs, and intimidation in the world can't teach a salesperson to sell. If Keith is intelligent and motivated—which, after all, was part of the hiring model—then having him do more of what he's already doing is unlikely to get him to improve his performance.

As noted in an earlier chapter, most sales managers got their jobs because they were naturally talented salespeople. They don't necessarily understand how or why they were successful, yet they are now charged with passing their intuitive selling skills onto their direct reports. The path many sales managers in this situation take to get salespeople up to speed is osmosis: "Watch how I sell, and learn (because I can't describe it)." Often intense during the first month or so after a new hire signs on, this kind of "training" tends to fall off precipitously shortly thereafter. The sales manager has other things to do—there's another new hire that needs to be exposed to the benefit of transference.

Skill-transfer results using "watch how I do it" approaches are disappointing. Transference is a poor substitute for sales process. And without process, selling resembles an art more than a science.

Assessing and coaching skills without understanding the basic mechanics of selling is next to impossible. When professional athletes experience slumps, there are standard ways of identifying and correcting problems. A professional golfer, for example, has several ways to identify swing flaws and correct them. First, there are generally accepted mechanics associated with a golf swing (head down, left arm straight, and so on). The golfer in question may view videotapes of a sound golf swing (either his or her own, or that of another player). Many have a "swing coach" who works with them. Even the process of identifying the problem—a problem on which the golfer and the coach can agree—gives rise to a surge of hope. This problem can be fixed! And this, in turn, gives the needed motivation to spend all that time on the driving range and playing practice rounds.

Is there a sales equivalent to the golf story? The answer is, "There *should* be, but it's hard to find." Consider a salesperson whose performance was previously at acceptable levels but has been in the doldrums for the past year and a half. Some harsh realities:

1. *There are few generally accepted and useful rules of selling.* There are general notions: listen, don't lead with product, selling begins when buyers say no, always be closing, and so forth. Some of these we (the authors) subscribe to, and others we take issue with; but at the end of

the day, our motivation in creating CustomerCentric Selling was that there was nothing close to a useful road map of how to sell, especially when compared to an activity such as hitting a golf ball.

2. *Selling habits have been developed through an unstructured series of individual trial-and-error experiences.* Instead of good "muscle memory," the salesperson has bad muscle memory, and self-diagnosis becomes extremely difficult. This makes it virtually impossible for someone to coach a salesperson out of a slump. As previously mentioned, Neil Rackham discovered that as sellers become more familiar with their offerings, they begin to lose patience and empathy in asking questions and listening to their buyers. This behavior is virtually impossible to self-diagnose.

3. *There is no "practice range" for salespeople.* If a golfer hits several bad shots on the driving range, ego aside, there are no negative consequences. In fact, it may help in isolating flaws. But salespeople have no "range" on which to experiment. They are under pressure to produce numbers (more so when they are in a slump), and they do not have the luxury of trying new approaches without potential consequences. A poor call reduces the number of prospects in the finite territory by one—and, in practical terms, for the duration of the salesperson's current employment.

4. *As it relates to development and improvement, salespeople live on remote islands.* One of the biggest challenges comes when the salesperson disagrees with his or her manager about a given course of action. There is no surge of hope like that experienced by the golfer and the coach. Slumping salespeople must work their way out of it alone. The sales manager is likely to make the problem worse if he or she applies pressure by demanding increased levels of activity (i.e., quantity) without influencing the quality of activity. Most people's performance degrades under pressure.

Assessment: What Doesn't Work

Sales management without sales process is largely a forensic (after-the-fact) exercise. Managers perform silver-medal autopsies after losses and during annual HR reviews. They wind up not helping either Joe or Keith, and—most likely—firing Keith or persuading him to move on.

But imagine if managers could be proactive instead of reactive. Proactive steps—corrective surgery—could reduce the need for autopsies. Why does it take a loss (or nagging from HR) for managers to act? We believe it is because most sales managers are merely driving numbers. Lacking the ability to assess and develop their people, they assess and develop their people's numbers instead. But this is exactly backward. If sales managers could develop their people, the numbers would take care of themselves.

First, let's look at flaws in the assessment process. Let's assume the annual evaluation requires sales managers to rank salespeople as one of the following overall categories (we've added our counterpoint in italics):

1. Consistently exceeds quota and provides leadership to the office. This exceptional salesperson who displays outstanding knowledge of offerings, possesses strong administrative skills, exhibits strong account control, and shows ability to disqualify poor opportunities from his or her funnel. Requires minimal guidance, and is a candidate for promotion into sales management.

   Sales management would be a breeze if these people could be cloned.

2. Meets or exceeds quota the majority of the time. This steady performer has a tendency to work identified opportunities and grow ongoing accounts. Sometimes gets entangled in low-probability opportunities. A more aggressive business development plan and more structured approach could bring performance up to the next level.

   Sales managers are happy to have people like this on the team. They need occasional coaching, but by and large they can be trusted to work on small to medium opportunities with minimal supervision.

3. Struggles to keep activity levels to a point where the pipeline reaches targeted levels. Requires extensive coaching, and requires managers to make joint calls whenever feasible. Needs extensive support on all opportunities and coaching on a weekly basis.

   This had better be a new hire on the way to becoming a 2. If he or she doesn't show progress within the next year, though, there will be a tough decision to make.

4. Has difficulty generating meaningful activity in territory. Marginal understanding of both offerings and industries called on. Micromanagement is necessary, both in reviewing activity from the previous week and in planning activity for the following week.

   Unless dramatic improvement is realized in the short term, it appears that either a hiring error has been made or the salesperson's skill or motivation has eroded. Unless things change, a performance improvement plan or termination looms on the horizon.

Selling is one of the strangest professions. Performance is measured exactly—sometimes to within hundredths of a percentage point. Companies calculate commissions to the penny. Many companies require managers to assign a single grade to reflect their assessment of a salesperson's perceived skill set that can influence his or her career path. But in reality, is this precision? Can a single grade reflect the skill set and abilities of a salesperson? We believe the answer is no.

Taken collectively, the skill set and personal characteristics required to consistently exceed quota are staggering. We know renowned doctors, lawyers, and professors who would starve as salespeople. They just don't have what it takes. For a complex offering, we believe a salesperson needs a minimum IQ of 120, strong verbal and written skills, the courage and confidence to accept a position where only a portion of his or her compensation is guaranteed, and so on. So can a sales manager effectively rate someone like this on a scale of 1 to 4? Not likely.

Performance Does Not Always Mean Skill Mastery

Let's assume that Ron was the third salesperson hired by a start-up company that is now publicly traded and has revenues of $150 million. Ron was involved in the initial large sale to an early-market buyer eight years ago. This sale validated the company's offering, and he received extensive support in that sales effort from the founder and other senior executives. For the past several years, Ron has averaged 225 percent of quota, largely by handling the growing requirements of three major customers. Ron's last cold prospecting call was made several years ago, when the thin condition of his pipeline drove him to make a call.

Ron has achieved legendary status, and preferential treatment, within the company. People wonder why he has never gone into management. The answer is simple. Ron has realized that his personal strengths and his quality-of-life goals all indicate that sales is the best position for him. Ron's manager treads lightly and consistently grades him as a 1. Failing to do so would probably prompt a call by Ron to the CEO complaining about his manager and the review, and necessitate changing the grade on the evaluation in HR's file.

According to his annual reviews, Ron is a 1 in the areas of need development, account management, negotiating, qualification and control, and so on. Peeling back the onion, however, it turns out that he is *not* a 1 in the skill of business development and prospecting—in fact, he is a 4. At this stage, it is impossible to tell if the problem lies in skill (cannot) or attitude (will not). In any event, Ron's manager is not doing him a favor by ignoring this glaring deficiency. Ron is, in effect, coasting. Smart salespeople know intuitively that they are worth what they can earn in their *next* sales position. If for some reason things go south with this company, Ron may face the challenge of finding and accepting a territory with a company where he does not enjoy sacred cow status and most likely will not be given the largest installed accounts to develop.

Five Selling Skills

As shown in the previous chapter, sales managers can be proactive in analyzing pipelines so that activity levels can be increased. This approach helps the manager influence the quantity of activity. We'd now like to show a technique for upgrading the quality of activity. To do so, we've distilled selling into five skills:

1. New business development
2. Solution development
3. Buyer qualification
4. Opportunity qualification and control
5. Closing and negotiating

These skills tend to come into play at different times in the buying cycle, as shown on the left side of Figure 18.1. On the right side are the deliverables that a sales manager can monitor to assess the skills of each salesperson.

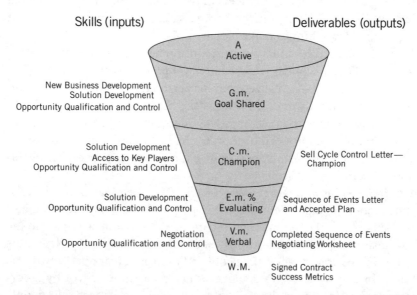

Figure 18.1 Funnel Management: Skills and Deliverables

The shapes of funnels can vary greatly by salesperson. The funnel of someone exhibiting high activity but low skill mastery in the area of business development could look like a martini glass, with many conversations (A's) needed to generate G's. As opportunities enter and progress through a salesperson's funnel over the space of a few months, if there are blockages where deals tend to stall, this points to a probable skill deficiency. We'd like to show how to assess funnel data so that skills can be assessed and—wherever necessary—the sales manager can come up with specific plans containing activities needed to shore up weaknesses.

Let's now assume that over a period of two or three months, there are bottlenecks in a salesperson's funnel—which, again, point to likely skill deficiencies. Look at Table 18.1.

An insufficient number of A's entering the funnel points toward a problem with business development. In response, the manager could set a minimum number of first contacts per week or month, but that would not address the quality of the effort. A proactive customercentric sales manager would do the following:

1. Ask to see the letters, faxes, and e-mails that the salesperson is using to generate interest. It could be they are not worded properly or are geared toward the wrong vertical industry or title. The manager could help write the documents and design a more effective strategy.
2. Ask the salesperson to spend some time with a peer who has realized great success in business development. It may be appropriate for the person who is struggling to listen to one of his or her peers making calls, or following up on leads, to see that person's approach.
3. The sales manager could role-play being a buyer taking a prospecting call from the salesperson.

Bottlenecks in getting prospects from A to C would point toward a lack of skill in getting buyers to share goals. The manager could spend time reviewing the following areas:

1. Review the menu of goals for each key player that the salesperson is using.
2. Help the salesperson generate and use the Success Stories that take a buyer from a latent need to sharing a goal.
3. Role-play with the salesperson to walk him or her through approaches to getting goals shared or problems admitted.

If opportunities stall at G status, there are two areas that are likely to need addressing. The first is that the salesperson lacks the ability to take a

Funnel Blockage	Potential Reasons
From "I" to "A" (Prospecting)	• Lack of new opportunities to call • Inadequate use of compelling scripts/tools • Difficulty aligning with buyer • Inability to get buyer to share goals or admit problems
From "A" to "G" or "C" (Solution Development)	• Calling too low to engage champion-level buyer • Issues on tools are too low-level • Poor goal identification and solution development skills • Poor understanding of how to negotiate access to key players
From "C" to "E" (Qualification)	• Issues on tools are too low-level • Poor goal identification and solution development skills • Poor understanding of how to set up or obtain decision-maker agreement to sequence of events
From "E" to "P" (Sales Process Control)	• Negotiates sequence of events with non-decision makers • Difficulty mapping Opportunity Organizational Chart • Cost versus benefit not quantifiable/not based on buyer's numbers • Implementation issues not addressed
From "P" to "V" (Negotiation)	• Lost control at the end of the sales cycle (no predecision review scheduled) • Unprepared for negotiation (no worksheet with polite no's and quid pro quo) • Unprepared to address buyer risk issues
From "V" to "W" (Closing)	• Out of alignment (closing too soon) • Logistical issues

Table 18.1 Analyzing Funnel Blockages

buyer from goal to vision, meaning he or she either is not using the correct Solution Development Prompter (SDP) or is having difficulty executing it. Again, the manager could review the material being used and could role-play with the salesperson. The manager could also make joint calls with the salesperson and demonstrate how to use the SDP.

Another reason for stalling at G status can be that the salesperson has difficulty getting prospects to agree to champion him or her and get the salesperson to the key players who need to be accessed. This difficulty can occur because the buyer's vision is not compelling (letters should be edited), there is not sufficient value in the mind of the buyer, or the salesperson is not able to defend or explain the need to meet with the key players requested. In such cases, the suggested approach would be to make joint calls—either face to face or via conference call. It is also possible that potential champions are being offered proof without the salesperson using a quid pro quo approach to getting access.

If a salesperson has opportunities that stall after qualifying a champion, there are several potential areas of difficulty:

1. If most of his or her champions are at relatively low levels, there may be difficulty relating to more senior executives. This skill can be developed via role-playing and making those executive calls jointly.
2. The salesperson may be having difficulty in gaining consensus and negotiating a sequence of events with the buying committee. The manager should have the salesperson take him or her to visit accounts where all key players have been met, but where no sequence of events has yet been finalized.
3. The salesperson may be attempting to qualify people at relatively low levels within organizations as champions. As stated earlier, a salesperson's quality of life will be better if he or she can get decision-maker–level champions. In such cases, access to key players is most often volunteered, rather than the salesperson having to ask or negotiate for it.

Once an opportunity reaches E status, the salesperson and manager should have at least a 50 percent chance of having the sell cycle result in an order. In our opinion, the single most important variable in determining win rates is which salesperson initiated the opportunity (again, caused someone who wasn't looking to change, to look). Having an agreed-on plan in place affords the manager visibility into whether the opportunity is moving forward. By evaluating the status at each checkpoint, managers take some ownership of and responsibility for determining that the transaction is winnable. As soon as it appears that things are not proceeding as planned, the manager and salesperson should strategize as to how to get things back on track. And as always, in some instances, it will be necessary to withdraw. This might have to be the manager's call.

Leveraging Manager Experience

The manager has to make a judgment call as to whether the pace of progress is satisfactory. This is a complex decision that takes into account whether the salesperson is dealing with early- or mainstream-market buyers, the size of the organization, the size of the opportunity, and the overall impact or risk to the prospect in moving forward. Here are some warning signs to look for:

1. The buyer starts to push dates back.
2. Access to key players becomes more difficult.
3. Line items in the agreed-to sequence of events are challenged or ignored.
4. Buyer requirements unexpectedly change, potentially influenced by competitors.
5. A key player leaves or is reassigned.

When managers are trying to decide at a given checkpoint whether to continue to compete, there is one bellwether question to consider: "Are we the vendor of choice for at least one of the key players—and if not, what can we do to get there?" If the ultimate answer is, "We can't get there," it may well be time to withdraw from the opportunity, rather than throwing time, effort, and resources into what is likely to be a losing cause, resulting in yet another silver medal.

Senior executives of sales organizations may want to monitor average discounting levels by district and salesperson to identify potential skill deficiencies in negotiating. A caution, though: if a potential problem is identified, it may not be the salesperson's. We worked with an organization that had a district manager in Boston who was a terrible negotiator. When he was brought in to "help" the salesperson on large transactions, the discounts offered wound up being far greater than those in other offices. (In fact, he had earned the nickname "Moon over Massachusetts" because of his propensity to discount.) For a period of time, his manager had to review and role-play the polite "no's" and get/gives prior to going to the negotiating meeting. There were a few instances where he had to walk prior to getting the business. Within three months, though, his discounting fell into the acceptable range.

Another statistic to track is the level of discounting based on the date of the order. Buyers expect the end of the month or quarter to give them better leverage in getting concessions. Whenever possible, an attempt should be made to schedule the sequence of events so that the decision date doesn't coincide with a quarter end.

Once a seller has asked for the business, the opportunity goes from an E to one of four milestones. Look at Figure 18.2.

W.M.	The seller got the order. The M reflects the total number of months it took to win. An analysis of the length of winning sell cycles can be helpful in isolating best practices. (The most important single variable often turns out to be how high the entry level within the prospect was.)
L.M.	The seller loses, either to no decision or to a named vendor. Tracking and analyzing the total months of losses may isolate common events that lead to losses, so that hopefully they can be avoided in future sales cycles.
V.M.	The buyer has provided a verbal commitment, but for some reason the contract or purchase order cannot be issued. In such cases, we suggest asking the buyer to sign a nonbinding letter of intent, so that when other vendors call, they can say they have already committed and the decision has been made.
P.M.	The proposal had to be issued prior to the decision's being made.

In our experience, time does not improve the likelihood of winning verbal commitments or getting proposals accepted. Once either is more than 30 days old, managers have cause for concern. When evaluating pipelines, we often see proposals out there for more than 60 days that are still assigned probabilities of 80-plus percent. Every month that a proposal doesn't close means that the chances of ultimately getting the order are decreasing.

In our experience, once a proposal is 30 days old, either it is heading toward no decision or the buyer has made a decision to go with another vendor and has elected not to give the seller the bad news. Even if you have had access to decision makers up to this point, after the proposal is in their hands, they usually don't want to talk with you. Either they haven't made a decision or they've made an unfavorable decision.

In other words, you relinquish a great deal of control once your proposal is delivered. Suddenly, the buyer has everything he or she needs, and access gets more difficult. Rather than wait and hope, consider taking some positive action if the proposal is out longer than you think is healthy for your chances of winning (30 to 45 days?). We suggest a take-back letter or a phone call withdrawing the proposal. If you opt for a letter, don't overnight it. The proposal has been out for over a month, and there is no sense in spending $11.95 to get the letter delivered the next day. Registered

m = # months; % = % complete: M = total # months

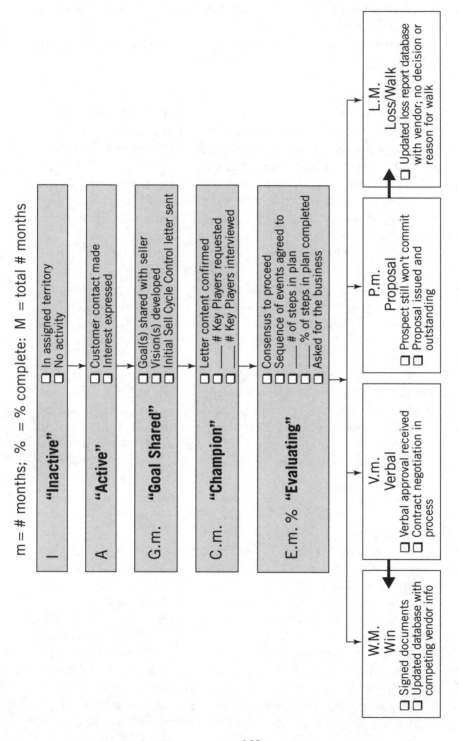

Figure 18.2 Grading Opportunities: Pipeline Milestones (m = no. of months; M = total no. of months; % = % complete)

mail will have the same impact and will cost significantly less. Figure 18.3 is a sample letter.

While some salespeople are terrified at the thought of withdrawing a proposal, the two most likely results are the following:

1. *The buyer does not call back.* At this stage, it is time to officially remove the opportunity from your forecast. Ultimately, it is better to get rid of deadwood in your funnel and pipeline, have a realistic view of what the next few months look like, and arrive at an appropriate business development plan.
2. *The buyer calls you back and asks why you have withdrawn the proposal.* This is an opportunity to determine whether the buyer is not going to buy, wants to buy, or would be interested in making changes to the proposal and trying to see if a favorable decision can be reached. If given a second chance, the seller now can focus on helping the buyer understand how to use your offering to achieve goals or solve problems.

April 28, 2009
Allan Campbell
XYZ Company

Dear Allan,

In reviewing my files, it has come to my attention that no action has been taken on the proposal we submitted to you on December 18, 2008. In rereading it, I understand why you may not have taken action. The proposal reflects a lack of understanding on my part of your primary business objectives. If you are willing, I'd like an opportunity to better understand if the usage of our CRM software can enable you to achieve your business objectives. The purpose of this letter is to make you aware of the fact that we are formally withdrawing our offer. Please call me if you have any questions.

Sincerely,

George Agnew
Sales Representative
CRM, Inc.

Figure 18.3 Sample Letter for Withdrawing a Proposal

Tomorrow Is the First Day of the Rest of Your Sales Career

In our workshops, we encourage salespeople and managers to be honest with themselves, and to assess and regrade every opportunity in their funnels and pipelines. When salespeople grade their opportunities against the new milestones, many discover that silver-medal opportunities get purged from their forecast—and fast.

Frequently, after our workshops, our clients hire us to participate in these kinds of regrading sessions. These are usually done via conference call between the first-level manager, the salesperson, and the CustomerCentric Selling consultant. A 45-minute session for each salesperson is scheduled for the first three months after the workshop. During each call with the salesperson, the top three opportunities are reviewed. In the first month, the CustomerCentric Selling consultant does most of the talking. (Especially during the first month, it is far easier for a CustomerCentric Selling consultant to disqualify opportunities, because he or she doesn't have any vested interest.) The second session is more of a sharing between our consultant and the sales manager. The client sales manager conducts the third session, with our consultant serving mainly as a safety net.

Most often, the overall value of the pipeline is reduced by 50 to 80 percent. That doesn't mean that 20 to 50 percent of opportunities are removed outright. Instead, it becomes clear that the opportunities are at either A or G levels. When we look at the value of the pipeline, we only look at E opportunities, which have been qualified to the point of having some visibility as to the potential close date. The mission of the salesperson is to get as many opportunities as possible to a level where the manager can grade them either a C or—ideally—an E. When existing opportunities are qualified to E status, some of the selling activities have already been done. The sequence of events is shorter, as the remaining activities amount to filling in the gaps, in contrast to starting with a new prospect.

To summarize: In assessing and developing salespeople, we advocate defining and sticking to a process. The CustomerCentric Selling process introduced in this book is an effective approach. It begins with the consistent positioning of offerings (through the use of Solution Development Prompters) and continues all the way through the development of salespeople—which, in the case of the salesperson, is the sales manager's job. Many of the same techniques that make a pipeline visible and predictable also contribute to improving the performance of the sales force—but only if the sales manager understands and accepts that responsibility.

Chapter 19

DRIVING REVENUE THROUGH CHANNELS

Over the past several years, many organizations have chosen to supplement their direct sales forces with—or even rely exclusively on—sales channels to drive top-line revenue. These indirect organizations include value-added resellers (VARs), distributors, and partners, to which we'll refer collectively as "channels."

These salespeople are not employees of the companies whose offerings they represent and sell. Microsoft is one of the most notable successes in driving a high percentage of their nonretail business through channels. Their channels have not only provided sales coverage but have also allowed Microsoft to minimize the hiring of technical support people to assist in implementations. This approach has been vastly different from that of many other technology companies, which have added support staff as direct employees.

In previous chapters, we've highlighted the challenges in providing a consistent buying experience with direct selling organizations. That challenge is heightened when selling through resellers that represent multiple vendors. Furthermore, there is a battle to gain mindshare (and wallet share) of the amount of effort resellers will spend promoting your offerings. There are two major ways to optimize mindshare:

1. Provide more attractive margins than competitors
2. Make your offerings easier to sell by providing Sales-Ready Messaging.

In this chapter we'd like to outline an approach that leverages Sales-Ready Messaging to serve as a differentiator to make positioning of offerings by resellers more consistent and to allow a superior customer buying experience.

Getting the Right Coverage

For companies that use both direct and indirect salespeople, one of the challenges is to define which market segments should be assigned to each, in order to maximize coverage and minimize conflict. We worked with a client that sold software ranging from under $10,000 to more than $500,000 that utilized both a direct and an indirect sales approach. We helped them define the desired coverage by working through the chart in Figure 19.1.

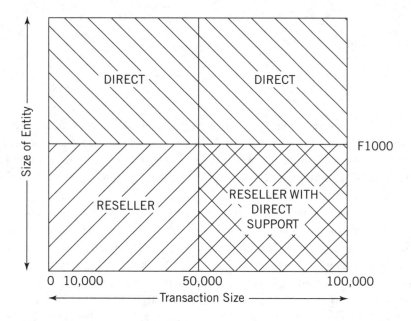

Figure 19.1 Desired Coverage

The criteria used to determine responsibility were account size on the y-axis (with the Fortune 1000 being a threshold) and opportunity size on the x-axis, with $50,000 or higher being designated as a major opportunity and below $10,000 being handled over the phone exclusively. Everyone was comfortable with his or her strategy, and we agreed that it was well thought out.

After we had collectively defined the desired coverage, the next logical question to ask was, "What does the actual coverage look like, today, in the field?" The room was quiet for a few moments. Finally, the most senior executive in the conference room volunteered his opinion—subsequently endorsed by everyone else—that the most extensive coverage was in the quadrant of non-Fortune 1000 accounts under $50,000 (see Figure 19.2).

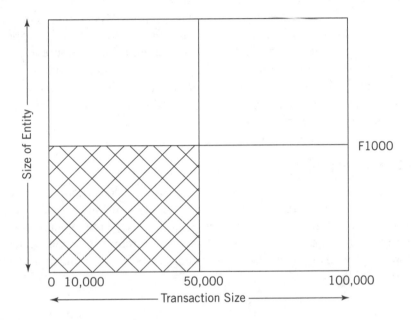

Figure 19.2 Actual Coverage

Further discussion brought out the fact that most of the company's salespeople (both direct and indirect) were engineers whose comfort level was calling on engineers—for the most part, non-decision makers. Interestingly enough, their direct salespeople were receiving an override on sales made by the channel. In some cases, in fact, direct salespeople were achieving quota while closing little or nothing themselves.

Gradually, it emerged that the firm's underlying problems lay in two areas. The first was that their direct salespeople did not know how to position their offerings for nontechnical businesspeople. Sales-Ready Messaging and a sales process were used to address this issue.

The second problem was inconsistency and conflict between the desired coverage and the compensation plan. While management can make their wishes known, the best way to influence a salesperson's behavior is to reinforce it with a commission plan structure. Part of the reason for the decision to implement an indirect channel was to decrease the cost of sales. But in their current situation, the company was actually paying duplicate commissions to both direct and indirect salespeople on most transactions.

By implementing our recommendations, direct salespeople were weaned from their overrides on sales by the channel over six months. After that time, the commission plan compensated them to pursue only Fortune 1000 accounts. Direct salespeople that were unwilling or unable to execute these enterprise sales efforts were encouraged to join VARs so that they could continue selling within their comfort zones for small to mid-size opportunities. The channel was given a different compensation structure, receiving 100 percent commission for sales to non-Fortune 1000 accounts that did not require sales support from the manufacturer. They could request support on sales of over $50,000, but in these cases they received only 80 percent of their sales commission.

Who's in Charge?

It is essential that the compensation plans for a sales organization reflect management's objectives. Even in the best of circumstances, however, the control that vendors can exert over channels is tenuous when compared with that over a direct sales force. They must attempt to influence actions without having authority. Control of channels is difficult due to many factors, including:

1. The majority of VARs sell offerings from multiple companies.
2. Some companies may compete with their channel on certain opportunities by trying to take the business direct.
3. The VARs' interests come first. Relationships work best when the manufacturer's offerings align with the VARs' business strategy and expertise. If the VARs' core business is consulting services, they will focus the majority of their sales efforts in this area. For such companies, representing products may be viewed as a way of generating consulting opportunities. Another VAR may want to generate a higher volume of product sales and have little or no appetite for consulting.
4. VARs representing multiple companies often focus on whatever vendor's offerings are easiest to sell at any given time (i.e., the "hot" product).
5. The methods used to sell are left almost completely up to the VARs, meaning that manufacturers are ceding the customer experience to individual salespeople who don't work directly for them.

6. Some VARs have relationships with a relatively fixed group of customers and may not exert much effort actively pursuing new accounts.

Poor design or execution of channel strategies are common, which—given the circumstances listed—shouldn't be surprising. Companies establishing indirect channels may fail to realize that in addition to handing over their offerings, they are inadvertently getting into the same business as CustomerCentric Selling—that is, providing sales training for their business partners. Most of them are not up to this challenge, with whatever training they provide treating their offerings as nouns.

Applying CustomerCentric Principles to Channels

In the same way many direct salespeople lead with offerings, many *channel managers*—that is, the people in the organization who are responsible for recruiting and supporting channels—are guilty of taking the same approach. The principles of CustomerCentric Selling can be applied to channels, and we'd like to discuss how the methodology can be used to empower business partners to see how they can increase top-line revenue. We believe that recruiting of VARs can be distilled to business goals, and therefore to conversations.

Calling at high levels is critical when recruiting new business partners. The decision to add to or modify the list of companies a reseller represents can cost significant resources and money. The majority of VARs are relatively small organizations. Whenever possible, calling on the owner of the business minimizes red tape, allows early qualification, and shortens the sales cycle. To gain mindshare and be in alignment with the buyer, the initial effort is to have the business owner draw the conclusion that he or she can improve bottom-line results by representing your company and its offerings. This is critical when you are attempting to recruit VARs representing multiple companies. Here is a sample Targeted Conversation List for the owner of a VAR selling software and services:

- Improve margins.
- Make good technology bets.
- Improve return on investment of relationships with vendors.
- Match offerings with their core competencies and customer base.
- Optimize the mix of services and offerings.

In an initial call, an attempt should be made to cause a business owner who isn't looking to change (the list of companies the business currently represents) to consider adding your company to the list. (By now, we assume that you recognize much of this language and approach.) When recruiting new VARs, it may be best to assume that you will have to displace an existing vendor the VAR is representing—presumably the one that is making the smallest bottom-line contribution. VAR owners have a finite capacity as relates to the number of manufacturers they can represent. From the VAR perspective, optimization of these companies will lead to the best bottom-line result. So your job is to help the buyer realize that your company belongs in that list of vendors that he or she chooses to represent.

Examples of characteristics the owner of a VAR could find attractive about a company and its offerings include the following:

1. A "hot" market space (e.g., e-commerce in 1998, customer relationship management in 1999, Sarbanes-Oxley compliance in 2002, or Electronic Content Management for health-care companies in 2009)
2. A unique offering that few, if any, other vendors have
3. An offering that is complementary to existing offerings used by their client base
4. An offering that is a good candidate for add-on business with their customer set
5. A product with a high degree of accompanying services (SAP, Oracle, and so on) if their focus is on professional services
6. Attractive margins or commission structure

A channel manager who is recruiting business partners should attempt to determine which characteristics represent their strengths and create a list of potential goals and Success Stories that will most effectively position the company. By doing a diagnosis first, ideally the business owner can be brought to a vision about the benefits of establishing a relationship.

Once you have gotten the attention of an owner who believes he or she can improve business results by joining forces with you, the next step is to provide an idea of how the owner will be successful. Especially for offerings with a mild to high degree of complexity, support of the channel partners is important. Once again, consider making a list of what you have available to offer partners. Here is a partial list:

1. Brand recognition
2. Advertising campaigns and promotions
3. Local sales staff available for making joint calls
4. Education and training for both your partners and their customers
5. Sales support
6. Lead generation

7. Web site or intranet to address frequently asked questions (FAQs)
8. Marketing programs and support (local and national)
9. Local technical support
10. 24/7 hotline
11. Quick turnaround of orders placed
12. Willingness to offer exclusive territories

In the same way that salespeople tend to spew opinions, many channel managers tell potential partners how great the support is going to be. But many VARs are "burn victims"; they remember that although past relationships sounded attractive while they were being sold, they ultimately turned out to be a series of broken promises and unmet expectations. Getting your proposed support down to the level of usage scenarios will be helpful in making sure both parties are on the same page.

Once the buyers believe that they can improve their business results and understand what support will be available, the last area to discuss is the usage of the actual offerings. This will require resources from both parties. As usual, many such recruiting attempts begin with a product "spray and pray." Yes, products ultimately have to come to the fore—but only after you've gained mindshare regarding the value of doing business, and have helped define the support that the partner will need (and that you can provide).

Fixing Broken Channels

In the early stages of a company's existence, recruiting efforts often concentrate more on the quantity than on the quality of channel partners. Eventually, though, quality has to come to the front of the line. Analyses of the contribution of each channel partner tend to show that a 90/10 rule applies. In other words, 90 percent of the revenue is generated by 10 percent of your business partners.

To encourage great VARs and (potentially) motivate poor performers, it is a common practice to establish three or more levels of partners, as defined by revenue thresholds that are either achieved or committed to. The designations platinum, gold, and silver have become fairly standard within the technology arena. The higher the designation, the better the treatment, which may include rebates, cooperative marketing funds, higher discounting levels, more favorable payment terms, earliest access to new offerings, and so on. Many vendors using indirect channels realize that they could improve their bottom lines if they were able to focus on top-producing partners. Attempting to pare the list can be a delicate situation, though, especially if an underperforming partner was one of the early companies to agree to become a VAR.

Assuming success in recruiting a channel that will provide you with the desired representation in the market, you still face the following challenges when working through indirect representation:

1. Gaining mindshare about what percentage of resources to allocate to your offerings
2. Making your offerings easier to sell than other suppliers'
3. Achieving consistent positioning of your offerings within the market-place
4. Qualifying opportunities before allocating resources
5. Forecasting top-line revenue despite being once removed from the salespeople
6. Once again, we believe that these and other issues can be addressed by integrating a sales process with Sales-Ready Messaging.

Both direct and indirect salespeople display a tendency to follow the path of least resistance. If a vendor can make the offerings easier to sell, with all other things being equal, it stands to reason that resellers will focus a disproportionate amount of effort on that product. Earlier, we discussed the challenge that a salesperson joining a company faces in positioning the offerings of his or her employer. For a VAR representing 10 or more companies, the challenge is staggering. It would be virtually impossible for a salesperson to fully understand and develop positioning for more than a handful of offerings. In addition, of course, direct salespeople aren't the only ones who are reluctant or unable—for example—to make effective calls at decision-maker levels.

For all of these reasons, and more, we advocate finding ways to give the indirect sales force some (or all) of the same training that the direct sales force receives. The reasons should be clear by now. Once a reseller understands how to execute a Solution Development Prompter (SDP), he or she develops the ability to have conversations with targeted titles within specific vertical segments. We believe that companies providing Customer-Centric Selling training and customized SDPs realize the following advantages:

1. They make their offerings easier to sell, thereby gaining mindshare.
2. More consistent positioning is achieved, and the manufacturer can influence the customer experience.
3. Product training becomes product usage training via SDPs and takes considerably less time, effort, and expense. By building Sales-Ready Messaging around new announcements, the channel is able to hit the ground running and consistently position those offerings. The prereq-

uisite would be having VAR salespeople master the CustomerCentric Selling vision development process.

4. After a VAR has been trained, there is now a consistent vocabulary and a set of debriefing questions that enable the channel manager to help decide which opportunities are qualified, and therefore worthy of sales support and resources.

5. If there is a sufficient level of trust that the VAR is providing funnel visibility, the channel manager has a way to more accurately forecast revenue.

6. If everyone is on the same page, it is easier to segment territories and to intelligently resolve the inevitable channel conflicts, either between VARs or between the VARs and the companies they are representing.

7. Training can be used as a "carrot" for VARs that are producing sufficient revenue—a way to enhance their performance while being subsidized by the manufacturer's cooperative funds. For underachieving partners, it can be used as a "stick"—in that to continue the relationship, they must invest in the training, perhaps on their own nickel.

8. Custom Sales-Ready Messaging for VAR new hires as well as for newly announced offerings can enable VARs to make effective calls with a shorter learning curve.

Organizations that successfully implement CustomerCentric Selling can turn the way their salespeople and their VARs' salespeople sell into a competitive advantage. Extending that concept, CustomerCentric Selling can provide companies using indirect channels an advantage that extends far beyond their offerings, margins, advertising campaigns, and so on.

Many companies have chosen to drive revenue through channels without fully understanding how to integrate product training and the sales process. From a senior executive perspective, the allure of a lower cost of sales, fewer direct employees, expanded coverage, and so on has often proved hard to resist. But positioning offerings, as we discussed earlier, is well beyond the scope of a traditional salesperson, whether direct or indirect. A compensation plan reflecting a manufacturer's objectives, Sales-Ready Messaging, and a repeatable sales process greatly enhances the probability of successfully leveraging channels.

Chapter 20

FROM THE CLASSROOM TO THE BOARDROOM

Many concepts discussed in books and classrooms appear viable until they are proven not to work in business situations. An engineering student spends weeks learning to make stress-strain calculations to simulate real-world conditions. Many disillusioned graduates learn in the field that this approach is seldom used because the results don't reflect reality. On the job, you make an educated guess during the design phase, build a test unit, subject it to stress and strain, and reinforce components that fail. Having said that, we would like to suggest a road map for implementing the CustomerCentric Selling sales process.

The difference between education and training is practice. We (the authors) have been intently watching Tiger Woods play golf since he burst onto the scene with his 1994 U.S. Amateur win. It has not had a meaningful impact on our individual golf games. Anything you want to get better at, you practice. Golfers take lessons and go to the driving range. Tennis players have a machine fire balls at them to hit back. Even professional baseball players take batting practice before each game. Sales, as a discipline we strive to improve at, should be no different.

In our workshops, true skill transfer takes place during role-playing. When closing our workshops, we make a point of acknowledging that the attendees and coaches expended significant effort, but that all we had accomplished was training. In fact, we also point out that when the workshop is over, the role-playing should not stop. Practice is the key to continuous improvement. Senior executives hire us because they want to implement a sales process. Training is an event during which skills are imparted. The expression "use it or lose it" could have been created to describe the crossroads traditional sellers face on completing one of our workshops. Changing selling habits that have been ingrained for 5, 10, 15, or more years is a daunting challenge.

When successfully implemented, the sales process becomes part of the culture of the adopting company and ultimately shapes the customers' experience. Implementation of the process requires extensive effort on the part of sales and marketing, but it also requires involvement and support by senior executives, ideally up to the CEO, to realize its full potential. Marketing programs, brochures, Web sites, and product development, to name a few areas, should change to align with the new concepts and approaches that CustomerCentric Selling introduces. The potential reward for companies successfully implementing a sales process is enormous, but we'd be setting unrealistic expectations if we told you it was easy. We have each had occasions where we turned down business because a lack of management support virtually assured that it would have been "drive-by" training. Because if management isn't managing people to the process, salespeople view compliance as optional.

Key to Implementation

First-level managers are the linchpins in implementing CustomerCentric Selling. Traditional salespeople are reluctant to change by trying new approaches. Many lack self-motivation. Others are afraid. Those who try and don't realize immediate success are sorely tempted to return to their old familiar ways. Salespeople need the support of their managers to make the migration from being either traditional or customercentric sellers to becoming CustomerCentric sellers. Two questions to consider if you're on the fence:

1. Would you prefer that a salesperson use this approach if you were on the other side of the desk as a buyer?
2. What would your win rate be when competing with a seller capable of executing CustomerCentric Selling?

Sales managers must learn and support the process. Their actions speak louder than their words. Verbalized support for the process rings hollow if they do not utilize the methodology while making calls with their salespeople. Failing to do so sends the wrong message to their direct reports. Salespeople are like your children in that they are hard to fool. A manager's behavior, much more than his or her words, shapes the behavior of the salespeople.

Suggested Approach

In order to gain acceptance and support by managers, the sales process (unlike engineering calculations) has to match your real-world selling environment. Here are some suggestions as to how to further evaluate CustomerCentric Selling:

1. Send a team of three people to a public CustomerCentric Selling workshop. This offers the following advantages:

   - Verification that the methodology represents a fit for your organization.
   - A foundation from which to discuss necessary modifications to the process and curriculum.
   - Attendees at public workshops can serve as role-play coaches if the company elects to have internal workshop(s).
   - The scope of effort in creating Sales-Ready Messaging can be determined.

2. Define the different types of sales that the process must handle, as described in Chapter 7. If the steps defined for a given sale don't reflect reality, your salespeople will resist implementing the process. We strongly suggest integrating the standard milestones described in Chapter 17 with your customized ones.

3. Create Targeted Conversations Lists for your offerings and vertical markets. Once the titles have been determined, create a list of potential business goals for each. This will determine the scope of the effort to support your sales staff in making calls on key players.

4. Create a library of Sales-Ready Messaging to "load the lips" of your salespeople. This should include Solution Development Prompters, Success Stories, phone scripts, and so on. Failure to do so means paying only lip service to the sales process. Sellers making key player calls without Sales-Ready Messaging have no choice but to wing it. The outcomes of these calls become the opinions of salespeople (see Chapter 4). In these situations, all bets are off as to qualification, and therefore the quality, of the funnel and ultimately the pipeline.

5. If possible, have sales managers attend a workshop first as students. These are the people most critical to the success of the sales process. This allows them two exposures to the methodology: once as a student and once as a role-play coach if you elect to have an internal custom workshop. In terms of commitment, seeing their managers in the back of the room sends a strong message to other attendees.

6. Train your salespeople and others who shape the customer experience. Most of our clients choose to train support or product people who make calls with salespeople as well. Because these people have the business and product usage knowledge and no sales background, many of them take to our process like ducks to water. For those within your organization who are not making customer calls but who need to understand the concepts, custom programs can be designed.

7. After the workshop, honestly regrade the existing funnels. Brace yourself for a rude awakening. The value of each salesperson's funnel is likely to be reduced by between 50 and 80 percent. It takes a strong stomach, but the sooner the manager and the salesperson get the funnel to reflect reality, the sooner they know what has to be done to build it to levels that will sustain quota achievement. As the CEO, CFO, or VP of sales, take the same attitude as a library that offers an amnesty program: Return your books (even if you took out *Gone With the Wind* in 1986), and there will be no fines. We just want the books back. That is to say: Without recrimination, this is a new day. Let's get the stale proposals, deadwood, and deadbeats out of your funnels and our pipeline. Instead of senior management discounting an unrealistic pipeline, we want the salespeople and the manager to do quality control much further upstream in the process.

   Sales managers are responsible for allowing opportunities to enter a salesperson's funnel and for grading those opportunities if they advance. Managers now share responsibility for those losses that take several months because during the execution of the sequence of events, they agreed to proceed at various checkpoints.

8. For the first 90 days, managers should work with their salespeople to get as many opportunities that remain in the funnel requalified to E status (Chapter 17). Once the salesperson has gained access to all key players and gotten consensus to execute a sequence of events, the visibility and probability of success dramatically increase. Many of these postworkshop evaluation plans are significantly shorter than ones done for new prospects, as many of the steps may already have been at least partially completed.

9. Reviewing opportunities with salespeople should be a relatively short, well-focused conversation. The debriefing questions in Chapter 14 become the basis for discussion. Generally speaking, the more lengthy the answers to the questions, the more tenuous your position on that opportunity. If the debriefing questions cannot be answered, the salesperson, with or without the manager's help, must make further calls on the buyer. Also, begin to track how the salesperson learned about the opportunity (proactively or reactively), as we believe that is the single most important variable in determining win rate. Our experience indicates that 75 to 80 percent of the gold medals awarded go to the salesperson that initiated the opportunity as Column A. Additionally, we find the amount of effort expended on Column B opportunities to turn them around is usually inversely proportional. In other words, we spend 80 percent of our time trying to turn around the 20 percent of the opportunities where our competition set the requirements.

10. Consider having your management team attend a CustomerCentric Selling Sales Process Implementation Workshop. This two-day session focuses on funnel and pipeline management and on assessment and development of salespeople. It amounts to a hands-on workshop for the topics covered in Chapters 17 and 18. We recommend scheduling this session 60 to 120 days after salespeople have attended workshops, so that managers have some real-world experience with the new methodology.

11. Any sales process should cover 90-plus percent of situations. The intent of our sales process is that *managers* make decisions on exceptions. There will be RFPs for which you understand that you are a silver medalist, but to which you elect to respond. It should be a manager's decision, and please be realistic about the probability assigned, as it most likely will not track with RFPs that you were able to wire.

12. Review compensation plans to verify that they support your objectives. Companies with long sales cycles should consider an alternative to the recoverable/nonrecoverable draw quagmire. After 60 days in the territory, why not have new hires earn bonuses by hitting predetermined milestone thresholds? Achievement of milestones must be verified by sales managers by auditing prospect and customer correspondence.

    Some CustomerCentric Selling clients keep their experienced sales reps hungry by having a percentage of their base salary paid on meeting targets for the E funnel on an ongoing basis.

13. When new offerings are in development, create key player menus of goals as a sanity check to minimize the chances of introducing a product in search of a market. Sometimes early-market buyers don't or can't bail you out, resulting in product write-offs, not take-offs. When introducing a new offering, make the creation of Sales-Ready Messaging part of the development costs. You may be able to reallocate funds from your product training budget.

14. Once or twice a year, review your most significant wins and losses, along with your competitive position. Sales process and Sales-Ready Messaging represent a journey more than a destination. Please be aware that what worked 10 months ago may have to be tweaked. In sales, the landscape is in almost constant flux.

15. Consider hiring CustomerCentric Selling consultants to help with the design and implementation of the sales process. Having been there and done that in several other organizations, they can provide an industry best-practices view as well as an objective outside opinion.

Making Your Sales Process a Competitive Advantage

During our careers, we have witnessed the maturing of technology as it relates to almost all business applications. The advances in accounting, manufacturing, engineering, and supply chain applications are astounding. Just as we may know more about the moon than about the deepest parts of oceans on earth, sales (perhaps the most essential business application) has resisted fully successful implementation of technology because it has not been codified in a repeatable process. We believe CustomerCentric Selling can enable you to remove that barrier.

Companies spend untold amounts of money honing their offerings to the point where they have what they perceive to be advantages over others in their market space, only to be sometimes disappointed with their results. Taking IBM's mainframe business as an example, during the 1980s and 1990s their offerings were seldom the fastest, the latest technology, or the cheapest. They did, however, do a tremendous job of gaining access to executive levels of their customers, often one or two levels higher than their competition, and winning by identifying and addressing key player business issues.

We hope that after reading this book, you have acquired a new outlook on sales and the belief that best practices can be applied to shaping your customer's experience. When asked the most common reason that salespeople lose, we say without hesitation: They get outsold. While implementation of a sales process is difficult, the potential rewards of making the way your organization sells a competitive advantage are virtually unlimited. CustomerCentric Selling can provide the way to achieve this advantage. Companies that successfully implement the process will have found a way to institutionalize a superior buying experience.

We wish you good luck and good selling!

Index

About the Authors

Mike Bosworth

Mike Bosworth is noted for founding and growing one of the most successful virtual businesses in the B2B arena. He founded Solution Selling® solo in 1983, began licensing his intellectual property to affiliates in 1988, and by the time he sold it in 1999, over 50 affiliates were contributing royalty income in excess of $2.8 million annually. His current focus is helping innovators brainstorm Internet business ideas at a conceptual level and, in many cases, participating in launching virtual businesses as an equity advisor. He also has a new book in progress on how sellers can harness the power of stories in building emotional trust with their buyers.

Bosworth is the author of *Solution Selling: Creating Buyers in Difficult Selling Markets* (McGraw-Hill, 1993) and coauthor of *CustomerCentric Selling* (McGraw-Hill, November 2003). Bosworth is a limited partner in a San Diego—based venture capital firm and is an advisory board member for a number of information technology ventures.

Mike Bosworth began his career in the information technology industry in 1972 as an application support person for Xerox Computer Services. He was their top new business salesperson in 1975, managed the "branch of the year" in 1979, and was promoted to national manager of field sales in 1980. From 1976 through 1982 he designed and delivered sales training programs for XCS. His years of field experience plus the knowledge he gained from working with Neil Rackham on the Xerox SPIN selling project inspired him to found Solution Selling in 1983.

Bosworth has a degree in Business Management and Marketing from California State Polytechnic University. In addition to his keynote speaking for professional associations and major corporations, he has been a featured lecturer at the Stanford Graduate School of Business, the Stanford Program on Market Strategy for Technology-Based Companies, the American Marketing Association Customer Message Management Forums, the Anderson School of Management at UCLA, the Paul Merage School of Business at UC Irvine, the University of Connecticut, and Rollins College, to name a few. He is certified (CMC) by the Institute of Management Consultants. He currently resides in Del Mar, California.

John Holland

Leveraging over 20 years' experience in sales, sales management, and consulting, John Holland coauthored and cofounded CustomerCentric Selling® (CCS) in 2002. His primary responsibility is continuing to evolve CCS intellectual property to reflect ongoing changes in how people and organizations buy.

As a sales consultant prior to launching CCS, Holland helped organizations design and implement standardized sales processes in such diverse sectors as professional services, technology, leasing, overnight delivery, logistics, language localization, office equipment, temporary housing, and financial services.

In 2003, Holland teamed with Mike Bosworth, who originally authored *Solution Selling*, to coauthor *CustomerCentric Selling*. In 2007, Holland coauthored *Relational Capital* with Ed Wallace.

Holland has had articles published in *Sales and Marketing Executive Report, Selling Power* magazine, and the *American Marketing Association* (AMA). He has spoken on various topics for organizations such as SMEI, IIDMA, AMA, and Software Success. He serves as a participant in CustomerThink's panel of experts and Cognizant's Customer Advisory Board.

Holland earned a degree in Mechanical Engineering from Northeastern University before starting his career with IBM's General Systems Division. He delivers keynote speeches and serves in an Advisory Board capacity with a limited number of companies, providing guidance on product direction, service offerings, and overall sales and tactical marketing strategies.

Frank Visgatis

As cofounder of CustomerCentric Systems, LLC, and coauthor of the CustomerCentric Selling® sales methodology, Frank Visgatis helps drive the overall direction and strategy for CustomerCentric Systems, LLC, leveraging close to 20 years of leadership experience. Visgatis knows how to conceptualize and execute a new business strategy into a winning company. He has done it numerous times—from cofounding a thriving commercial and residential real estate holding company to turning a small private consulting practice into one of the most successful sales training providers in the country. His ability to identify trends and changes in the sales ecosystem has helped change the dynamic of interaction between sellers and buyers through the development of CustomerCentric Selling® and Sales-Ready Messaging®. Visgatis' vision has propelled CustomerCentric Systems, LLC, to being one of the industry's top providers of sales process consulting, sales training, and Sales-Ready Messaging®.

Prior to cofounding CustomerCentric Systems, LLC, Visgatis had been helping companies since 1993 in the "high-difficulty" marketplace operate more productively through the implementation of definable, measurable sales processes. He has worked with companies such as EMC, The Math-Works, REL Consultancy, Giga Information Group (now part of Forrester Research), FAST Search and Transfer (a division of Microsoft), Galileo, Worldspan, and Orbitz, to name just a few. He has personally trained thousands of salespeople in North America, Latin America, the United Kingdom, Europe, and Asia. In July of 1999, Visgatis merged his own highly successful sales training and consulting practice with John Holland and Gary Walker to form Vision Group. In January 2002 the three partners, along with Michael T. Bosworth, the original author of the Solution Selling® sales methodology, joined together to form CustomerCentric Systems, LLC, and develop the CustomerCentric Selling® sales methodology.

Visgatis attended both Bryant University and the University of Massachusetts School of Management prior to his start in the high-tech business in the mid-1980s.

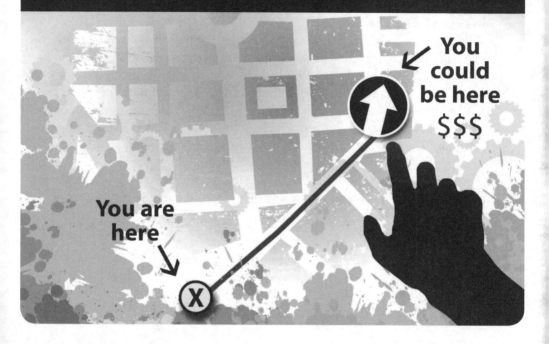